D1385448

DAVID A. COLLINS

THOMAS
CORNEILLE

Protean Dramatist

MOUTON & CO

STUDIES IN FRENCH LITERATURE

VII

THOMAS CORNEILLE:
PROTEAN DRAMATIST

by

DAVID A. COLLINS

Kalamazoo College

1966

MOUTON & CO.

LONDON THE HAGUE PARIS

Printed in The Netherlands by Mouton & Co., Printers, The Hague

ACKNOWLEDGMENTS

In the preparation of the present study it has been my pleasure to work under the supervision of Professor Hunter Kellenberger for whose guidance I am deeply thankful. It was he who first suggested the topic to me and who has since offered valuable criticism which has contributed vitally to whatever positive merits the study may possess.

I am grateful to many others as well for a variety of reasons: to my father and Kalamazoo College for grants-in-aid; to Professor Harcourt Brown for reading the revised manuscript and making many helpful comments; to Professor Charles Leighton, my colleague at the University of New Hampshire, for proofreading parts of the manuscript and offering considerable incidental assistance; to Miss Dorothy Jones, and Messrs. Ezra Fitch and Hugh Pritchard for important bibliographical errands; and most of all, to Vera whose encouragement and patience have been a genuine inspiration.

CONTENTS

INTRODUCTION

STUDIES ON THOMAS CORNEILLE

The only significant studies in which Thomas Corneille's contributions to the seventeenth century French theater are discussed at length are H. C. Lancaster's *History of French Dramatic Literature in the Seventeenth Century* [1] and Gustave Reynier's *Thomas Corneille: sa vie et son théâtre.* [2] Aspects of Thomas' work are treated at least briefly in numerous literary studies including most recently Dr. Lacy Lockert's *Studies in French Classical Tragedy* [3] as well as his *The Chief Rivals of Corneille and Racine,* [4] Professor Clifton Cherpack's *The Call of the Blood in French Classical Tragedy,* [5] and Professor Jacques Scherer's *La Dramaturgie classique en France.* [6] Those who have treated the French theater in particular and literary historians generally have usually seen fit to devote a number of pages to the younger brother of the great Corneille. The brothers Parfaict [7] and Petit de Julleville [8] gave him a place of merit among his contemporaries. In his *Histoire de la littérature française au XVIIᵉ siècle* [9] Antoine Adam briefly

[1] Baltimore, 1929-42. Subsequent references to this work will be abbreviated *History*, followed by a Roman numeral indicating Part and a page number. See bibliography for full information on all works consulted.

[2] Paris, 1892. Hereafter indicated as *Thom. Corn.*

[3] Nashville, 1958; subsequently abbreviated as *Studies.*

[4] Nashville, 1956; subsequently abbreviated as *Rivals.*

[5] Baltimore, 1958.

[6] Paris, 1950; subsequently abbreviated as *Dramaturgie.*

[7] François and Claude Parfaict, *Histoire du Théâtre français* (Paris, 1734-49). Subsequent references will be abbreviated as *Histoire.*

[8] L. Petit de Julleville, *Histoire de la langue et de la littérature française* (Paris, 1897).

[9] Paris, 1949-56. Hereafter cited as Adam.

describes his contribution to the various phases of dramatic evolution taking place in the latter half of the century. Thomas Corneille has also figured with sporadic prominence in the background of studies centered on Racine,[10] de Visé,[11] Quinault,[12] and quite naturally Pierre Corneille,[13] to name but a few.

Only recently a curious book was published under the title *Descendance de Thomas Corneille*.[14] It is primarily a genealogy tracing the dramatist's descendants to the present day. Although this book has only tangential interest to the present study, its publication has some significance as the outcome of a modest revival of interest in Thomas Corneille's theater. Under the auspices of the Cercle Pierre et Thomas Corneille, several of the latter's plays have been produced in the last few years at Barentin near Rouen. *Timocrate, Le Geôlier de soi-même, Le Festin de Pierre, L'Amour à la mode, Le Baron d'Albikrac, Le Comte d'Essex, Don Bertrand de Cigarral, Le Feint astrologue,* and *Le Galant doublé* have been produced since 1956; and presumably others are to follow.

PURPOSE AND METHOD

Our general purpose is to re-evaluate Thomas Corneille's serious dramatic works in an attempt to disengage his peculiar talents from the morass of condescending judgments which accrue to his reputation. It has been both affirmed and denied that he would have fared better if he had not had to withstand constant comparison with his brother and Racine. The fact is that his popularity did not suffer appreciably from this association during his lifetime, but it has since his death. A close examination of his plays has persuaded us that, due allowances made for obvious weaknesses, his merits as a dramatist have been underestimated. We propose to make an analytical survey of his plays, treating some of them briefly but omitting only those which are

---

[10]   Among others, Raymond Picard's *La Carrière de Jean Racine* (Paris, 1956) and René Jasinski's *Vers le vrai Racine* (Paris, 1958).

[11]   Pierre Mélèse, *Donneau de Visé* (Paris, 1936).

[12]   Etienne Gros, *Philippe Quinault* (Paris, 1926).

[13]   Among others, Louis Herland's *Corneille par lui-même* (Paris, 1954).

[14]   Louis van Renynghe de Voxrie (Bruges, 1959).

peripheral works involving spectacular devices, machines, or musical accompaniment.

While the study of Thomas Corneille's dramaturgy is an important aspect of our discussion, we do not intend to deal with dramaturgy for its own sake by cataloguing the various devices that he used. We propose rather to make a general appraisal of the plays as dramatic compositions, paying particular attention to dramaturgical technique where its effects have significant bearing on total dramatic interest. For this reason discussion of particular techniques will vary according to the nature of individual plays. For example the use of *quid pro quo* is persistent in the comedies and identity plays but less important in the so-called Cornelian plays and virtually non-existent in the later tragedies. The comedies call for more technical analysis than the tragedies, whereas the latter demand more attention to characterization. In brief, each play will be treated on its own merits for its most significant aspects. We hasten to add, however, that there is an underlying unity in Thomas' works, or at least obvious threads of cohesion, which will be emphasized in the following manner: first, by grouping the plays into four meaningful categories which correspond roughly to their dates of appearance; and secondly, by tracing in the conclusion on a more generalized level the organic continuity of the total production. While our four groups generally include the same plays as those of Reynier, his principles of classification have been modified and revised. We have made no attempt to study sources in themselves beyond a few occasional remarks which present new evidence or suggest a shift of emphasis. At the risk of incurring the wrath of some "Baroquistes", we have purposely avoided the term *baroque* to characterize Thomas Corneille's dramatic vision. Since the application of this term has been stretched in recent years to encompass a wide variety of features in authors as divergent as Montaigne and Baudelaire, we concur with Henri Peyre's admonition to exercise restraint in its use.[15]

Except for the 1692 edition of his plays, in which he modernized the spelling, Thomas Corneille made no revisions of his works. The

---

[15] See "Common Sense Remarks on the French Baroque" in *Studies in Seventeenth Century French Literature*, ed. Jean-Jaques Demorest (Ithaca, N.Y., 1962).

choice of an acceptable text is not complicated therefore by the existence of variants. We have used the edition of 1738 as the source of documentation of quotations from the plays.[16] All brief references are documented in parentheses subsequent to the first mention. Except where an intermediate source is used the spelling has been modernized, and the French version of proper names is used in referring to characters unless the reference is outside the context of the plays.

A LONG AND VARIED CAREER
(BIOGRAPHICAL SKETCH)

During his lifetime Thomas Corneille enjoyed considerable prominence. Between 1655 and 1680 he was among the five most respected playwrights in France, including in this group the aging Pierre, Racine, and Molière. In a brief preface to his commentaries on *Ariane*, Voltaire concluded: "C'était d'ailleurs un homme d'un très grand mérite, et d'une vaste littérature; et si vous exceptez Racine, auquel il ne faut comparer personne, il était le seul de son temps qui fût digne d'être le premier au-dessous de son frère." [17] Both Lancaster and Lockert have insisted that our view of the French theater in the latter half of the seventeenth century has traditionally been distorted by nearly exclusive emphasis on the contributions and worth of Racine to the neglect of lesser figures. Lancaster in particular stresses the need to remove Racine from the hallowed vacuum in which he has been placed and to show him, as it were, in context. To illuminate the portion of this context which concerns Thomas Corneille, it will be useful at the outset to situate him in his milieu.[18]

Thomas Corneille was born in Rouen on August 20, 1625, nineteen years after his famous brother. Their father, also named Pierre, was

---

[16] *Poèmes dramatiques de T. Corneille* (Paris, 1738). 5 vols. In quoting from introductory "Epîtres" and "Au lecteur", we have on two occasions used original editions in the case of *La Devineresse* and *Bradamante* (see note on Thomas Corneille in bibliography).

[17] From the commentaries on Corneille (1764) in *Œuvres complètes*, éd. Moland (Paris, 1877-83) Vol. 32, p. 305. Subsequent references to Voltaire's comments will be documented by this edition abbreviated as *Œuvres*.

[18] For biographical information on Thomas Corneille we rely chiefly on Reynier's *Thom. Corn.*

what we would call today a supervisor of woodlands and waterways for the area of Rouen. In the footsteps of his brothers Pierre and Antoine, Thomas gained early recognition for his poetic efforts at the Jesuit college of Rouen where at about age fifteen he is said to have composed in Latin verse a play which pleased his director so much that it was substituted for the one already chosen for performance at graduation ceremonies.

After the death of his father in 1639 until he completed his study of law at the University of Caen in 1646, he was counseled and guided by Pierre whose growing reputation during these years must have inspired Thomas with visions of glory. Having been tutored in Spanish by Pierre, Thomas set out around mid-century, as Pierre had a few years earlier, to adapt Spanish *comedias*, a type of play then very much in vogue on the Parisian stage. Meanwhile he was officially made a lawyer in 1649 and a year later married Marguerite de Lamperière, the younger sister of Pierre's wife.

His early dramatic efforts were undistinguished but enjoyed moderate success at a time which proved to be auspicious for a young and vigorous dramatist. The decade beginning 1650 was witnessing a change of generations. Rotrou died in 1650, Tristan l'Hermite in 1655, and DuRyer in 1658. With Pierre Corneille in temporary retirement from 1652 to 1659, Racine not yet writing and Molière returning to Paris only in 1658 with his best plays yet to appear, the way was relatively open to newcomers. After a run of eight light comedies from 1649 to 1656, Thomas produced his amazingly successful *Timocrate* (1656) which established him as a leading dramatist. Louis XIV himself complimented him. Meanwhile Thomas had ingratiated himself with a circle of admirers including the comtesse de Fiesque and the comtesse de Noailles whose influence both on him and in his behalf contributed much to the success of his gallant tragi-comedies beginning with *Timocrate*. From 1656 to 1672 he supplied nineteen plays to the Hôtel de Bourgogne and the troupe du Marais.[19]

The presentation of his *Camma* in 1661 brought such crowds that the players initiated a fourth weekly performance on Thursdays in addition to the regular times on Sundays, Tuesdays and Fridays. The

[19] For a complete list of plays, dates of first performance and publication, see Appendix.

following year Pierre and Thomas moved to Paris where they were lodged by the duc de Guise to whom Thomas had dedicated *Timocrate*. After the death of the duke in 1664 the brothers apparently remained together in Paris until after 1681.

In 1664 the modest claim to nobility which had been bestowed upon their father at the time of the *Cid* was revoked by an order of the king to retract all titles of nobility granted in Normandy in the previous thirty-four years. The brothers filed protests and, five years later, received letters confirming their titles. Thomas added to his name the designation écuyer, sieur de l'Isle by which he was frequently identified in distinction to Pierre's simple "Corneille".

ASSOCIATION WITH THE THÉÂTRE DE GUÉNÉGAUD

After Molière's death in 1673 his acting company was reconstituted to become the troupe de Guénégaud to which came also, at the king's behest, some of the best actors of the Marais. The new company sought out Thomas Corneille who began turning his plays over to them starting with *La Mort d'Achille* in 1673. His relationship with the Guénégaud proved to be the closest bond he made with any theater troupe and probably the most lucrative. It also marks the beginning of a series of collaborative works. The actors of the Guénégaud had acquired with their building a number of elaborate stage machines and requested Thomas to produce a play which could put them to use. In collaboration with de Visé he composed *Circé* (1675),[20] a lyric tragedy which enjoyed such success that the company voted to award Thomas a bonus of sixty louis.[21] The troupe then asked for another spectacular which Thomas, again with de Visé, prepared for presentation on the heels of *Circé* in November, 1675. This play was *l'Inconnu* to be followed in August, 1676 by a third machine play, *Le Triomphe des dames*. By this time Thomas had spanned nearly the entire range of theatrical productions; and so it was not surprising that the composer Lulli, having broken off relations with his librettist Quinault, should

[20] Dates in parentheses refer to the year of first performance.
[21] See entry of May 8, 1675 in the *Registre* of Lagrange cited in Reynier, *Thom. Corn.*, p. 49.

seek out Thomas as the most likely competent dramatist to make an adaptation of the opera *Psyché*, which was presented in a new form in 1678. But opera was not to Thomas' taste and, when asked to collaborate a second time, he refused until the king expressed a desire that he should cooperate. Eventually three others, Boileau and Fontenelle officially and Quinault unofficially, claimed collaboration in the new opera, *Bellérophon*, which was staged in 1679. Later the same year Thomas and de Visé wrote and presented *La Devineresse*.

De Visé's influence in Thomas Corneille's life had begun around 1673 when he was instrumental in securing Thomas' services for the troupe de Guénégaud. A highly self-assertive and energetic man, de Visé advertised his own and Thomas' plays in his newly formed periodical, the *Mercure galant*, begun in 1672. In 1682 Thomas and de Visé signed an act of association by which Thomas was recognized a full partner of the *Mercure*. He participated actively in its publication from about 1677 to 1700.

In the thirty-five year period 1650-85, the most prolific author of comedies next to Molière was Thomas Corneille. The fact is all the more significant because in the same period he also wrote more tragedies than any one of his contemporaries. In a letter of July, 1658 to the abbé de Pure, Pierre Corneille amicably chided Thomas on his disappointment at producing only one play for the season: "Mon frère vous salue, et travaille avec assez de chagrin. Il ne donnera qu'une pièce cette année." [22]

He was early esteemed a worthy competitive dramatist, as is evidenced by the fact that he was twice placed in competition with Scarron whom Thomas surpassed at his own game, that is, in creating a role for the buffoon-valet Jodelet (see below p. 44 ff).

LE FESTIN DE PIERRE

A further mark of esteem came to Thomas Corneille through his role in reviving a play by Molière. When Molière's widow decided to

---

[22] Reproduced in Pierre Corneille, *Œuvres*, éd. Marty-Laveaux (Paris, 1862-68) Vol. X, pp. 481-482. All subsequent quotations from works of Pierre Corneille refer to this edition abbreviated as *Œuvres*.

restage *Don Juan*, she turned to him for a new version, which he gave under Molière's original title, *Le Festin de Pierre* (1677). While remaining as faithful as possible to the original text, Thomas nevertheless altered a few scenes which had been found objectionable by the censors and rendered the prose into verse, under which form the play was given for one hundred and seventy years until Molière's prose original was finally restored.[23]

WORK WITH THE ACADEMY

When Pierre Corneille died in 1684, Thomas was chosen to fill his chair at the Académie française. Henceforth his efforts in the field of drama diminished as he took up scholarly pursuits for the Academy. His first work as a savant was to produce in 1687 his notes and commentaries on the *Remarques* of Vaugelas. This effort was later enlarged into the *Observations de l'Académie française sur les Remarques de M. de Vaugelas* (1704). A tireless worker he also compiled for the Academy a supplement to its Dictionary in the form of a *Dictionnaire des termes d'arts et de sciences* which appeared in September, 1694.

Elected to the Académie des Inscriptions in 1701, he proceeded to work on another encyclopedic undertaking, the *Dictionnaire universel géographique et historique*, which was completed in 1708. By this time Thomas was virtually blind and left Paris to spend his final months at Les Andelys where he died in December, 1709.

VARIETY OF THOMAS CORNEILLE'S THEATER

By virtue of the remarkable variety of tone and technique in his works, Thomas Corneille is more representative of seventeenth century French theater, taken as a whole, than either his brother or Racine. No other dramatist of his age could boast of covering more ground than he. Light comedy of intrigue, *tableaux de mœurs*, gallant tragi-comedy, farce, Cornelian drama, tragedy of deep feeling, machine spectacle

---

[23] For a comparison of the two plays see Aaron Schaffer, "Thomas Corneille's Reworking of Molière's *Don Juan*", *Modern Philology*, XIX (1921-22), pp. 163-175.

plays, and finally operas; he left little unexplored. The sources from which he derived his materials were no less varied: the Spanish *comedia*, contemporary French novels and drama, recent English history, Cassius Dio, Diodorus, Plutarch, Ovid (whom he translated), Homer, Livy, Procopius, Justin, Appian and others. A prolific and successful playwright, he wrote in the course of over forty years some forty-two dramatic pieces; and, if existing evidence is correct, he had the greatest financial success for a single play as well as the most popular first run performance in the entire century.[24]

Much of Thomas's strength as a dramatist lay in the area of dramaturgy, that repository of devices and methods which are the very heart of the playwright's craft. He came to learn very well what made a play function and appeal. Particularly conscious of the technical aspects of composition, the problem of dramaturgy doubtless occupied much of his time; for he consistently strove to give his plays an air of verisimilitude by arranging scenes logically, observing a proper lapse of time between events, justifying encounters of characters as well as their exits, entrances and motivations. His sense of timing, his flair for creating situations of dramatic irony, his ability to exploit all the potential consequences of a *quid pro quo*, his frequent use of suspense, in brief the strictly dramatic aspects of his art were the acquisitions of an exuberant apprentice. To illustrate his development of a dramatic method, we shall in the first chapter deal with Thomas Corneille as a writer of comedies and shall attempt to show how, as a practitioner of the lighter genre, he perfected most of the techniques he was to use later in tragedies, for basically much of his approach can be traced to characteristically comic devices.

A survey of his productions leads one to suspect that he catered obsequiously to the changing tastes of his age with a determination to stay in vogue. There is no doubt that this is to some extent true. But in many respects, though not always to his credit, Thomas led the fashion rather than following it. The most notable instance was his exploitation of the romanesque identity play, a type of precious and complicated tragi-comedy, the first and most famous of which was

---

[24] *La Devineresse* (1679) brought Thomas over 5600 francs and his *Timocrate* (1656) is said to have been performed over eighty times during the winter season 1656-57.

Timocrate, followed eventually by *Bérénice* (1657), *Darius* (1659) and *Pyrrhus* (1663) the most complicated of them all. These four plays, which constitute the subject of our second chapter, evinced a genuine ability to invent and present characters in a suspenseful and fast-moving plot. With a taste for contrivance that was being refined on the precious casuistry of Mlle de Scudéry's heroes and heroines, Thomas' audiences delighted in the gallant titillations which the surprise and deception of these tragi-comedies could give them.

Probably realizing the limitations of this type of play, he next sought to inject his tragedies with some of those traits for which his brother had become famous. In *Commode* (1657) he created a ruthless tyrant who curiously prefigures most of his subsequent heroes. This play has an importance far exceeding its dramatic merit. *Commode* is unique in French classical tragedy, for it sums up a tradition of conspiracy plays at a time in which conspiracy was more likely to be amorous than political. Quinault's *Amalasonte* (1657) and *Cyrus* (1658) give witness to this trend. We have chosen Commode as the key figure of an anachronism produced by the clash of the new sensibilities of the 1650's with the more sober rationale of the 1630's and 1640's, a conflict that will be examined in our third chapter in connection with Thomas Corneille's mid-career tragedies. Despite the ambiguous ring of the term, we have chosen the word Cornelian to describe this group of plays for reasons which will become apparent in later discussion. The first tragedies to enlarge on the conspiracy theme in *Commode* were *Stilicon* (1660) and *Maximian* (1662) in which are portrayed two scheming courtiers whose political ethics compare in turpitude to those of Pierre Corneille's Ptolomée. In 1668 and 1669 Thomas produced two plays which bear unmistakable similarities to two of his brother's plays. In *Laodice* (1668) he used Cléopatre of *Rodogune* as the model for his villainous heroine, and in *La Mort d'Annibal* (1669) he borrowed three of the roles and the same setting that appeared in *Nicomède*. A sixth tragedy, *Camma* (1661), completes the Cornelian plays, in which Thomas devoted his dramaturgical competence to an intensified study of moral problems.

Insofar as Thomas Corneille has survived as a literary figure in France, he has done so on the strength of a half-dozen tragedies and a few comedies. His *Ariane* (1672) and *Essex* (1678), having been frequently included in editions of Pierre Corneille's plays, are probably the best known to us today. And indeed in his own time as well as throughout the eighteenth century, these two plays figured longest in the repertory of the Théâtre Français. Voltaire in his commentaries on *Ariane* evinced genuine admiration for the younger Corneille's talent. In the following century, Nisard singled out *Ariane* for special praise and compared it favorably with Racine's *Bérénice* and *Phèdre*. His enjoyment of *Ariane*, he observed, was due to:

toute la préférence que je donne aux beautés de sentiment sur les autres beautés de l'art. *Ariane* me tire des larmes si vraies que je n'avise pas qu'il y en ait de meilleur aloi; et ni Bérénice, ni Phèdre, ni Hermïone ne me rendent moins touchante l'amante délaissée de Thésée.[25]

It is significant that *Essex* and *Ariane* have been the two plays to be honored by posterity as those which represent Thomas' best work, for the very choice of his most nearly Racinian plays pays tribute to the tremendous prestige which has been accorded to the style and manner of Racine. It does not follow, however, that Thomas owed very much to Racine as a model. In some instances it is worth pointing out that Racine might well have borrowed ideas from Thomas. The latter's *Persée et Démétrius* (1662), appearing two years before Racine's *Thébaïde*, dealt with the theme of feuding brothers in competition for a throne. The well known dilemma of Andromaque was represented in *Camma* wherein, as Lancaster has pointed out (*History*, III, p. 441), a widowed queen, faced with the prospect of losing her child if she does not agree to marry the insistent usurper, finally agrees to the marriage. Like Andromaque, Camma intends to kill herself after the ceremony. Hermione's bribing of Oreste is anticipated by several years in *Camma* wherein Hésione proposes to marry Sostrate if he will first murder Sinorix, who has scorned her. The *dilemme d'Andromaque* or some variation of it appeared in *Commode* where Helvie reluctantly agrees to marry Commode in order to prevent her father's death, and was to recur in *Maximian*. In *Antiochus* (1666) Thomas used the triangular love relationship in which father and son woo the same woman, a situation exploited by Racine in *Mithridate*.

---

[25] Désiré Nisard, *Histoire de la littérature française*, 12 éd. (Paris, 1884), Vol. IV, p. 161.

It is not our purpose to belabor the point further by enumerating the situations, themes and devices which Racine might have borrowed from Thomas; many of the similarities were doubtless coincidental, and much of Thomas' material, too, can be traced to other dramatists. Nevertheless he played a significant role in creating an atmosphere in which Racine could flourish. In our fourth chapter we shall attempt to show in three of his later tragedies, how Thomas himself fared competing with Racine in a type of play toward which he had been evolving quite independently.

Genuine originality was not easily achieved under French classical dogmatism. It was common practice to borrow ideas, lines, sometimes entire scenes from some predecessor or contemporary and present them as one's own work. Just as seventeenth century playwrights invoked the authority of an ancient source as a stamp of authenticity and dignity for the events of a dramatic piece, so some of these playwrights, less fastidious at times, were content to seek in predigested form both their data and the manner in which these data were informed. Thus, for example, did Pierre Corneille in writing *Le Cid* imitate very closely several sections of Guillen de Castro's *Mocedades del Cid*. Quinault was a shameless borrower of material. His *Mère coquette* and *Rivales* are obvious reworkings of de Visé's *Mère coquette* and Rotrou's *Deux Pucelles*.

Dramatists were quick to realize that a successful play might, with a little reworking, name-changing and modernizing, be repeated for a new audience with the freshness of an original work. It is thanks precisely to the recurrence of identical themes in the course of several generations of playwrights that the student of literature can detect, in at least one form, the evolution of attitudes, ideals and customs. The comparison is in fact facilitated by the similarities of basic situation, for contrasts and variations between original play and its later adaptation are the more discernible for having sprung from the same set of premises. It will be our purpose later to make such comparisons between *Cinna* and *Commode*, *Rodogune* and *Laodice*, and *Nicomède* and *Annibal*.

The line of demarcation between plagiarism and imitation was at best rather tenuous. Yet it would be incorrect to state that, because a considerable repertory of themes and practices had accumulated in the first half of the century, many of which were bound to be revived, the later dramatists of the century were little more than furbishers of old plays. It has frequently been contended that classic doctrine, insofar as it was codified, was formulated in its essential aspects by mid-century and that the contribution of the generation of Racine and Boileau was rather one of refined taste.[26] If Racine and his contemporaries were not original in creating a brand new product, they must nevertheless be credited with perfecting the old.

In his later years Thomas departed from the classical mould to collaborate in writing a kind of play quite different from his earlier productions. The change is a significant demonstration of the ease with which he could adapt to new tastes, an ability which Jules Wogue has described as one of Thomas' distinctive traits:

Quand on aime les imbroglios compliqués, il compose des pièces inextricables; quand on aime le burlesque, il est encore plus burlesque et cynique que Scarron... à l'époque où l'on pratique volontiers l'inconstance en amour, il écrit *l'Amour à la mode*, lorsque l'on juge la Voisin, il met à la scene *la Devinerese*, etc. Il a deux traits en commun avec son frère: la préoccupation de l'actualité, ainsi que l'art de bien nouer et de bien dénouer les intrigues.[27]

Molière and Racine, too, made a studied effort to give their audiences what was wanted and expected. Besides the general public, the tastes of certain noble patrons often had to be considered. It is not surprising, therefore, that any dramatist of this period, merely to survive professionally, should have sought to give expression to contemporary interests. The very success of his art depended to some extent upon his ability to grasp the transient infatuation of his public. Beyond this ability Molière had the vision and psychological insight to infuse his plays with more enduring qualities as well. Thomas Corneille did not probe so deeply, but he came to develop in his later comedies a keen sense of timeliness. It is very likely that his association with Donneau de Visé in publishing the *Mercure galant* contributed to his journalistic flair.

[26] Adam has chosen 1640 as the year beyond which no significant changes in classical doctrine occurred (I, p. 577 ff).
[27] *La Comédie aux XVIIᵉ et XVIIIᵉ siècles* (Paris, 1905), p. 154.

COLLABORATION WITH DE VISÉ

Beginning with *la Devineresse* (1679) he produced in collaboration with de Visé three plays which deal with the conspicuous issues of the day. At the moment that *la Devineresse* was being performed, the actual events which it portrayed were under deliberation in the *chambre ardente* in an effort to determine the fate of the famous sorceress, Catherine Monvoisin, known as la Voisin. Along with several others suspected of practicing various forms of sorcery, la Voisin was arrested in March, 1679, tried in the following months and finally executed in February, 1680. Thomas Corneille and de Visé could not have chosen more felicitously a subject better calculated to public interest. Too many well known people, including Mme de Montespan, were involved in the affairs of la Voisin not to have created curiosity about a play purporting to deal with the impostures of a sorceress. The identification of the play's protagonist, Mme Jobin, with la Voisin was inevitable.[28] The great success of the comedy fully attests to the authors' opportunistic perspicacity and to Thomas Corneille's ability to improvise a clever dramatic sequence from the disparate elements given him by de Visé.

The co-editors of the *Mercure galant* were soon to collaborate on two more plays, the texts of which unfortunately no longer exist. In 1681 appeared *la Pierre philosophale*, a satirical treatment of Rosicrucians. The play had but two performances. More successful was *l'Usurier*, staged in 1685 and dealing with *la question d'argent*. Judging from what was said about the play in contemporary accounts, one may conclude that its authors had gone far to expose the abuses of bankers and "riches roturiers" and in so doing created a lively defensive reaction among those who saw themselves too closely identified

---

[28]   The authors made the gesture of a protest against a precise identification but admitted the possibility of coincidental resemblances. In the "Au Lecteur" one reads:

Tant de gens de toutes conditions ont été chercher les devineresses, qu'on ne doit point s'étonner si on a trouvé lieu de faire quelques applications. Il est pourtant vrai (et on se croit obligé de le protester) qu'on n'a eu aucune vue particulière en faisant la pièce; mais comme dans cette sorte d'ouvrage, on doit travailler particulièrement à corriger les défauts des hommes ... on n'en tirerait aucun profit, s'il était déguisé de telle sorte qu'il fût impossible que personne s'y reconnût.

in the play.[29] It appears to be the first play produced in France dealing extensively with questions of banking, and as such testifies at an early date to the incipient stages of a socio-economic problem which was to become the subject of numerous plays in the eighteenth and nineteenth centuries.

There is some question whether Thomas collaborated with de Visé on *Les Dames vengées* (1695). Reynier (p. 246) claims he did and interprets the play as a retort to Boileau's *Satire X, Sur les femmes* (1692). The play tells how an upright heroine, Hortense, avenges her sex against the promiscuous Léandre who falls genuinely in love with her. Failing to recover in time from his frivolous and scornful attitudes toward women, Léandre loses Hortense to a convent. According to Reynier the comedy attests to its authors' sympathies with the "Modernes" whose cause was being supported, particularly after Boileau's satire, by a strong feminine contingent. But even if Thomas did not help compose this play his proclivity toward an essentially modern point of view is evidenced by the fact that since 1674 he had abandoned conventional sources for his comedies in favor of current events.

Thomas Corneille played an important role in the evolution of seventeenth century French drama. He never did rise to Racine's height of genius in exploring the emotions although his later tragedies were noteworthy attempts in this direction. Nor did he succeed in equaling his brother's portrayal of the man of destiny summed up in the phrase: "Je suis maître de moi comme de l'univers." But in the course of seventeen tragedies, he produced a number of striking portrayals, including some which he introduced to the French stage. He strove for and, we believe, achieved an autonomy of creativeness which has all too often been buried under the laurels of Pierre Corneille and Racine.

---

[29] See Mélèse, *Donneau de Visé*, pp. 177-180.

I. APPRENTICESHIP IN COMEDY

ANTECEDENTS

With his initial play, *Les Engagements du hasard* (1649),[1] Thomas Corneille stepped into a milieu of vigorous dramatic activity. Since the early 1630's the work of a new group of playwrights had begun to consolidate a public interest in drama, particularly in Paris where two major theater companies, the troupe du Marais and the Hôtel de Bourgogne, were regularly performing their plays. A growing stability in political life and social institutions under the ministry of Cardinal Richelieu doubtless contributed much to create an atmosphere in which dramatic art could flourish. The playwrights themselves, in addition to providing fodder for histrionic talents, had begun, following the tradition of the Pléiade, to contribute as well to the formation of an *ars poetica* which was to become an important part of French classical doctrine. Attempts to apply the critical standards of modified Aristotelian poetics to contemporary drama may be witnessed in Jean Mairet's preface to *Sylvanire* as early as 1631. From the excitement surrounding the presentation of Pierre Corneille's *Le Cid* six years later there developed an increased awareness not only of dramatic craftsmanship but also of public spectatorship. The insults and polemics of this famous *querelle*, enhanced and dignified by the adjudication of the newly founded French Academy, constituted a candid advertising campaign which, in the present day, might well elicit envy from a professional huckster.

[1] Where the dates of first performance are conjectural, we have accepted the authority of H. C. Lancaster (*History*) and S. Wilma Deierkauf-Holsboer (*Le Théâtre du Marais*, Paris, 1954) who concur in every instance. For a complete listing of dates see Appendix.

The dramatist most successful in substantiating his critical opinions with creditable works was Pierre Corneille. But he was by no means alone. A fair selection of the serious productions posterity has chosen to honor most from the years 1630 to 1650 must include, in addition to Mairet's *Sophonisbe* (1632) and Corneille's *Cid*, the latter's *Horace* (1640), *Cinna* (1640-1) and *Polyeucte* (1642?); DuRyer's *Alcionée* (1637), *Saül* (1640) and *Scévole* (1644); Tristan l'Hermite's *Mariane* (1636) and *La Mort de Sénèque* (1643-4); and Rotrou's *Venceslas* (1647) and *Cosroès* (1648).

Of the plays that have endured from this period the pre-eminence of tragedies over comedies bespeaks a gravity matching the serious concern that dramatists were experiencing in regard to the proper function of their art. Was it to be based on an appeal to an essentially rational sense of curiosity or, on the contrary, to an emotional one? Professor Georges May has demonstrated rather convincingly that dramatic taste in the generation of Pierre Corneille tended toward the rational appreciation of tragedy whereas the generation of Racine preferred a deeply emotional involvement in tragic representations.[2]

Accepting this thesis, one can begin to account as well for the popular emergence in the 1640's of a highly rationalistic form of comedy whose appeal was anything but emotional. We refer to a rash of light comedies adapted from plays of Calderon, Rojas, Lope de Vega and other Spanish writers. D'Ouville, Rotrou, Scarron, and eventually, Boisrobert and Thomas Corneille were the chief exponents of the *comedia* in France. The nature of these plays was such as to demand a constant attention to external details which, with little regard for *vraisemblance*, were intended to create complicated situations of frivolous humor. It was this tradition that Thomas Corneille followed in his first play.

THE IMBROGLIOS OF SPANISH INSPIRATION

Since our main concern is with Thomas Corneille's serious drama, we do not wish to involve the reader in a detailed treatment of all the comedies. No attempt will be made to observe a strict chronological

[2] Georges May, *Tragédie cornélienne, tragédie racinienne* (Urbana, 1948).

presentation or to analyze plot and structure beyond the point which is useful to demonstrate significant stages in the dramatist's development. For this reason the comedies, all but one of which are of Spanish inspiration, will be grouped for summary treatment.[3]

COMEDIES OF SPANISH INSPIRATION:
LES ENGAGEMENTS DU HASARD

Throughout his long career, Thomas never tired of making adaptations of *comedias*. From *Les Engagements du hasard* in 1649 to *Don César d'Avalos* in 1674, he repeated the same type of situation from play to play with only minor variations. The plot of *Les Engagements du hasard*, taken from Calderon's *Casa con dos puertas mala es de guardar* and his *Empeños de un acaso*, is typical. It describes a veritable hodgepodge of episodes tied loosely together by a love interest and animated by a series of *quid pro quo* occurring in such rapid succession as to make their contrived nature all too obvious. In Acts IV and V a closet is used no less than seven times to hide first one suitor then another as suspicions are successively created, allayed, duplicated and finally dispersed to allow the reconciliation and marriages that everyone knew had to occur. Heroines, disguised under a "coiffe abattue", coquettishly force their lovers into ironic avowals of love for a person who does not exist. The utter confusion of relationships thus created is a feature that Thomas Corneille was to use later in his identity plays, especially in *Pyrrhus*, as we shall see.

The embroiling complexity of *Les Engagements du hasard* is well expressed by the stupefaction of a valet, Clarin, who, when asked where one of the heroines is hiding, confesses:

> Je ne sais ce qu'il faut répondre cette fois,
> Et j'ignore, Monsieur, tant ce succès m'étonne,
> Si vous me demandez la mauvaise, ou la bonne,
> La fausse ou bien la vraie; et dans un tel souci,
> Pour ne me point tromper, l'une est là, l'autre ici.
> (V, 9)

---

[3] For more detailed information and analysis of the Spanish comedies of Thomas Corneille, one is referred to Ernest Martinenche, *La Comedia espagnole en France* (Paris, 1900) and Georg Michaelis, *Die sogenannten "comédies espagnoles" des Thomas Corneille* ... (Berlin, 1914), and for all Thomas' comedies to Lancaster, *History* and Reynier, *Thom. Corn.*

Despite obvious weaknesses there are certain devices in the play which Thomas was later to perfect into clever techniques of dramatic construction.

His ability to create a *quid pro quo* and extract from it all the possible consequences in an orderly, minute fashion is notable. But his fascination with this technical problem led him to neglect the more important considerations of verisimilitude in human relations. Anyone reading *Les Engagements du hasard* would properly conclude that its author, although very conscious of craftsmanship, needed lessons in the art of simplicity.

LE FEINT ASTROLOGUE

In his second comedy, Thomas Corneille showed a little improvement. He took the subject of *Le Feint astrologue* (1650) from Calderon's play of the same name, *El Astrologo fingido*. In Thomas' play a valet, Philipin, claims that his master has powers of clairvoyance and prescience. Taking advantage of the misunderstandings which abound in the comedy, Don Fernand and Philipin astound the other characters with feats of necromancy. A staple situation involving two pairs of lovers is swept into the background to make way for their cavorting and a display of burlesque erudition which prefigures Sganarelle's verbal gymnastics in Molière's *Médecin malgré lui*. Like Sganarelle, Don Fernand amusingly overwhelms his victim, Léonard, with a conjurer's vocabulary:

Fernand: Pour vous dire en deux mots, Monsieur, ce que j'en pense,
　　　　 Vénus aux amoureux promet beaucoup de biens,
　　　　 Et Saturne peut tout sur les Saturniens:
　　　　 Mais la triplicité de cette conjoncture,
　　　　 Ainsi que l'union d'Hécate avec Mercure,
　　　　 Combinant leurs aspects, ou les rétrogradant
　　　　 Sur l'horizon fatal d'un bizarre ascendant,
　　　　 Pourrait paralaxer sur un cerveau si tendre...
Leonard: Ce discours est si haut que j'ai peine à l'entendre.
　　　　 De grâce, en ma faveur, pour éclaircissement,
　　　　 Expliquez-vous un peu plus populairement.
Fernand: Ce sont termes de l'art.

(II, 3)

A suppleness in the dramatist's style and a crispness in the movement of characters from one equivocal situation to another in this play account for Thomas' ability to evoke momentary laughter. But the humor is such that it requires constant renewal with each successive scene.

One need not look far to find the source of Thomas' early deficiencies. They lay inherent in the Spanish originals which he chose to adapt but failed to predigest. Ernest Martinenche has called attention to the irony of the fact that Thomas used two Spanish plays as a basis for *Les Engagements du hasard* whereas either one would have been more than sufficient (*La Comedia espagnole*, p. 340 ff.). Still an apprentice eager to learn the rules of dramatic art, Thomas Corneille labored all too conscientiously to capture the flavor of his models with the result that his dramaturgical method made itself unduly conspicuous in the fabric of his plays. One comedy in particular reveals an obsession for technique.

LE GALANT DOUBLÉ

The entire plot of *Le Galant doublé* (1660) is devoted to illustrating a dramaturgical device. The hero, Fernand, in an effort to lead a double life, barely succeeds in deceiving anyone. Instead all his contrivances are aimed at establishing the misconceptions which would enable him to play a double role and court two ladies simultaneously. He never quite succeeds in convincing the other characters of his dual existence. Hence any potential human interest the play might have possessed is shrouded in dramaturgical tergiversation. The action does not support the meager love interest so much as it illustrates the difficulty of the hero to achieve a double identity. In other words, Thomas used the very plot of his play to create a device which, if he had wished, he might have taken for granted as a hypothesis of the initial situation in the comedy.

In only two such productions did he achieve something of a success several years later. These plays, *Le Baron d'Albikrac* (1667) and *La Comtesse d'Orgueil* (1670), take us well into the period of his major tragedies and for this reason represent an interesting differentiation in his conceptions of the two genres. While his tragedies were progressing toward structural unity, which was to culminate in the stark simplicity of *Ariane* (1672), the comedies remained at least as complicated and multiform as *Les Engagements du hasard* and *Le Feint astrologue*.

LE BARON D'ALBIKRAC

Le Baron d'Albikrac and *La Comtesse d'Orgueil* are frankly amusing, for each portrays an eccentric character interesting in his own right. The former satirizes an amorous widow who at age sixty fancies herself in great demand among the young nobles of her acquaintance. La Tante, as she is called in the play, develops a passion for young Oronte who is in love with her niece, Angélique. With the aid of a friend, Léandre, and this friend's servant, Oronte contrives to postpone the elderly widow's ardent advances all the while striving to preserve her good will, for he will need her consent to marry Angélique. (Thomas later repeated this situation in his tragedy, *Théodat* [1672].) First Léandre feigns interest in La Tante, but failing to divert her attention from Oronte, finally has his servant LaMontagne impersonate le baron d'Albikrac who is supposed to have been courting the old lady by correspondence. He appears and humorously mistakes Angélique for her aunt whose age he surmises to be twenty-one. Not easily put off, La Tante plans to foist the alleged baron on Angélique. This contretemps necessitates the invention of a fiction whereby Oronte is made out to be the long lost secret nephew of la Tante, hence a blood relation and unable to marry her. The denouement is brought about by a series of ruses involving so many peripeteias that the deceivers cannot keep abreast of their own deceit.

To appreciate the visual effects of the play, one must imagine a stage setting representing a parlor adjoined on both sides by rooms which in turn communicate with others to form a circuit. A character scurries off stage to perform an assigned task and returns moments later to discover that his commission has already been superseded and annulled by another. Meanwhile at least one other character has set out to mitigate the impressions, by now false, of the first character who in turn is on his way to a new assignment. One thinks of the effect that might be made by a performance taking place on a carrousel.

LA COMTESSE D'ORGUEIL

Similar in structure and plot is *La Comtesse d'Orgueil* in which the role corresponding to that of la Tante is given to a vain marquis who is foiled in his attempts to win his brother's sweetheart. The role of the comtesse, like that of Albikrac, is conjured up and impersonated by a servant as a decoy to divert the marquis, and the play concludes in much the same manner as *Le Baron d'Albikrac*.

At one point in *Albikrac*, the action becomes so thoroughly confused that Thomas uses a scene (V, 2) merely to inform the characters of the backlog of events that they have been unable to assimilate owing to their frenzied activities. In both these plays, ruses are compounded to the point of canceling one another's effects. This is a fair indication that Thomas was crowding more into these comedies than he could conveniently handle. The result was that his technique impeded the progress of the plots.

There is perhaps symbolic significance in the fact that the character represented by the title role never appears on stage in either *Le Baron d'Albikrac* or *La Comtesse d'Orgueil*. Thomas appears to have considered most important not the character he portrayed, but the one whose absence, or supposed presence, is essential to the machinations of the plot. In a sense the titles announce the functional device of the intrigue in much the same manner that *feint astrologue* reveals with greater candor the method by which the author intended to create his humorous situations.

DON CÉSAR D'AVALOS

Don César d'Avalos (1674) presents a variation on the theme of mistaken identity but in most respects recreates the impressions of *La Comtesse d'Orgueil*. Situations from *Les Engagements du hasard* are also repeated. The hero, having lost his baggage and papers of identification en route to conclude an arranged marriage, arrives to find his fiancée being pursued by an impostor who has usurped his identity. The plot describes his struggle to regain his name and fiancée who, meanwhile, has fallen in love with him, unaware that he is her intended husband. The impostor is exposed, and Don César marries his beloved.

Don César d'Avalos enjoyed meager success, but *Le Baron d'Albikrac* and *La Comtesse d'Orgueil* survived their first run performances by more than a century to be shown at the Comédie Française 134 times and 59 times respectively. If it were possible to establish the date of *Le Baron d'Albikrac*, one might argue that Thomas supplied Molière with situations for *L'Avare*; but since the reverse may be true, no useful purpose will be served in pursuing the matter until clear evidence is revealed.

By making reference in *Albikrac* (II, 10) to the investigation of nobiliary titles, in which he was involved himself, and in *La Comtesse d'Orgueil* to the morals of gay clerics, Thomas adopted the practice of alluding to contemporary situations to raise incidental points of topical interest. We have seen how in his final comedies, such as *La Devineresse*, he was to expand such allusions to comprise entire plays.

LES ILLUSTRES ENNEMIS

Of all Thomas' plays, the one which has probably the most characteristically Hispanic flavor is *Les Illustres ennemis* (1655), produced in competition with Scarron's adaptation of the same original, Rojas Zorrilla's *Obligados y ofendidos*.[4] In it Thomas exploited the theme of honor by creating a situation in which the two heroes become friends and defend each other only to discover later that honor requires them to seek each other's death. The play offers a curious example of the kind of paradoxical situation which Thomas was to use as the staple element in his identity plays, for the friendly enemies of this comedy find themselves in a predicament not unlike that which was to occur in *Timocrate*.

---

[4] Boisrobert, too, entered the competition. For the probable order in which the three men composed their respective adaptations, see Lancaster, *History*, III, p. 69 ff.

Despite the stereotyped nature of his adaptations from the Spanish, Thomas Corneille began as early as 1650 to show signs of originality. Not content merely to imitate, he began to embellish by imposing a form of Gallic wit on the French speaking Spaniards who peopled his plays. *Don Bertrand de Cigarral* (1651) and *Le Geôlier de soimême* (1655), as we shall see shortly, present individuals who stand out in pleasant contrast to the conventional roles of *Les Engagements du hasard*.

L'AMOUR À LA MODE

For the most part, however, his early comedies interest us today not for their intrinsic value as drama but insofar as they reflect tastes and attitudes of Parisian audiences in the 1650's. In the year following *Le Feint astrologue* he varied his treatment of Spanish subjects by creating a comedy of manners under the title *L'Amour à la mode* (1651).[5] The hero, Oronte, is a spokesman for those careless lovers of the Don Juan tradition who would

> Pour ne risquer rien en pratiquant les femmes,
> Les adorer en gros toutes confusément,
> Et les mésestimer toutes séparément.
> Voilà la bonne règle.
>
> (IV, 1)

Oronte's motto, reiterated in various forms throughout the comedy, has led numerous readers of the play to see in it a lack of moral earnestness characteristic of the period of the Fronde. It is alleged that Mlle de Rambouillet typified this spirit of fickleness when she chose to witness a performance of *L'Amour à la mode* in preference to Pierre Corneille's *Pertharite* (Lancaster, *History*, II, p. 6).

INFLUENCE OF THE SALONS

The fact that Thomas was at this time a promising young playwright and had begun to frequent the gatherings of some eminent society

---

[5]   Derived from Antonio de Solís' *El Amor al uso*.

ladies of the day suggests that part of his early success was fostered by the good wishes and support of fellow socialites assembling in the refined atmosphere of the salons. From Reynier we have the following account:

Thomas avait été fort recherché dans les sociétés élégantes, particulière-ment dans celles où régnait encore le goût du romanesque et du précieux et qui continuaient, à leur manière, les traditions de l'Hôtel de Ram-bouillet. Après avoir été le protégé de la comtesse de Noailles, de la comtesse de Fiesque, de la duchesse de Montpensier, il avait été fort bien accueilli dans le salon de Mme Deshoulières qui, plus jeune que Mlle de Scudéry, recueillit vers 1665 l'héritage de l'illustre Sapho: il y avait fréquenté Pellison, Benserade, Ménage, Conrart, Fléchier, Quinault, dont il était le rival très courtois, Perrault et Charpentier... le duc de la Rochefoucauld, le duc de Montausier. (*Thom. Corn.*, pp. 71-72)

There are clear indications in his plays that his association with the salons gave him a taste for gallant *badinage*. *L'Amour à la mode* is the first to show what will turn out to be a vigorous obsession with the sinuosities of *précieux* logic, particularly as it was applied to love.

LE BERGER EXTRAVAGANT

The influence of the salons may also account for Thomas' selection of his next play, *Le Berger extravagant* (1652), which is unique in being the only comedy he wrote, excepting those of which he was co-author, that does not have a Spanish source. It is based on an earlier novel of the same name by Sorel. A revival of interest in pastoral literature, discernible in the years immediately preceding the play, helps to explain why Thomas decided to portray a fatuous shepherd frolicking about in a sylvan milieu inhabited by would-be rustics. A new edition of d'Urfé's *L'Astrée* appeared in 1647 to be followed in 1650 by the publication of DuRyer's *Amaryllis*, which had existed previously only in manuscript. Tristan's reworking of a comedy by Rotrou resulted in the production of another *Amarillis* (1652) called a pastoral by its author and played with great success. The hero of Thomas Corneille's play is reported to have witnessed one hundred performances of *Amarillis*, a play described by one of the other characters as a "vilain spectacle".

The most interesting innovation of *Le Berger extravagant* is Thomas' use of a play within the play. In previous comedies he had given certain characters the means of duping others with the help of minor connivances. In *Le Berger extravagant* several members of the cast purposely assume a basic error and begin to play their roles accordingly. The inner action begins in Act III where Lysis' fellow shepherds agree among themselves to honor his disguise as an innocent, persecuted young maiden.

The conspiracy against Lysis is deliberate and concerted. He alone is ignorant of the ruse being perpetrated on him, although within this deception he is given to believe that he is deceiving the others under his feminine disguise. Before his entrance in scene 2 of Act III, Hircan, one of the courtly shepherds and the producer-director of the inner play, explains to Angélique how things are to take place. She joins in the fun and suggests a distribution of roles:

> Donc à bien réussir votre esprit s'étudie.
> La diversité plaît dans une comédie;
> Et j'ose m'assurer que la nôtre ira bien,
> Les uns bergers, moi nymphe, et vous magicien.
>
> (III, 1)

Since *Le Berger extravagant* on its first level of presentation is already a highly affected performance, the actors playing the role of courtiers who in turn play at being shepherds and shepherdesses, the further illusion begins to endanger the basic reality of the play. So frivolous has the action become at this point that Corneille took the precaution of warning the audience that the whole matter is to be taken in jest:

Angélique: Le rare passe-temps que vous nous préparez!
Hircan: S'il ne vous charme pas, du moins vous en rirez.
> (III, 1)

Just as the bewhiskered Lysis is about to enter, assured that Hircan's magic makes him look like a shepherdess, Charite momentarily loses countenance and has to be sobered by Angélique:

Charite: Le plaisant personnage!
Angélique: Vous gâterez la piece à rire davantage.
            Que chacun se contraigne.
> (III, 3)

And again after Lysis has exposed the horrible misfortunes of his ill-fated youth Charite exclaims:

> O le plaisant récit!

and has to be reminded by Lucide:

> Ils ont mon frère et lui concerté ce qu'il dit.
>
> (III, 4)

Charite's irrepressible urge to laugh, an urge which an actor must normally suppress categorically during the action of a play, in these instances is a manner of establishing direct rapport between audience and actor, since, by laughing while the others are soberly playing their inner roles, Charite is reducing herself to the spectator's point of view. She thus becomes a prompter of the audience and intermediary between spectator and stage action.

It is questionable whether the device makes for good theater. Certainly in serious drama it cannot be made obvious. In a comedy as lighthearted as *Le Berger extravagant*, however, it is permissible and, in its fashion, effective. What interests us most here is what it reveals about Thomas Corneille's dramatic self-consciousness, that is, his awareness of the fact that somehow his play must make a special appeal to the audience beyond that afforded by the mere objective presentation of a series of humorous events.

LE CHARME DE LA VOIX

Thomas Corneille was to experience one theatrical failure before achieving startling success with *Timocrate*. In *Le Charme de la voix* (1656?), generally recognized as one of his weakest plays, he adapted another *comedia* while admitting ironically in his dedicatory épître, that the reason for his own play's failure lay in the fact that he remained too faithful to his model:

J'ai rendu si religieusement jusqu'ici ce que j'ai cru devoir aux auteurs Espagnols qui m'ont servi de guides dans les sujets comiques qui ont paru de moi sur la scène avec quelque succès, qu'on ne doit pas trouver étrange, si leur en ayant fait partager la gloire, je refuse de me charger de toute la honte qui a suivi le malheur de ce dernier, puisqu'en effet j'eusse peut-être moins failli, si je ne me fusse pas attaché si étroitement à la conduite de D. Augustin Moreto, qui l'a traité dans sa langue; sous le titre de *Lo que puede la apprehension* [sic] (I, pp. 490-491).

He goes on to explain that he had opposed the project from the beginning but had surrendered to the insistence of a friend. In self-defense he maintained that the Spanish original was to blame,

> ... que quelque soin que l'on apportât à les justifier [les caractères] pour le faire paraître avec quelque grâce sur notre théâtre, il serait impossible d'en venir à bout, sans faire voir toujours ceux qui sont intéressés dans cette intrigue plus capricieux que raisonnables (p. 491).

His diagnosis stands valid today, for the comedy demands highly contrived circumstances indeed in order to sustain the strange motives of the principal characters.

The proposition of the play is simply that a man is capable of falling in love with a lady upon hearing her sing, and nothing else. He need know nothing more about her, may not even be able to recognize her physically. But upon hearing her voice, he is absolutely convinced of his love. Considering the fact that the hero, having been charmed by a feminine voice before the events of the play begin, does not match the voice with its possessor, Fénise, until the last scene of Act V, one may well conceive that the execution of the plot involved numerous detours.

Despite the fact that *le Charme de la voix* abounds in *quid pro quo*, the play gives evidence of Thomas Corneille's effort to infuse his comedies of this period with the sobriety of potentially tragic events. The comic action conceals only slightly a problem of dynastic succession. Fédéric, father of Fénise, represents serious interests of state and is constantly invoking reason of state to support his policies. Much of the simple *badinage* characteristic of earlier plays has been eliminated. *Le Charme de la voix* may be viewed as a step in Thomas Corneille's evolution toward tragi-comedy.

TWO EARLY TRIUMPHS:
DON BERTRAND DE CIGARRAL AND
LE GEÔLIER DE SOI-MÊME

After *Le Feint astrologue*, Thomas produced one of his best comedies, *Don Bertrand de Cigarral* (1651). Since this play epitomizes some of

Thomas' best comic verve and a typical sampling of dramatic devices, we shall analyse it in some detail. Like its predecessors, *Don Bertrand* was based on a Spanish original, Rojas' *Entre bobos anda el juego*, but does not show the diffuseness characteristic of his first two adaptations.

Don Bertrand is a crude miser, not an unworthy predecessor of Molière's Harpagon in many respects. Like Harpagon Bertrand plans to marry a young lady whom he will accept without dowry. He makes every effort to minimize the expenses of the wedding as Harpagon will, and he is bested in his marital plans, not by a son as in *L'Avare*, but by a cousin who, however, like Cléante, depends on the inheritance of the old miser. Molière was familiar with Thomas' play, for his troupe offered it eleven times between 1659 and 1661.[6]

Although Thomas violated the unity of place by moving the action from Madrid in Act I to a country inn for the other four acts, he created a well unified plot. For the first time he gave to his plot a pivotal character around whom all the events revolve. Bertrand, though not physically present in Act I, is its central figure since the nature of his letter to Don Garcie and the colorful reports of his valet, Guzman, do as much to describe him as an actual confrontation on stage would do. The rather disgusting portrait which Guzman draws of him in scene 2 is well motivated, moreover, for not only must the audience be informed of his character but also Isabelle who, until now, has heard nothing about her recently chosen fiancé.

Through Acts II and III Bertrand is shown doing his best to expedite the marriage. Beginning in Act IV, having come to suspect that Isabelle is lacking in mental stability, Bertrand has the problem of getting rid of her. Despite the reversal in his tactics, there is no real violation of unity of action since everything he does is motivated by his greed and contributes to his portrayal as miser.

Two scenes of this play illustrate particularly well the progress Thomas Corneille has made in the use of deception. Upon meeting his young fiancée, Bertrand has the impression that she is not endowed with much imagination and wishes to test her reactions by having his

[6] Between 1681 and 1705, *Don Bertrand* was performed at the Comédie Française seventy-seven times, making it one of the most successful comedies in France before Molière's (Lancaster, *History*, II, p. 757).

cousin, Alvar, tell a love story. Alvar is only too pleased to relate under the guise of pure fiction the circumstances of his first encounter with a beautiful lady, how he had saved her from an attacking bull, fallen in love with her, and how, later, to his chagrin he was asked to second a friend who was to be married to this very lady. Isabelle listening to this account is quick to penetrate the anonymity of the tale and realize that she is the lady in question and Alvar, the hero. What is masterful in this scene is the manner in which Bertrand is included in the story without his realizing it.

This technique or some variation of it is not rare in seventeenth century French drama. Many are the declarations of love which are preceded by a long discussion in the most general and non-committal terms, but it is not usual to preserve the anonymity beyond the point where the individuals involved understand the key to it. This Corneille succeeded in doing first by having Bertrand be the one to request that a story be told and by keeping him present while it is related. Suspense is aroused during the long *récit* by Alvar because each line makes more imminent the possibility that Bertrand will discover Alvar's and Isabelle's love for each other. Alvar brings the events from the past to the immediate present in such a way that it becomes a fine distinction at one point whether he is still relating his story or is acting and feeling it in reality. In his narration he says of the hero:

> Il soupire, il lui parle [à la dame], et devant son rival,
> Sans qu'il s'en aperçoive, il lui conte son mal.
> Elle en paraît surprise, il l'attendrit sans doute,
> Avec émotion il voit qu'elle l'écoute;
> Mais sa seule espérance est dans le désespoir,
> Puisqu'elle s'abandonne à son triste devoir.   (II, 4)

The fact that this *récit* is rendered in the present tense facilitates the confusion which Thomas Corneille purposely created between the past events recounted and the present moment in the play. The couplet above beginning "Il soupire" and ending "son mal" serve, then, the double function of stage directions and dialogue. Isabelle, when asked to comment on the adventure continues the fiction and opines that the lady of the story, too, is worthy of pity and is in love with her rescuer. In so saying Isabelle actually exceeds the limits suggested by the *récit*, for she takes it upon herself to inject an element of certainty which Alvar had not permitted himself. Nothing in Alvar's story had given evidence of the lady's feelings toward her fiancé. Nevertheless, Isabelle asserts:

> De cette dame ainsi le malheur est extrême,
> Car enfin elle perd ce que sans doute elle aime;
> Et pour comble de maux, dans son affliction
> On la livre à l'objet de son aversion.

(II, 4)

Here Isabelle is either projecting herself into the fiction or, surely having guessed by now what Alvar is talking about, is protesting in her own behalf and giving him assurance of her love for him. Alvar replies:

> Que dites-vous, Madame? Ah! s'il osait le croire,
> Qu'en un si grand malheur il trouverait de gloire.

This spirited reaction to her encouraging comments should have aroused suspicion in Bertrand's mind but he is too obtuse to realize that a love scene is unfolding under his very eyes.

Molière was to exploit this device on several occasions notably in *Le malade imaginaire* (1673) where Cléante, under the pretext of presenting "un petit opéra qu'on a fait depuis peu" for the amusement of Angélique's father, fiancé, and father-in-law, declares in song his love for Angélique, who in turn sings her affections to him.[7] Molière does not improve upon Corneille's use of the situation, however, for the scene from *Le Malade imaginaire* lacks the virtue of being integral with the plot. It is, rather, supplementary to the play in the manner of an *intermède* in which no new action develops. Cléante and Angélique are both already aware of their mutual love and have declared it to each other before this scene begins. On the other hand in Corneille's play, Alvar and Isabelle had not had occasion to make their declarations privately. There is therefore no prearranged contrivance or complicity between them when they meet in the presence of Bertrand. They must improvise. The effect of their doing so, Alvar's surprise at seeing Isabelle, the cleverness with which they make their avowals despite this surprise create an irony of situation which is in the best tradition of comedy.

[7] Molière used similar situations in *L'Etourdi*, *l'Ecole des maris*, *L'Amour médecin*, *Le Sicilien*, and *L'Avare*.

The second scene in which Thomas Corneille gives evidence of his improved craftsmanship appears in Act V and requires a brief introduction. At the end of Act II Bertrand's sister Léonor, an eccentric, husband-seeking spinster who faints seven times a day, has invited Alvar to visit her during the night. Instead of doing so, Alvar meets with Isabelle and is forced to hide in her room upon the approach of Félix, who also has come to court Isabelle. By mistake Félix knocks on Léonor's door and declares his love for her, thinking he is speaking to Isabelle. Léonor in turn believes she is talking with Alvar, whom she was expecting. Bertrand arrives and discovers Alvar, who, in the hope of diverting his suspicions from Isabelle, pretends to be wooing Léonor, who by now is lying on the floor in a faint. Léonor regains consciousness just in time to catch the last words of Alvar and is left at the end of this act thinking that he loves her. In Act V, however, Félix explains to Léonor the confusion of the previous night telling how he mistook her for Isabelle and how she mistook him for Alvar. He concludes with the following words which Bertrand arrives just in time to hear:

> Oui c'est moi
> Qui cette même nuit vous ai promis ma foi,
> Et me suis engagé de tout mettre en pratique
> Pour vous soustraire au joug d'un pouvoir tyrannique,
> Abuser Don Bertrand, vous tirer de ses mains;
> Et faire réussir de plus justes desseins;
> Mais j'ai cru qu'en effet . . .
>
> (V, 5)

At this point Bertrand interrupts and, under the misconception that what he has heard applies to his sister and Félix, tries to give her to him. At the end of scene 5 and in all of scene 6, then, one sees a clever use of *quid pro quo* in a double sense. No sooner is one misunderstanding dissipated than another is being created to replace it. Yet the two are organically intermingled, for Félix' explanation serves at the same time to clarify the situation for Léonor and falsify it for Bertrand.

Don Bertrand has the advantage of a closely woven plot. Although it would have been possible to eliminate Léonor and Félix, they are useful to create the confusion necessary for the night meeting of Alvar and Isabelle. The use of asides is diminished in this play, and the obvious tricks of disguise, *cachette*, lost rings, intercepted letters are eliminated. Thomas depended instead on more refined techniques to bring about the desired misunderstandings. He has passed in *Don Bertrand* from physical *trucages* to the use of deliberate acts on the part of characters (Guzman's extinguishing a candle) and propitious timing (Bertrand's arrival in time to overhear Félix).

With the exception of two long speeches, the dialogue is lively, and each of these speeches has its redeeming feature. The first is the long *récit* by Alvar, which remains absorbing because of the presence of Bertrand who might at any moment pierce through its fiction. The second is a long discourse by Bertrand on his noble qualities spoken to Don Garcie in an effort to prove what a desirable match Bertrand is for his daughter. In addition to the purely comic nature of the utterances, Thomas took a further precaution to keep the scene from dragging. He had Bertrand prepare the audience with the following preamble:

Bertrand: M'interromprez-vous point?
D. Garcie: A quoi bon?
Ber.   Mon dessein
          Est de parler longtemps.
D.G.   Parlez jusqu'à demain.
Ber.   Posément?
D.G.   Posément.
Ber.   Et vous saurez vous taire?
D.G.   Tant que vous parlerez.
Ber.   Écoutez donc, beau-père.
                                        (IV, 1)

Follows the sixty-nine line self-description by Bertrand which Don Garcie interrupts only to be hushed by Bertrand in much the same manner as that of the protesting Cinna being silenced by Auguste. Bertrand reprimands Don Garcie for breaking in:

          Vous avez l'humeur prompte.
          Soyez de par le diable attentif à mon conte,
          Ecoutez jusqu'au bout, vous parlerez après.
                              (IV, 1)

Dramaturgically speaking *Don Bertrand* represents a climax in Thomas Corneille's early career. Like Jodelet in *Le Geôlier de soi-même*, produced four years later, Bertrand is sufficiently picturesque and absorbing to compensate for a certain amount of background complexity and even profit by it. Some of the speeches uttered by the title character, vulgar though they may be, give witness to Corneille's ability to turn out natural, comic verse well suited to the physique and temperament of the character he sought to portray. As an individual Bertrand stands out, in his fashion, as one of the most memorable theatrical personalities of the young Corneille. The most useful lesson that Thomas learned from *Don Bertrand* was to focus attention on a central figure. A few years later he produced another successful comedy by following this lesson. As if to capitalize on the peculiar talents of the popular comic actor Jodelet,[8] he created a comedy around the laughable exploits of a buffoon disguised as king.

LE GEÔLIER DE SOI-MÊME (1655)

Le Geôlier de soi-même, based on Calderon' *Alcaide de sí mismo,* was first played with great success in competition with Scarron's less successful version of the same original. A number of the changes made by Thomas Corneille might well have been suggested by Scarron whose *Gardien de soi-même* preceded Thomas' by several months.

Two general observations should be made at the outset in regard to *Le Geôlier de soi-même.* First, it represents a further step in the evolution of its author's taste for the tragi-comic paradox soon to reach fruition in the romanesque tragedies. Secondly it is significant in demonstrating that he was capable of building his best comic situations around a prominent central figure. We have observed how his first two plays lacked a point of focus owing to the proliferation of trivial events distributed among conventional characters. *Don Bertrand, Le Geôlier* and to some extent *le Baron d'Albikrac,* on the other hand, represent his efforts to intensify the comic impact by concentrating it into one figure.[9]

---

[8] Stage name of Julien Bédeau whose long career in Parisian theater began in 1610 at the Théâtre du Marais. Here he played the role of Cliton in *Le Menteur* and *La Suite du Menteur.* He also performed at the Hôtel de Bourgogne, notably in several of Scarron's plays whose titles frequently included the name Jodelet.

[9] Fontenelle in his *Vie de Corneille* saw fit to mention *Don Bertrand* and *Le Geôlier de soi-même* along with *Le Menteur* as the best examples of comedy

His continuing preoccupation with the paradoxical situation, suggested here in the title, is not surprising in view of his predilection for the use of *quid pro quo* as a dramaturgical device. For the paradox is only rendered possible by a protracted *quid pro quo* or several minor ones. In *Les Illustres ennemis* he had created in gradual stages the concept of friendly enemies. His approach in *le Geôlier de soi-même*, as we shall see, is more candid and direct.

Act I is devoted to establishing a context in which a paradoxical situation may occur. Fédéric, prince of Sicily, having just killed Rodolfe, prince of Salerno, in a tournament, has discarded his armor to take shelter in the country château of the king of Naples. Here he is received by Isabelle, sister of the man he has just killed. She is unaware of Fédéric's identity but learns of her brother's death at the hands of an *inconnu*. Meanwhile Jodelet, having come upon Fédéric's armor, dons it and decides to play nobleman. After a humorous scene in which Jodelet is unable to answer the question, "Qui va là?",[10] three guards overpower him and take him to the château believing they have surely captured Rodolfe's killer. All this action is lively and to the point. The seeds of *a quid pro quo* have been sown, Jodelet having been incorrectly identified. When in Act II he cultivates a taste for his royal role and the luxurious treatment it brings him, he decides to play upon the error for all its worth with a view to satisfying his gourmandise:

> Mais pourquoi m'obstiner à ne me point connaître?
> Puisque chacun ici d'une commune voix
> Soutient que je suis prince, il faut que je le sois . . .
> Quand c'est pour mon profit, j'ai la mémoire bonne,
> Je prétends festiner du matin jusqu'au soir.
>
> (II, 6)

He casually insults the king of Naples and is placed under the surveillance of Fédéric, hence the sense of the play's title. Jodelet's bumptious behavior in the context of a royal court at a moment of

---

before Molière (*Œuvres complètes*, Paris, 1818 V. II, p. 341). *Le Baron d'Albikrac* has been the most frequently reprinted of Thomas' comedies in collections entitled *Chefs-d'Œuvre de T. Corneille*.

[10] Enrique: Qui va là?
Jodelet: La vilaine enquête que voilà!
          J'avais réponse à tout hormis à qui va là. (I, 8)

crisis produces a comic of antithesis analogous in our present day to an imagined situation in which the three stooges might cut their capers at a meeting of international heads of government.

If the primary action is little more than slapstick, the background in which it occurs is, on the contrary, potentially tragic. A prince has been killed. The killer is loved by both the victim's sister and cousin. There is a question of a peace treaty between the two kingdoms involved, Naples and Sicily. War is imminent, however, for Fédéric's brother is in the harbor of Gaita ready to attack. Fédéric, unidentified, is in the enemy's hands. At one point the Neapolitan king considers marrying his daughter Laure to the supposed offender, Jodelet, in an effort to cement relations between his country and Sicily.[11]

Having established the paradox of *Le Geôlier de soi-même*, the author proceeded to derive from it various humorous episodes. Just as he had played upon the ignorance and vanity of Don Bertrand to develop a love scene before his very eyes, so does he profit from Jodelet's eccentricity to produce a similar scene. Fédéric makes gallant speeches to Laure in behalf of Jodelet, who supposes himself to be Fédéric:

> Aussi puis-je assurer que chacun ne sait pas
> Combien pour Fédéric vos vertus ont d'appas.
>
> (IV, 4)

Laure replies encouragingly:

> Pour payer une si belle flamme,
> Je puis à Fédéric ouvrir toute mon âme.
>
> (IV, 4)

Eager now to speak for himself but unable to compete with Fédéric's elegant language, Jodelet fumbles to find the proper formulae:

> Hé bien, je la veux trouver laide;
> Elle est sotte, elle est grue, elle a l'esprit bourru,
> La taille déhanchée, et le corps malotru,
> Elle a l'œil chassieux, le nez fait en citrouille,

[11] While marriage for political purposes is common in the seventeenth century both in literature and in real life, the Spanish source is responsible for the more specific idea of a marriage to amend for a wrong committed against the family of the girl. Revenge by means of union is illustrated in works of Cervantes, Tirso, Castro and others. Thomas' *Illustres ennemis* contains another example of it.

La bouche... Pardonnez si je vous chante pouille,
Ma Reine, ce faquin m'a tout colérisé,
Il en sera, ma foi, déchambellanisé;
Vous me plaisez pourtant, et je vous trouve belle.

(IV, 4)

He readily apologizes for this outburst, explaining that he had wanted
to show Fédéric that he could speak for himself. Fédéric assures him
that kings have ambassadors for such menial chores as lovemaking
whereupon Jodelet, having become hyperconscious of royal decorum
in his brief tenure, consents to let Fédéric speak for him. He insists,
however, that the third person not be used. Fédéric could ask for
nothing better, for now he is free to declare his love directly. Jodelet,
however, not to be easily outsmarted, feels that Laure, too, should have
an ambassador in order to leave her free to attend to more tangible
aspects of their relationship:

S'il est vrai, comme il l'est, qu'il soit de ma grandeur
Que je vous parle ici par un ambassadeur,
J'entends que de tout point ma grandeur s'accomplisse;
Et que vous répondiez par une ambassadrice,
Tandis qu'ils jaseront, les poings sur nos côtés,
Nous ferons guerre à l'œil sur nos deux gravités.
Reculez donc d'un pas.

(IV, 4)

Reynier finds it strange that Thomas Corneille should have created
for Jodelet this dominant role so incompatible with romanesque tastes
just at the moment of his closest association with the salons of Mme
de Fiesque and Mme de Noailles and on the eve of *Timocrate* (*Thom.
Corn.*, p. 218). But he overlooks Thomas' numerous concessions to
the romanesque in the setting and circumstances in which Jodelet indulges in his antics. The play begins on a note of mystery: an *inconnu*
has killed a prince of the blood in a tournament. This unusual event
is followed by a curious coincidence in the best romanesque tradition:
an *inconnu* appears shortly afterwards at the castle of the royal family
of Naples. Suspense is generated by the revelation that an enemy
prince has become a favorite at the court in which he is being sought
as a murderer. A flash-back reveals how Fédéric and Laure had
secretly fallen in love with each other's pictures, another romanesque
cliché. Discussions of love and personal merit center on questions dear

to the salons such as the following: At what point does admiration become love? Can the majesty of a prince be concealed by clothes? And in a final melodramatic flourish the Infant, Fédéric's brother, arrives just at the propitious moment in the harbor of Gaita. This was indeed ample sustenance for those of Thomas Corneille's spectators who were delighting in the intricate adventures of Mlle de Scudéry's *Grand Cyrus* (1648-53) and who were to revel in the precious sentimentality of Quinault.

COMIC STYLE

The peculiar merit of *Le Geôlier de soi-même* lies in the fact that Thomas was able to combine so skillfully a background which would appeal to his sophisticated admirers with a heavy dose of buffoonery calculated to satisfy the grosser appetite of the pit. Nor is it certain that the refined taste of the salons was incompatible with a rather hearty sense of humor. After all, the *habitués* of the Hôtel de Rambouillet enjoyed tossing Voiture in a blanket. Much of the humor in Thomas' play comes from Jodelet's social *gaffes*, something a refined society, particularly a self-conscious one, could always enjoy.

Before we proceed to Thomas' tragedies, it will be useful to summarize his accomplishments as a writer of comedy. He obviously does not stand in the same class as Molière whose genius dominates the French comic stage in the decade or so before his death in 1673. We must rather place Thomas Corneille on a lower level, comparing him with Scarron in the fifties and with such minor luminaries as Quinault in the sixties. Viewed in this light, his position is an honorable one. The esteem he held among his contemporaries, the variety of his comic art, his ability to manipulate plot for creating movement, suspense and dramatic irony, and eventually his conscious and successful efforts to infuse comedy with living contemporary issues make him an interesting figure.

With his first eight comedies from 1649 to 1656 he explored in breadth an impressive number of dramatic techniques. He developed a sense for staging which enabled him to achieve a reasonable compromise between the disunity of his Spanish models and the constraints imposed by French dramatic tastes. By various suggestive means,

Thomas protracted the locus of action beyond the confines of the physical stage all the while preserving unity of place. One violation of this unity, as noted above, occurs in *Don Bertrand de Cigarral*. However, the closet in *Les Engagements*, the open sylvan décor of *Le Berger extravagant*, the large house in *Le Baron d'Albikrac*, and, in all the plays, the expected arrivals, imminent departures, and reports of voyages produce an illusion of spatial extension quite in keeping with the comic deception of the plots.

Yet Thomas' predilection for paradoxical situations and *quid pro quo* are symptomatic of a basic weakness in his dramatic method. Except in *Don Bertrand* and *Le Geôlier* he failed to recognize the importance of characterization. For all his dynamic agility, he had hardly begun to exploit the potentialities for comic effect inherent in the psychological portrayal of human foibles. Professor Adam, while defending Thomas Corneille's craftsmanship, attributes to his comedies an absence of moral concern:

Les critiques qui n'ont lu ni Scarron, ni Boisrobert, ni Quinault, ni Thomas Corneille, ont imaginé que ces auteurs mettaient sur la scène des intrigues invraisemblables et des personnages chimériques, ils ont cru qu'avant Molière notre théâtre n'était qu'arbitraire et fausseté. La vérité est différente. Les scènes finement observées, les traits et les mots justes abondent chez ces auteurs méprisés. Mais la comédie, dans leur esprit n'a pas d'autre ambition que de divertir. Leur défaut essentiel, c'est la gratuité (Adam, III, p. 405).

In light situation comedy Thomas successfully rivaled his most talented contemporaries; and, by assiduously cultivating the external aspects of his craft, appealed to a widespread taste for rationalistic theater.

But a display of his deeper talents did not become apparent until he was well into his tragic productions. These, as we shall see in the following chapter, began on a note of glaring triumph. Measured by dramaturgical standards, his first tragedies differ only slightly from the comedies immediately preceding them. Yet Thomas Corneille caught hold of a secret ingredient and played it for all it was worth. He raised what was basically a comedy of errors to a prestigious drama of mystery and gallant heroics. In the process a type of hero emerged who, despite the mystery of his identity and perhaps even more because of it, constituted a strong focal point for a series of marvelous adventures.

II. THE ROMANESQUE IDENTITY PLAYS

> Sa naissance inconnue est peut-être sans tache:
> Vous la présumez basse à cause qu'il la cache;
> Mais combien a-t-on vu de princes déguisés
> Signaler leur vertu sous des noms supposés
> Dompter des nations, gagner des diadèmes,
> Sans qu'aucun les connût, sans se connaître eux-mêmes?
>
> (*Don Sanche d'Aragon*, I, 1, 49-54)

THE HERO INCOGNITO ON THE FRENCH STAGE

The foregoing lines from Pierre Corneille's *Don Sanche* (1649) reveal the basic ingredients of a type of situation which enjoyed great success in mid-seventeenth century French theater as it did in Spain and England as well. Mistaken identity as a basic hypothesis of plot construction was by no means new with Pierre Corneille although he made interesting innovations with it, notably in *Héraclius* (1646).

The technique can be traced to Greek tragedy, for, in its fashion, Sophocles' *Oedipus Rex* was an identity play. Aristotle's stress on this play and on recognition scenes in general gave critical respectability to a theme which the medieval romances often exploited, as in *Yvain*. As a device, mistaken identity is related to a family of dramaturgical practices, an obvious and superficial level of which occurred in medieval mystery plays as allegory. An actor representing truth or some other virtue, perhaps even carrying a sign to facilitate identification, was hardly expected to deceive the spectator. But, if only from simple convention, spectators thought of the player as intermediary to the abstract quality he sought to portray. The actor was important insofar as a transfer of identity from himself to the personified abstraction could occur. Strictly speaking, such a transfer did not involve mistaken identity but, theoretically, willful transcendance of the actor by the spectator. Still, in the allegory there was implied a latent form of deception which may be seen as a threshold to later developments.

In seventeenth century comedy, the technique has made enormous progress. In the comedies discussed in the previous chapter, characters used deliberate physical disguise to deceive other characters. Although the concealment was temporary and usually a spontaneous contrivance good for only one or two scenes, it represented a refinement in technique over the mysteries. Characters from the comedies took on a disguise in response to a situation arising from the internal events of the play. Nevertheless, false identity remained a device, not a theme. The distinction is significant. As long as the transfer of identity was taken for granted as in the mystery plays or intended only as a means of temporizing as in the later comedies, it was subservient to the play's argument. The condition necessary to convert the device into a theme was produced when the spectator, the hero, other characters or some combination of these became victims of a situation involving false identity rather than remaining superior to it and in control of it.

Mistaken identity as a dramatic theme appears to have become popular in France along with the pastoral vogue, particularly after d'Urfé's *L'Astrée* (1607-27). Playwrights of the period were tempted to use the "device" of self-discovery as a dramatic means symbolically appropriate to the portrayal of a hero in quest of self. Now this was on a more elevated plane than the use of false identity merely as a comic device. In this conversion to a theme, the plays themselves were usually converted to tragi-comedy, a transformation we can see as early as Du Ryer's *Alcimédon* (1632) and Scudéry's *Prince déguisé* (1634).

The former recounts the adventure of Alcimédon and Phénice who, having been separated as young lovers, meet years later under different names and, unaware of each other's identity, fall in love once more. Their sense of guilt at the thought of abandoning their former attachments is dispelled by recognition and identification before the play is half finished. A new conflict arises in Act III, and the question of identity loses importance.

On the other hand, Scudéry's play is more typical of the later tragi-comedies that concern us in this chapter. *Le Prince déguisé* places the hero incognito at the court of an enemy queen with whose daughter he is in love. This queen promises her daughter to whoever will deliver to her the head of her enemy, who, of course, is the hero himself. This is precisely the situation of Timocrate, as we shall see shortly.

Another variation is illustrated by Pierre Corneille's *Don Sanche* in which the hero, to his own surprise as much as anyone else's, is identified as heir to the throne of Aragon. The same author's *Héraclius* and Quinault's *Astrate* portray unknown heroes at a court, of which, as it turns out, they are the rightful rulers.

This type of play was by far the most popular to fall under the heading of Romanesque tragedy, which flourished in the 1650's and early 1660's. For different reasons, Thomas Corneille and Quinault were its foremost exponents. The latter is usually credited, and properly so, with giving the identity play a dimension of sentimentality in the figure of the sighing, helpless lover. Thomas Corneille, although not exempt from a similar attribution, managed on the whole to preserve a heroic vision in his protagonists. Their heroism was usually placed at the service of an amorous ideal, but a vestige of self-respect kept them from love prostration. In conjunction with the identity plays, we shall briefly illustrate Quinault's sense of lyric tragedy as compared to Thomas' romanesque tendencies.

Several reasons have been suggested to account for the vogue of the romanesque in general as well as the particular manifestation of it which concerns us here, the tragedy of false identity. Chief among the reasons commonly advanced is a socio-political one: after the Fronde there was a general relaxation marked by a return to the genteel, sociable pursuits of an elite grown weary of internal wars. The seriousness of political tragedy was abandoned in favor of burlesque and, occasionally, pastoral drama. Tales of love and heroic adventure from the pens of La Calprenède and Mlle de Scudéry made love the pervasive theme of novels and tragedies alike. No longer was love represented as a foil to greater passions as in early Cornelian tragedy but as an ennobling force akin to medieval courtly love. Thomas Corneille's heroes and heroines strive for moral perfection not in spite of their love but because of it. The common manifestation of ennobling love may be seen in the contests of generosity between lovers which we shall see in the identity plays. Above all there was an attempt to classify and describe the various stages in the progression of love. It was an age of amorous cartography. Considering both comedy and tragedy during the years 1650-1680, one may run the gamut of conceptions of love from the capricious coquetry of *L'Amour à la mode* to the anguished lamentations of Phèdre.

In view of the predilection on the part of dramatists and novelists to represent the anatomy of love, it was an astute technique to use the figure of the prince incognito as a central dramatic character. Much in the manner of Condillac in his description of nascent sensations in a statue, dramatists of mid-seventeenth century came more and more to exploit an equally objectified figure in the form of unidentified hero. Like the statue, the unknown protagonist represented a *tabula rasa* on which unprejudiced reactions could be recorded in gradual stages. Thus Quinault's Astrate can be seen falling in love with Elise who, unbeknowns to him, has had his father and brothers put to death. Conversely, Elise falls in love with him, ignorant of his right to bear the scepter which she sways. Owing to Astrate's mistaken identity their sentiments are allowed to flourish without the restraint which enlightenment would naturally impose.

Two further reasons suggest themselves to help explain the success of identity plays. The first has to do with the notion, flattering to the noblemen of the audience, that true merit is invariably shown to coincide with nobility of rank. So entrenched was this conception (whether in fact or fancy is difficult to know), that in *Don Sanche*, to mention one example, the disguised prince, Carlos, was imposed upon to disavow what he supposed to be his humble ancestry on the grounds that his valor belied any but a noble lineage:

> Et le vrai sang des rois sous le sort abattu
> Peut cacher sa naissance et non pas sa vertu;
> Il porte sur le front un luisant caractère.
>   (IV, 3, 1315-17)

A seventeenth century nobleman watching *Don Sanche* or any of a number of plays of a similar nature, while admiring the deeds of the *inconnu*, must have been agreeably disturbed by the absence of a noble title which would correspond to the magnitude of the deeds. A taste for chivalric romances still persisted in the seventeenth century. The arrogant attitude of Don Lope and Don Manrique in *Don Sanche*, exaggerated though it may be, implies a solid belief in the principle that true personal worth is necessarily sanctioned by noble birthright. The denouement of the play would seem to prove their point.

A final reason for popular acclaim of the identity play inhered in the dramatic potentialities which it contained. The most obvious advantage lay in the readiness with which suspense could be created, usually in the first scene, and sustained throughout the play. The variety of manners in which the hero was handled could well be the subject of an entire study. We mention but a few as an indication of the wealth of dramatic possibilities in the genre.

The dramatist could divide characters into any number of combinations depending whether he chose to develop a sequence of revelations or a grand single exposure of the disguised hero. He had a further choice in determining the order in which characters were to learn of the identity and at what point of the play to inform the audience. On this last matter, the playwright had to consider the attitude he wished the spectators to adopt with respect to the hero, whether one of complicity, suspicion, or complete uncertainty. It mattered, for instance, whether the hero himself did the informing or another character.

Most important was the unidentified protagonist's relationship with himself, for from this relationship the dynamics of the plot were largely determined. Hence in Scudéry's *Prince déguisé* we see a hero, Cléarque, who knows his identity but conceals it at first from all except a friend. Scudéry made him an active hero by virtue of Cléarque's privileged state of knowledge. From the vantage point of secrecy, he controls events more than he submits to them.

The contrary is true in the case of DuRyer's *Alcimédon* where there are two unknown figures, neither of whom is at first aware of his own or the other's identity. This situation, which recurs in Thomas Corneille's *Bérénice*, tended to produce a relatively inactive hero too occupied by seeking out his own identity to direct events toward exterior goals. Don Sanche is exceptional in this regard, for he is active though he does not know who he is. The explanation for his surefootedness lies in the fact that he thinks he knows his identity and is not troubled by gnawing uncertainty. *Astrate* offers an example of the ignorant hero, a victim of events until it is too late to affect them.

Having once started using false identity as a theme, dramatists did not feel constrained to limit the incognito to one character. Frequently the marvel which accounted for the survival and reappearance of a prince was an exchange of children that had taken place some twenty years before the events of the play. In *Héraclius*, thanks to the sacrifice of the governess Léontine, the legitimate heir has been brought up as the son of the ruling usurper. The latter's son is thought to be the child of Léontine. Uncertainty is prolonged by informing some characters but not others and by placing the correct information at the disposal of a person who finds it advantageous to remain enigmatic. The final disclosure of identity is deferred by an intermediate revelation which later turns out to be false.

Yet another refinement could be made by passing the hero through two changes of identity each requiring a realignment of attitudes and reactions. Such is the case in *Don Sanche* and Thomas Corneille's *Bérénice*.

False identity was a peculiarly apt nucleus for dramatic interest, for around it many secondary motifs and themes could be grouped. Sometimes these motifs were causal, sometimes sequential. Common among them were the combat of generosity and the head motif, examples of which we shall presently examine. The latter involved the promise of a widowed queen to award her daughter in marriage to whoever would deliver up the head of her enemy. Invariably this head belonged to the disguised prince. If he was clever and persuasive like Timocrate, he might manage to win the princess by surrendering the requested head, his own, still attached to the body.[1]

Like the adaptations of Spanish comedias, the identity plays appealed primarily to a rational sense. The composing and disentangling of plot challenged the ingenuity of playwright and audience respectively. Here was a type of performance which elicited active mental participation from the audience and at some point in the play made the spectator an accomplice after first treating him as a dupe. For the

---

[1] For a succinct delineation of the themes commonly used as subsidiaries to false identity see Barbara Matulka, ed. *Le Prince déguisé*, by Georges de Scudéry (New York, 1929), pp. 1-27.

spectator, transition from ignorance to enlightenment held the same type of appeal that one experiences upon finding the solution to a problem. Essentially the identity plays were precisely that — problems to be solved for intellectual entertainment and enhanced by an heroic illusion.

TIMOCRATE (1656)

Beyond its appeal to a public nurtured on romanesque *invraisemblance*, *Timocrate* owed its amazing success to more durable qualities of purely dramatic interest which make for valid theater in any age. It is not high tragedy, nor was it meant to be. A careful analysis of its structure reveals a tightly knit, fast-moving drama which by no means warrants the scorn with which modern critics have generally treated it.

The basic problem confronting the hero is how to win the hand of a princess whose mother, the widowed queen, has sworn vengeance on him and promised the princess to whoever will deliver up his head. Their countries are bitterly hostile and at war. His first step is to win the queen's respect and her daughter's love by disguising himself as an adventurer and performing prodigies of valor in defending their kingdom. In the process he creates and solves a further problem. His success at overcoming the first obstacle by the use of disguise produces the awkward impropriety of a princess in love with a person of lower estate. This difficulty is dissolved by her overriding respect for the hero. Meanwhile the queen's oath remains, along with the paradoxical situation it creates as Timocrate finally establishes his identity. This last problem is solved in stages concluding with the queen's abdication. Throughout the play, action is enlivened by the shifting fortunes of war between the two countries.

Timocrate's exposition simultaneously reveals and conceals. The hero is in fact presented in the second scene but is not known until Act IV, scene 8. The reason for this delay lies in the nature of the play and the effects which Thomas Corneille chose to make. Earlier revelation of Timocrate's identity would have implicated the audience into the basic secret of the plot and softened the impact of the *coup de théâtre* by limiting the surprise to the actors. The spectator is not certain of the identity of Timocrate although a few ambiguous innuendos may have led him to suspect Cléomène who, as early as Act II, has said:

> Oui, du même moment que la fortune ingrate
> Eût semblé se résoudre à flatter Timocrate,
> Comme victime due à ce fameux accord,
> Cléomène sans doute eût achevé son sort.

(II, 4)

Thomas Corneille sought a psychological reaction of maximum impact by postponing the essential revealing fact so as to intensify the eventual surprise. According to Thomas Corneille's dedicatory *épître*, few people were able to guess the identity of Timocrate. A notable exception was the duc de Guise, whom Thomas Corneille complimented in the following terms:

Je me souviendrai toujours avec admiration de cette merveilleuse vivacité, qui vous fit découvrir d'abord les intérêts les plus cachés de Cléomène, et développer dès ses premiers sentiments le secret d'un noeud qui pendant quatre actes a laissé Timocrate inconnu presque à tout le monde.

(II, p. 185)

Except for the secret of Cléomène's identity the essential facts are exposed in the first two scenes. In the first is presented Nicandre, a prince of Argos, registering happy surprise upon hearing of Cléomène's return. We learn of Timocrate's presence in the harbor, of his father's past rivalry with Argos, of Nicandre's love for princess Eriphile, and of the presence of neighboring kings Léontidas and Cresphonte, who have been summoned by the queen to support her against Timocrate. In scene 2, Cléomène tells of the request of the Cretan ambassador for an audience, and Nicandre reviews the traditional animosity between Argos and Crete. In scene 3 the queen holds council in order to decide on an answer to Timocrate's ambassador. In the course of deliberations a steadily rising interest culminates in the queen's key decision to seek Timocrate's death, a decision which affects subsequent actions of the characters and poses the chief condition of what will later become the queen's dilemma.

Act II presents no new action but develops the relationship between Cléomène and Eriphile. Thomas Corneille has his hero and heroine digress on the subtleties of *précieux* love and makes Cléomène defend his ambivalent attitudes toward Eriphile, who is at the same time

resentful for having been made the victor's reward and angry that
Cléomène has supported Timocrate's demand for her hand. Both
Reynier and Lancaster have pointed out the similarity of her parting
words to Cléomène and those spoken by Chimène to encourage
Rodrigue to do his best in battle. Says Eriphile:

> Va, tu n'ignores pas ce qu'a promis la reine,
> Combats, vaincs, et surtout n'expose pas ma foi
> A refuser ailleurs ce qui n'est dû qu'à toi.[2]
>
>   (II, 4)

Act III is pivotal to the action, for it contains the battle which, after
two reversals of fortune, concludes with a temporary Argive triumph.
The progress of the battle is reported in much the same manner as in
Mairet's *Sophonisbe* and Pierre Corneille's *Horace*. First Cléone, a
confidante, reports that Trasile has been captured, hence a victory for
Argos. Then the queen reports the deaths of Cresphonte and Léontidas at the hands of Timocrate. This disaster is followed shortly by
the news that Nicandre has been captured. Argos is in despair when
unexpectedly Nicandre reappears telling of Timocrate's clemency
toward him. Argos' hopes are completely restored as Cléomène appears
announcing that he has captured Timocrate. To avoid ending the act
on a note of finality, Thomas Corneille included a brief scene where
Nicandre, in gratitude for his release, resolves to liberate Timocrate
in return.

Thomas Corneille prolonged suspense through Act IV by an ironic
complication. Cléomène is forced into a position which terminates in
his admission of identity. He had engaged one of his Cretan subjects,
Trasile, to play the role of captive Timocrate. However, Trasile, unaware of his master's ruse, refuses to acknowledge that the captured
party is Timocrate. The scene is comically ironic, for Cléomène is seen
imploring his faithful subject to support him by an apparent betrayal,
one of several minor paradoxes of the play. The first two speeches of
this scene illustrate the ingenuity with which Thomas Corneille
handled his characters. As Trasile is brought in to testify:

---

[2] Other lines reminiscent of *Le Cid* are "Si c'est vaincre en effet, c'est
triompher sans gloire (III, 6) and "Et dans mon ennemi confondant mon
amant . . . (V, 4).

Trasile: Quoi? Madame, on persiste en la même imposture?
            On ose soutenir qu'on ait vaincu mon roi,
            Qu'il soit entre vos mains?
Cléomène: Oui, Trasile, et c'est moi.
            Vous-même oserez-vous soutenir le contraire?
            Parlez, il n'est plus temps, Trasile, de vous taire,
            Ai-je trompé la reine, et trahi mon espoir,
            Jurant que Timocrate était en son pouvoir?

                                           (IV, 7)

Cléomène is improvising a kind of double talk intended to inform Trasile of his plans at the same time that he keeps them hidden to the queen. However, his "Oui, Trasile, et c'est moi" does not bring about the desired effect. Trasile is understandably confused by his master's behavior. In a comedy this would have been the place for an aside or a stage whisper. But even if Thomas Corneille had been willing to take such a license, he could not have done so without revealing the secret one scene earlier than he in fact did.

The clarification thus brought about, although serving to explain Cléomène's previous defense of Timocrate, only creates a new problem, for now the queen must decide how to fulfill her pledges. Hence Timocrate's exposure produces a shift of obstacles by confronting him with a new peril for the last act. The queen's procrastination in making a choice is counterbalanced by the impatience of the populace to have Timocrate's head. The queen handles matters one at a time. First she decides to fulfill part of her oath by marrying Timocrate and Eriphile. She will then have Timocrate put to death. This course of action would indeed fulfill her promises to the letter and, if carried out, give the play a tragic ending. However, a final *coup de théâtre* relieves the queen of all responsibility for Timocrate's fate as Nicandre in a melodramatic flourish permits the Cretans to enter the city and restore the victory to Timocrate.

As we stated in the introduction of this study, Thomas Corneille never completely abandoned the comic vein even when writing tragedies. The three comedies preceding *Timocrate* do indeed show an evolution toward more serious drama, not so much because they were purged of all comic effects, but because Thomas Corneille supplemented the comic with potentially tragic events as background. In writing *Timocrate* the reverse is true, for he made the minimal gestures indispensable to tragedy while preserving the techniques of comedy. His characters are noble (there are four sovereigns in the play), there is immediate peril to the throne of Argos as well as to the life of the king of Crete. The moment is one of crisis since the Cretan fleet and ambassador are in Argos with an ultimatum. A momentous decision is imminent. Surely these features announce a tragic plot. And yet something is missing, or it is perhaps more exact to say that too many things are present which detract from the tragic tone. The complications of the intrigue, reversals of fortune, the psychological gymnastics of the hero and Nicandre, the mystery and uncertainty of Timocrate's identity, the paradoxical situation created by the Argive queen's oaths, and her ingenious manner of acquitting herself of them require so much attention that the tragic is overshadowed.

Although the rules of tragedy did not permit the use of physical disguise, a patently comic device, Thomas Corneille remained as close as possible to comedy by using the substitution of a character for another. This substitution is not precisely a replacement, however, for, if Cléomène's presence is required in the palace of Argos, he is simultaneously required in his capacity as Timocrate to be at the head of the Cretan forces in the harbor. The physical impossibility of this feat demanded a certain dramaturgical dexterity and meant a necessary sacrifice of one of the identities of the hero. Thomas Corneille chose to give the first four acts to Cléomène while perpetuating the illusion by brief *récits* and reports from messengers that Timocrate is a separate entity.

Also in the nature of comedy is the happy ending, comprised of the reconciliation of enemy parties and the projected marriage of Timocrate and Eriphile. Upon reaching the final scene, one is tempted to view the whole play in retrospect as a series of obstacles placed in the way of the lovers. The pervasive quality of Timocrate's speeches is one of gallant *badinage* characterized by an exaltation of love as the prime virtue. He says to Eriphile:

> Renoncer pour l'amour au soin de sa fortune,
> N'est que le faible effet d'une vertu commune;
> On a vu mille amants dans ses moindres douceurs
> Trouver la pente aisée au mépris des grandeurs,
> Et pour l'objet aimé, sans que rien les étonne,

Quitter parents, amis, sceptre, trône, couronne;
Mais il est inouïe peut-être avant ce jour
Qu'aucun ait immolé l'amour même à l'amour.

(II, 4)

Timocrate can think of no greater superlative to describe the depth of his love than to say that he would sacrifice it to nothing short of love itself. This strange rhetoric, a form of question begging, is best understood by interpreting the second *amour* to mean the unselfish love that springs from abnegation. A very noble sentiment indeed, since Timocrate appears to be working in the best interests of Eriphile. But what coquetry we soon discover it to be when Cléomène turns out to be Timocrate. The latent pathos is destroyed as the paradox is made clear. Reynier has criticized Timocrate's callousness in killing so many men, including two kings, just to bring his courtship to fruition. He has suggested that Timocrate could have simplified the situation and avoided bloodshed if, once having won Eriphile's heart as Cléomène, he had made himself known under his true name (*Thom. Corn.*, p. 126). We feel that the solution was not so simple as Reynier claims, however. It is very questionable that the queen of Argos would have accepted Timocrate as her son-in-law without being forced to do so. We learn in the exposition, as in the novel, that she is a vindictive sovereign, compelled to avenge the death of her late husband. For some time before Timocrate's arrival she had been mobilizing her military forces for an invasion of Crete. Moreover, at the council deliberations (Act I, scene 3), she might have opted for peace but refused. Her bitter animosity toward Crete was at least as strong as her esteem for Cléomène. For Timocrate, in his capacity as defender of Crete, the risk would have been too great. There is little doubt that Timocrate suffers as tragedy because it lacks the moral seriousness characteristic of this genre at its best. Nevertheless, Lockert has defended the play against the charge of moral absurdity:

The story of his [Timocrate's] twin roles, in which he drew his sword now on one side and now on the other that he might win his heart's love, is of course sheer stuff of romance. Yet how else could he have won her? . . . It might even be asked further: How else could he so well and promptly have brought about a lasting peace between Argos and Crete? As matters stood, the implacable Queen of Argos was sure to re-open the war once more as soon as she believed that she had a chance of success. Disregard the impracticality of Timocrate's course, suppose he could go through with it successfully as he is represented as doing, and he is justified in it from the point of view of State policy as well as from that of love. It is not as regards political morality that the play is absurd.

(*Studies*, p. 14)

The role of Nicandre is one of considerable dramatic importance to the play and poses some interesting problems. Thomas Corneille first uses him to help make the exposition and prepare Cléomène's arrival. Subsequently he has the ungracious role of playing alternately friend and rival to Timocrate. He is placed in the ironic position of summarizing Timocrate's career in the presence of Timocrate himself (I, 2), a procedure which, except for the hero's incognito in this case, was unacceptable dramatic practice. The most curious aspect of Nicandre and one which has been overlooked in previous analyses of the play concerns his unwillingness to identify Timocrate in Act III. It must be recalled that Nicandre, fighting for the queen of Argos, was captured by Timocrate and then released. Shortly after Nicandre's return to the queen, Timocrate appears in Argos as the familiar Cléomène and reports, in Nicandre's presence, how he has captured Timocrate. Nothing seems irregular to the spectator at the time this action occurs. In fact if at this point one had entertained the slightest suspicion that Nicandre was Timocrate's accomplice, this scene and the action immediately following would have belied it. Only later when Timocrate is revealed does one become aware of Thomas Corneille's earlier trickery. One then wonders why Nicandre remained silent. Was he already an accomplice? If not, why did he not expose Cléomène as Timocrate? With these questions in mind, further reflection reminds us that, at the time of his capture, Nicandre had had ample opportunity to recognize the Cretan warrior. In reporting to the queen, he had observed Timocrate closely:

> J'y vois le Roi de Crète encore tout armé,
> Sitôt qu'il m'aperçoit, il hausse la visière.
> Je découvre l'éclat d'une mine guerrrière,
> Et tel que sur un teint et vif et coloré,
> La chaleur du combat ne l'a point altéré.

(III, 5)

If it were not enough that Nicandre was so close as to be able to see "un teint vif et coloré", how could he have failed to recognize him when, before taking leave of each other, they embraced:

> Nous voguons tant qu'enfin n'osant plus avancer,
> Avant qu'on nous sépare, il me fait l'embrasser.
>
> (III, 5)

And yet when Cléomène appears in the following scene, Nicandre gives no indication of recognizing him as Timocrate. With the advantage of hindsight one can conclude that Nicandre had been won over, had already decided to betray Argos. Thomas Corneille's deception consisted in giving him speeches that do not so indicate, however, for Nicandre rather appears to oppose or at least question Cléomène's claim of triumph as well as his pretentions to the hand of Ériphile. Sarcastically he asks Cléomène:

> L'ambition déjà vous fait-elle ignorer
> Qu'à moins d'être né prince on n'y peut aspirer?
>
> (III, 6)

And even after the Queen's assent to Cléomène's claims, Nicandre remains skeptical:

> Mais, Madame, est-ce lui que nous en devons croire?
>
> (III, 6)

Furthermore, when Cléomène leaves the scene and Nicandre is left alone to confide to the audience, he still does not admit that Timocrate and Cléomène are the same person.

There is no credible excuse for Nicandre's reticence unless we are willing to accept the compromise which Thomas Corneille made with the rules of his art. The blatancy of *invraisemblance* is attenuated by the peculiar nature of the device which makes it possible, for temporarily the device serves as its own antidote. That is, as long as Nicandre does not disclose Timocrate's identity, there seems to be nothing amiss since the audience has no way of knowing how it is being deceived. Once Timocrate is revealed, however, the question of Nicandre's silence quite naturally arises. But by this time it does not matter so much, since the surprise of revelation has been successfully executed. The violation of credibility is realized only upon retrospection and must be charged not to Thomas Corneille's dramaturgical ineptitude, but to his willingness to take a calculated risk in sacrificing dramaturgical correctness to dramatic interest. He was determined to keep his audience in ignorance at any cost until what he thought was the proper moment.

Lockert has criticized Thomas Corneille's dramaturgy on the grounds that the author showed "a tendency to relegate crucial plot details to the intervals between the acts instead of having them occur before the eyes of the audience, or offstage while the act is playing" (*Studies*, p. 19). Lockert's statement is general. When measured against *Timocrate*, it seems not to apply at all. Between Acts I and II absolutely no action occurs, nor is there anything after Act II except the departure of the Argive forces for battle. Following Act III, Arcas goes to the prison cell of the captive Cretan supposed to be Timocrate. He reappears with Nicandre at the opening of Act IV to tell of the supposed Timocrate's reluctance to be freed. The action occurring in the interim is readily summarized in Arcas' first speech and does not constitute "crucial plot details" although the information which he reports is significant. Since Arcas had closed the preceding act, Thomas Corneille had somehow to indicate that time had elapsed. To achieve this effect, despite his violation of the sequence of scenes, he had Act IV open in the midst of a conversation, implying that Arcas and Nicandre had parted and reconvened. When Act V opens, it is the following morning. Timocrate has been taken to prison, a fact known and presented at the end of the preceding act. The populace is up in arms eager to hasten his death. It was customary to report the activities of the populace and not to try to represent them on stage since the problems involved in attempting the latter were too numerous. In brief we can see no important action relegated to the wings which could possibly have taken place on stage without weakening the dramaturgy in some other more important respect.

Along with his use of reversals of fortune and hidden identity, Thomas Corneile sought to create suspense by tempting his audience with prognostications based on partial knowledge. A play which starts with an oath, a promise, a curse, an oracle, a dream, or some other ominous prediction frequently portends a gloomy denouement. It is an effective dramatic device since the spectator, forewarned of what to expect, is called upon to fit successive events into a logical pattern which will fulfill the terms of the prognostication. Ostensibly one would expect that the use of an oracle, a promise or an oath would be most useful to a dramatist interested in preparing his public rather than in surprising it. And yet the information given in the prognostication, semantically absolute though it may appear, usually allows of various interpretations. An apparently benign prediction can turn out to be a baleful one and vice-versa. Probably the greatest suspense is achieved when the prognostication seems to foretell a tragic event but actually produces a happy one. Such is the case in *Timocrate*.

The play is made to turn on the fulfillment of two oaths made by the queen of Argos. One is that she will kill Timocrate if it remains in her power to do so, and the other, that she will give Eriphile in marriage to Timocrate's conqueror. It does not occur to her that the execution of one of these oaths might preclude or make extremely difficult the execution of the other. However, the moment of dilemma arrives; a choice must be made. Cléomène has, in a sense, captured Timocrate yet they are the same person. In these circumstances the queen decides to unite Eriphile and Timocrate in marriage and then kill Timocrate. When Nicandre's treason results in a definitive Cretan victory, it appears that one of the queen's oaths will have to be revoked. It then becomes important to recall the exact wording of the oaths in order to see if the terms have been satisfied. Thomas Corneille made a particular point at various points in the tragedy of emphasizing the oaths and particularly the one involving Timocrate's death. He has the queen repeat it as if to bid the audience not forget. Originally she had sworn:

> Et j'atteste aujourd'hui les dieux nos souverains,
> Qu'il payera de son sang s'il tombe entre mes mains,
> Oui, tant que dans ces lieux j'aurai le nom de reine,
> Si d'autres intérêts affaiblissent ma haine,
> Puissent ces dieux vengeurs, pour le dernier des maux,
> Sous les loix de la Crète assujetir Argos.

(I, 3)

She later reiterates the same sentiments with elaborations:

> Oui, dieux, de cet état protecteurs redoutables,
> Des serments voilés vengeurs impitoyables,
> Pour obliger ma haine à ne fléchir jamais,
> Oyez-moi répéter ceux que j'ai déjà faits.
> Tant que reine en ces lieux j'aurai quelque puissance,
> Si de hâter sa mort mon devoir se dispense,

> Puisse votre courroux, par de justes fureurs
> Exposer tout Argos aux dernières horreurs.
>
> (III, 5)

Henceforth references to the queen's oaths are frequent, their inviolability emphasized. First Nicandre:

> Mais sait-il que sa prise importe à Cléomène,
> Que son amour l'expose aux serments de la reine?
>
> (IV, 1)

A few scenes later the queen is obliged to reaffirm her promise of the princess' hand to Cléomène:

> Non, Cléomène, non, la princesse est à vous,
> Ayant reçu sa foi vous êtes son époux,
> Et tout ce que le temple a de cérémonies
> Ne rendra pas demain vos âmes mieux réunies.
> Nous devons par respect ce dehors à nos dieux.
>
> (IV, 5)

Five more references to the oath [3] make it very evident that Thomas Corneille attached a high degree of importance to this device, which he conceived as especially amenable to the creation of a dilemma.

The prosody of *Timocrate* is not outstanding although stylistic effects are varied and often effective. To express emotional turmoil, Thomas Corneille had recourse to stances, seldom heard in tragedy of this period but still used occasionally to set off an introspective soliloquy such as Eriphile's in Act I, scene 1. For rapidity of movement he introduced nearly an entire scene of stichomythia used, as is characteristically the case, to develop an exchange of testy remarks, here between Nicandre and Cléomène (IV, 3).

The Argive queen has some of the most expressive lines as, for example her apostrophe upon learning Timocrate's identity:

> Ô devoir, ô vengence, ô serment téméraire!
> N'ai-je engagé le ciel à servir ma colère,
> Que pour lui voir offrir à mon cœur alarmé
> Timocrate haï dans Cléomène aimé?

---

[3] La Reine: Oui, quand de mes serments, l'inviolable foi ... (IV, 8)
La Reine: Les dieux dont l'intérêt fait agir mes serments ... (IV, 8)
Cléone: L'effroi qu'il a conçu des serments de la reine ... (V, 1)
Eriphile: Et qu'après un serment que la vengeance anime ... (V, 4)
La Reine: L'irrévocable arrêt d'un aveugle serment ... (V, 5)

> Fatal accablement d'une illustre famille!
> Puis-je donner la mort à qui je dois ma fille,
> Ou si je suis contrainte à ce funeste effort,
> Puis-je donner ma fille à qui je dois la mort?
>
> (IV, 8)

The queen's conflict is further emphasized in later lines in which her dilemma is underlined rhetorically by antithetical utterances stressing the irreconcilable aspects of her sentiments:

> Vous m'avez fait aimer ce que j'ai cru haïr.
>
> (IV, 8)

> Car enfin si je dois ma fille à Cléomène,
> Je dois en même temps Timocrate à ma haine.
>
> Ô trop sensibles coups d'une rigueur extrême
> J'aime ce que je perds et je perds ce que j'aime.
>
> (V, 5)

Professor Lancaster has made light of the queen's conflict which he calls a "rather ridiculous struggle between her desire to reward Cléomène and her promise to punish Timocrate although she knows them to be the same person" (*History*, III, p. 186). We feel that this criticism is made without sufficient consideration for the sentimental shock involved. Why, indeed, should the queen not be perplexed in her decision? If on the one hand she might have had additional incentive for revenge having learned of Cléomène's imposture, on the other hand her respect and admiration for him were personal and direct as opposed to her official and, as it were, theoretical hatred of Timocrate, whom she had never met. It seems to us not at all strange that her struggle should exist and with all the more poignancy *because* Timocrate and Cléomène are the same person.

Timocrate was the smash hit of the century at the time of its production, yet critics have been almost unanimous in condemning it on the grounds that it is morally superficial, psychologically unsound, and incredibly melodramatic. These charges are at least partly true if *Timocrate* is compared with full-scale tragedy of the century. Certainly the play raises no serious moral issue and love, in the form of a refined gallantry, is the motive power of Timocrate's every gesture. For these reasons it is fairer to judge the play not as tragedy, but as tragi-comedy, a term which Lancaster has already seen fit to apply.[4]

With the exception of Nicandre's strange silence, the events of *Timocrate* are cleverly arranged for maximum dramatic interest. As an assimilator of dramatic techniques used in his age, Thomas Corneille proved himself in this play to be an eclectic marvel. Various analogies have been pointed out by Lancaster, Martinenche and others. In addition to those already mentioned earlier are the following: Eriphile's reluctance to marry a subject is reminiscent of the Infanta's attitude in *Le Cid*; the council scene re-echos those of *Cinna, Pompée* and *Don Sanche*; the queen's abdication in order to avoid discharging a disagreeable duty is similar to Venceslas' abdication; Eriphile's sermon to Nicandre on the duties of a subject remind one of speeches in DuRyer's *Alcionée*; the clandestine activities of Nicandre in Act V resemble Attale's in *Nicomède*. With all the variety of devices that enter the composition of *Timocrate*, the main lines of the play remain remarkably clear and simple. The plot may be summarized as Timocrate's effort to win Eriphile by playing the double role of enemy and lover. Above all *Timocrate* attests to a vitality refreshing by its ingenuous appeal to imagination and idealistic fantasy.

BÉRÉNICE

Capitalizing on the success of his *Timocrate*, Thomas Corneille composed a second play along similar lines in *Bérénice* (1657). The plot of *Bérénice*, based on the episode of Sésostris and Timarète in the sixth book of the *Grand Cyrus*, is considerably more complicated than that of *Timocrate*. The latter involves one unknown figure, the former, two. *Timocrate* has one scene of recognition, *Bérénice* has three. Whereas Timocrate was aware of his identity, Bérénice and Philoxène are unaware of theirs. Reynier's conjecture that the mediocre success of the play was due to a lack of complications seems dubious:

S'il plut médiocrement, malgré ses défauts, c'est parce que l'intrigue n'en était pas assez compliquée. On attendait de l'auteur de *Timocrate* d'autres coups de surprise, d'autres mystères longtemps soutenus; on fut fâché

---

[4] *History*, III, p. 184. The line between tragedy and tragi-comedy was not a firm one as Pierre Corneille's change in the designation of *Le Cid* suggests.

de ne trouver là qu'une histoire déjà très connue et si régulièrement, si mathématiquement conduite, que, la première situation étant donnée, les autres devaient nécessairement suivre.   (*Thom. Corn.*, p. 130)

A public well acquainted with Mlle de Scudery's novels might indeed have found *Bérénice* "mathématiquement conduite". The fact remains that it contains more fortuitous, unforeseen events than *Timocrate*, as a brief summary of the plot will illustrate.

Philoxène, believed to be the son of the King of Lydia, and Bérénice, supposed daughter of Araxe, have fallen in love at the court of Léarque, King of Phrygia. The King intends that Bérénice should marry Anaxaris, a favorite, and would attach Philoxène to the throne through an alliance with Philoclée, Léarque's sister. Word is brought that the Lydian King, having discovered that Philoxène is not really his son, has placed a real son, Alcidamas, on the throne. It is now supposed that Philoxène is the son of Cléophis, formerly his preceptor. Philoxène's abasement makes him the equal of Bérénice who now fears, however, that Araxe will be opposed to her marriage to Philoxène, the prospect of which momentarily looked brighter owing to the likelihood that Philoxène was no longer a suitable match for Philoclée. It is then revealed that Bérénice is not the daughter of Araxe but of King Léarque himself. For reasons of state policy Léarque now opposes the marriage of his daughter to Philoxène. Meanwhile Anaxaris has been hovering over Philoclée and Bérénice hoping to marry the one who will bring him the more power. Having declared his love to each of these women in turn, he has aroused the suspicions of Araxe. In a desperate move Anaxaris carries off Bérénice but is apprehended by Philoxène, who is finally recognized as Atis, the rightful ruler of Phrygia. Bérénice and Philoxène will marry and Philoclée will be given to Alcidamas of Lydia.

Rather than accept Reynier's explanation for the failure of *Bérénice*, we would suggest that its weakness may be attributed to the lack of a cohesive central figure. Timocrate was aware of his identity. He was a "héros prodigue", appearing in all acts and always in an aura of mighty accomplishments. Philoxène embodies all the conventional virtues of the gallant warrior but is less imposing because not in control of his own fate. His identity is too easily lost and regained, too easily manipulated by explanations of events which had taken place a score of years before the action represented in the play. Moreover, although we are verbally assured of his warring prowess, he does nothing to demonstrate it in the course of the tragedy. On the other hand he spends much time declaiming his love to Bérénice, debating the virtues of earned distinction as opposed to inherited nobility, and registering surprise over his changes of identity.

When he first learns that he is not Philoxène, he accepts his fate with self-respecting grace, proud that his past actions have not belied the noble title mistakenly conferred upon him:

> Quoi? Par l'accablement d'une âme lâche et basse
> L'on me verrait, Seigneur, mériter ma disgrâce,
> Et cédant au revers qui désabuse un roi,
> J'aiderais au destin à triompher de moi?
> Non, non, à quelque excès que son caprice monte,
> Il m'ôte un rang bien haut, mais je le perds sans honte;
> Et cet abaissement arrivé par hasard
> N'est qu'une faible injure où je n'ai point de part.
>
> Pour n'être plus son fils, suis-je moins Philoxène,
> Et le dehors, sujet aux derniers accidents,
> Peut-il mêler quelque ombre à l'éclat du dedans?
> Si toujours la grandeur et d'âme et de courage
> Fut d'un illustre sang le précieux partage,
> C'est beaucoup d'avoir su la posséder au point
> D'avoir été cru prince, et de ne l'être point.   (II, 6)

However upon learning later that he has been dispossessed not only of a royal father but of Cléophis as well, Philoxène displays a consternation which is frankly humorous despite the despair which it should normally imply:

Cléophis: Et ce vaillant héros qui passait pour le sien
           N'est en effet, Seigneur, ni son fils, ni le mien.
Le Roi: Et qui donc?
Cléophis: C'est de quoi je n'ai point connaissance.
Philoxène: Dieux! Quel astre fatal éclaira ma naissance,
           Si sans m'en éclaircir le funeste embarras,
           L'on m'apprend seulement ce que je ne suis pas?   (V, 10)

His sheer bewilderment makes him a far less forceful character than was Timocrate.

At this point Thomas Corneille missed an opportunity to make something of his hero. There is no feeling that the foundations of Philoxène's world have been shaken, as well they might have been, by his loss of identity. Like a resourceful *honnête homme*, he takes it all in rather good grace and makes the necessary adjustment. There is no hint of a tragic event, no philosophical questioning of the situation, only a momentary shock.

Nor does the role of Bérénice have the power to excite dramatic interest. Despite her stoic abnegation, her generous sentiments and her youth, she is essentially a wisp in the hands of those who surround her. Indeed her weakness as a dramatic character springs ironically from her strength of soul. Her filial obedience becomes a dull resignation to her father's wishes. Her unwillingness to take advantage of the force of Philoxène's love in her own interest becomes excessive modesty.

It is clear that Thomas Corneille was seeking to represent paragons of *précieux* virtue. But in the process this virtue became so self-conscious and discussion centering upon it so prominent as to prevail over the very action which had given rise to its exercise. The very style betrays an intellectual dehumanization of the emotions, which are represented here as abstract nouns in combat with one another quite independent of the human beings involved. Witness for example the long contest of generosity between Philoxène and Bérénice, each trying to surpass the other in nobility of sentiment. Philoxène comes to Bérénice prepared to release her from any commitment to him by renouncing any claim on her love:

> Votre foi par Araxe à mes voeux engagée
> Combat pour moi sans doute et vous tient partagée;
> Mais comme un sort nouveau veut un cœur différent,
> Mon amour la reçut, mon respect vous la rend.
>
> (IV, 3)

Bérénice, however, is not disposed to receive his renouncement, for it implies, she feels, that she did not have the constancy to remain faithful to Philoxène when his fortune was running low:

> Si pour y renoncer ta force est assez grande,
> Attends du moins, cruel, que je te le demande,

> Et te voyant du ciel injustement trahi,
> Mérite d'être plaint, et non d'être haï.
>
> (IV, 3)

He feels it a crime to engage her love when duty demands that she extinguish it. But her ideal is more exacting, for she requires that their love, however unrequited it might remain, continue to exist:

> Ose m'aimer encore pour vivre malheureux.
> Cette double disgrâce à qui ta raison cède,
> Ne trouve dans la mort qu'un indigne remède.
> N'en cherche point la honte, et loin de recourir,
> Tâche à me disputer la gloire de souffrir.
>
> (IV, 3)

Earlier Bérénice had shown similar indignation for not being allowed to display her steadfastness. A generous withdrawal on the part of Philoxène had, she thought, preëmpted her own chances for a display of virtue:

> Quoi, ma flamme, peut-être à s'expliquer trop prompte,
> D'un si sensible outrage a mérité la honte,
> Et d'un fatal revers l'indispensable loi
> Vous souffre une vertu dont vous doutez en moi!
> Est-ce ainsi qu'en m'aimant vous m'avez dû connaître?
>
> (III, 1)

This ostensibly fragile love affair, tenuous though it appears at times owing to a hypersensitive heroine and an over-generous hero, sustains the entire plot. All the perils arise and are dissipated in relation to love. There is a question of dynastic succession, reason of state is invoked, personal honor figures prominently; but basically *Bérénice* is a tale of young lovers.

Although the action of the play is interrupted from time to time to allow for explanations (V, 10, for example) and nearly gratuitous discussions of principles (III, 3), *Bérénice* has its dramaturgical merits. The digressions are not entirely devoid of connection to the main action, for they serve as *scènes à faire* or as pauses during which the impact of a recent surprise may be absorbed. Stances, by now rarely used, had served a similar purpose in earlier tragedy. Moreover, in the case of Act V, scene 10, in which Philoxène is revealed as Atis, the very climax of the tragedy is prepared in two brief *récits* by

Cléophis and Araxe. Even though no action is developed in their speeches the import of their messages commands the attention of the audience.

The nature of the story which Thomas Corneille dramatized and the surprises he sought prompted him to use a technique involving spurts and delays. Act IV, scene 1, for instance, contains the king's decision to forbid Bérénice's marriage to Philoxène. Scenes 2 and 3 are given to commentaries on this decision and the reactions it provokes. Conversely in Act V there are three scenes of preparation (3, 4, and 5), during which, as one shortly learns, the principal action (Anaxaris' abduction of Bérénice) is taking place off stage.

In any but an identity play, explanations of the kind contained in the *récits* of scene 10, Act V would properly belong in the exposition. Their postponement until the denouement can only be justified by the nature of the play itself and the peculiar sacrifice it requires in technical precision in favor of dramatic surprise. Pierre Corneille, having given Thomas the prototype of the identity play, was nevertheless more conservative than his brother with respect to dramatic composition. Surprise revelations in *Rodogune, Héraclius,* and *Don Sanche,* for example, are presented with greater verisimilitude and preparation. In *Rodogune,* although it is never revealed which one of the brothers enjoys the *droit d'aînesse,* it is known that the queen holds this information. Moreover, the identity of Antiochus and Seleucus is not precisely the question since their histories are summarized in the first act. In *Héraclius,* more properly called an identity play, the rumor that Héraclius, a son of the former emperor, has survived is made known from the first scene. The uncertainty surrounding his identity is not in itself intended to surprise so much as to provide a basis for the psychological reactions of Phocas, Héraclius, Martian, and Pulchérie. The existence of an heir to Aragon in *Don Sanche* is reported near the end of Act III, and his eventual recognition occupies the two remaining acts. The result is that, while Corneille admitted in his *examen* the intent to surprise, the shock is attenuated by a longer treatment of preparatory details.

Such is not the case with Thomas Corneille's *Bérénice* in which Atis is, so to speak, pulled out of a hat for the purpose of concluding a highly unlikely romance. The explanation necessitated to justify the

final turn of events has the value of a *deus ex machina*. It is reported
how, twenty years earlier through the efforts of Cléophis and Araxe,
acting independently, Atis had been reared with Cléophis' son. Upon
the latter's death Atis replaced him, survived a shipwreck, was re-
covered floating in a basket on the sea and was finally brought to
Phrygia. This sort of information, logically coherent though it may be,
is hardly satisfactory in a drama purporting to be tragic. It is probably
this sort of contrivance Lockert had in mind in criticizing Thomas
Corneille's dramaturgy.

Anaxaris, the villain of the play, commands greater interest than
either hero or heroine. His role provides the only genuine action as
such, for he is constantly trying to maneuver into the position most
favorable to his interests. Bérénice and Philoxène, on the other hand,
are too noble to act. Their gestures are largely reactions to events
taking place around them whereas the ambitious Anaxaris behaves in
a positive, if unscrupulous, fashion. Having been named as a potential
mate for Philoclée in Act I, he first appears in the opening scene of
Act II telling Bérénice of his love for Philoclée. In the following
scene, alone with his confidant, his true sentiments escape: he is really
in love with Bérénice, but ambition prevails and he will court
Philoclée. The latter enters and skeptically hears Anaxaris' amorous
declarations. He remains on stage for the rest of the act as a silent
but now meaningful witness to the reversals of fortune affecting
Philoxène. Allowed to go unnoticed for several scenes in Act III and
half of Act IV, he then reappears to solicit Philoxène's help in paying
court to Philoclée. Meanwhile, however, the king has decided that
Bérénice should succeed him on the Phrygian throne. Upon hearing
of this reversal from Philoclée, Anaxaris visibly pales, for Philoclée
remarks:

> C'est par l'ordre du roi qu'Araxe m'a fait voir.
> Que je ne puis sans crime en conserver l'espoir.
> Eh bien, puisqu'il le faut, cédons une couronne,
> Il semble qu'à ce mot ton courage s'étonne,
> Il s'émeut, il chancelle, et se laisse accabler
> D'un coup dont ma vertu dédaigne de trembler.
>
> (IV, 6)

He protests on the grounds that his reaction was one of sympathetic disappointment for her, but the following scene reveals that he was indeed stricken and will now take drastic measures to win Bérénice. In much the same way that Nicandre had concluded Act III of *Timocrate* on a note of suspense,[5] Anaxaris brings Act IV of *Bérénice* to a close with an ominous but secret resolution:

> Viens, dans peu tu sauras à quoi je me résous.
> (IV, 7)

In Act V he tries to force Bérénice's hand by insisting that the people demand their marriage. When this does not work, he has recourse to abduction, which is discovered soon enough to bring about his destruction and the only opportunity for Philoxène actively to demonstrate his valor by saving Bérénice.

Beyond the fact that he is the principal instigator in the play, Anaxaris also holds the dubious distinction of being Thomas Corneille's first genuine villain, a role which the dramatist was to amplify to more significant proportions in succeeding tragedies.

Another theme occurring for the first time in *Bérénice* is the *cri du sang*, that curious, instinctive power of communication which was supposed to exist between members of the same family.[6] Léarque first experiences premonitions of his relationship to Bérénice in Act I, scene 1 when he observes, speaking to Araxe:

> Ce n'est pas que mon cœur, qu'un secret instinct presse,
> Ne penche vers ta fille avec tant de tendresse...

And later in the same scene as Bérénice approaches, he assures Araxe with unconscious irony:

> La voici qui s'avance; adieu mais souviens-toi
> Qu'ici j'agis pour elle en père plus qu'en roi.

More attention is directed to the blood relationship when Araxe mysteriously encourages Bérénice not to abandon hope of making an advantageous marriage:

---

[5]   Pour hâter un glorieux dessein
Viens prendre pour Iphite un ordre de ma main. (*Timocrate*, III, 7)

[6] Clifton Cherpack in his *Call of the Blood in French Classical Tragedy* (Baltimore, 1958) has discussed this theme in some detail as found in Corneille, Racine, Voltaire and others. Of Thomas Corneille's plays, he has treated *Bérénice, Darius, Pyrrhus,* and *Stilicon* (see pp. 59-65).

> Je connais mieux ton sang que tu ne fais toi-même,
> J'en vois jusqu'à la source, et j'y sais pénétrer
> Ce qu'à tes yeux le ciel refuse de montrer.
>
>   (I, 2)

More conclusive evidence, in the form of a letter, is required to convince Léarque that Bérénice is really his daughter, and he has to admit that nature's voice in itself does not suffice to invalidate the long accepted supposition that Bérénice was Araxe's child. He explains:

> Oui, ma fille, le sang par un vif caractère
> Me traçait dans tes yeux l'image de ta mère,
> Et ces aimables traits imprimés dans mon sein
> Cherchaient à prévenir ce gage de sa main.
> Mais sans un tel secours [la lettre] la nature muette
> Ne pouvait de ton sort se faire l'interprète,
> Et son aveuglement affaiblissant ses droits,
> Lui faisait dans mon cœur méconnaître sa voix.
>
>   (IV, 1)

In this play then the force of instinct is at best subliminal, for in the case of Philoxène it doesn't work at all. Upon being told that he is Cléophis' son, Philoxène attributes the older man's kindnesses to him as expressions of paternal affection:

> Et dans ce que pour moi Cléophis a su faire
> Je vois paraître enfin toute l'ardeur d'un père.
>
>   (II, 6)

But it turns out that Cléophis is not his father.

In Bérénice the theme of the call of the blood is not exploited in a consistent fashion; its chief use is as a dramaturgical device to prepare for the recognition of the heroine.

In toto, Bérénice may be said to be one of Thomas Corneille's weakest romanesque plays. The lack of a striking character, the passiveness of hero and heroine, the incredible circumstances of their early years and the fact that many precious lines are used to account for these circumstances are the chief reasons for its lack of success. Except for the death of Anaxaris, who arouses little sympathy anyway, there is no reason to consider *Bérénice* as tragedy. As in *Timocrate* the main peril is not one involving life and death but the conclusion of a marriage.

Thomas Corneille's natural inclination to use comic devices and his great concern for dramaturgical intricacies, a heavy dose of romanesque literature and the success of *Timocrate* had led him to compose *Bérénice*. But its failure led him temporarily to turn away from the situation of false identity. Later the same year he wrote *La Mort de l'empereur Commode* where for the first time, as we shall see in the following chapter, he portrayed a serious event with tragic dimensions. But he was not yet disposed to abandon the type of plot which had made him famous, for after *Commode* he returned to the romanesque imbroglio and created a new problem of identity, this one involving Darius.

DARIUS

Although the historical elements of *Darius* (1659) have been traced to Justin, Diodorus and Plutarch, the general tenor of the play and the dramatic techniques it embodies were not new to Thomas Corneille for, as Lancaster has pointed out, his *Bérénice* contained the same devices (*History*, III, p. 189). In an article on the sources of *Darius*, Raphael Levy has suggested that an episode from *L'Astrée* was Thomas' starting point (*Romanic Review*, XX, [1929], 35-41). Certainly there is enough resemblance between the play and a section of the famous novel to make this rapprochement plausible. The episode that Levy isolates, Part IV, Book X, however, does not bear the striking resemblance with *Darius* that more recent plays did. That the play is romanesque in tone, if not textually inspired by d'Urfé, is undeniable. But in the final analysis it must be acknowledged that the essence of the play derives immediately from *Bérénice* and was ultimately derived, as was also probably the case for *Timocrate* and *Pyrrhus*, from Pierre Corneille's *Héraclius*.

Darius has in common with *Bérénice* the fact that the hero, under an assumed name, is living at the court of which he is the legitimate ruler and has fallen in love with the daughter of the ruling usurper. In both plays a deceitful favorite of the throne pays court alternately to the usurper's sister and daughter in the hope thereby of securing his position for a *coup d'état*. His deceit is finally revealed and a conspiracy thwarted by the recognition of the hero, who will marry the King's daughter and reclaim the throne.

So close in outline are the plots of *Bérénice* and *Darius* that Reynier saw fit to discuss only the former in detail, grouping the latter with several other of Thomas Corneille's plays in a summary treatment. Certainly there is little reason to repeat the same observations in connection with each play, but differences there are, chiefly in the manner of handling effects.

In *Darius*, Thomas Corneille paid closer attention to preparatory devices, possibly realizing that his exclusive reliance on surprise revelations in *Bérénice* made for an excess of gratuitous action. In the first scene, for example, the rumor is spread that Darius, believed killed by Ochus, is alive. In Act II, he informs Amestris of his identity. By revealing him early, Thomas Corneille created an entirely different mood from that of *Bérénice*. For despite other striking similarities, *Bérénice* and *Darius* differ markedly in this one important aspect. Having informed the audience of his hero's identity, Thomas Corneille forfeited the opportunity to surprise the better to create situations of dramatic irony. To accomplish the latter, he needed the complicity of his spectators. What *Darius* loses in shock reactions, it gains in suspense. From Act I, scene 2 it is known that Mégabise conspires to claim the name and fortune of Darius. The scene in which he solicits Darius' support is one of the best in the tragedy especially since Darius, under the name of Codoman, is on the point of revealing himself to Mégabise:

Mégabise: Ochus n'est que son père [de Statira] et Darius son roi.
Darius: Quoi? vous connaissez donc...
Még.   Oui je puis bien connaître
          Sous quel astre fatal son malheur le fit naître,
          Si Tiribase, hélas!
Dar.   Vous m'en dites assez.
          Je ne demande plus si vous le connaissez;
          Mais j'atteste les dieux qu'à taire sa naissance...
Még.   Non, non, je n'ai de vous aucune défiance;
          Et vos serments en vain cherchent à m'assurer
          D'un cœur à qui le mien aime à se déclarer.
          Admirez seulement quelle rare conduite
          A su de mon tyran arrêter la poursuite;

> Et par ma fausse mort l'abuser à tel point,
> Qu'il croit ma vie un songe, et ne s'en émeut point.

Dar.   Quoi? Que me dites-vous?

Még.   Ce que je dois vous dire,

> Qu'Ochus jura ma mort pour s'assurer l'empire;
> Et qu'à me la donner Tiribase commis,
> M'ayant sauvé le jour, me fit croire son fils.

Dar.   Vous êtes Darius?

Még.   Oui, ce Darius même

> Sur qui la tyrannie usurpe un diadème.

(II, 5)

Codoman proceeds to offer his support to Darius and thus seemingly encourages Mégabise in his plot to overthrow Ochus. Codoman can do this in good faith merely by speaking in the third person:

> Et lorsqu'à Darius on doit une couronne
> J'ose sur moi des dieux appeler le courroux,
> Si je n'ai pas pour lui la même ardeur que vous,
> Si de son premier sort l'abaissement extrême
> Ne m'intéresse pas à l'égal de lui-même;
> Et si dans mes souhaits rien m'est plus précieux
> Que de revoir ce prince au rang de ses aïeux.   (II, 5)

From this point on the interest centers on the predicament of Darius; and the audience, now committed to view matters through his eyes, feels more psychologically engaged in the outcome.

We have seen how, when Thomas Corneille sought to conceal information from his audience during most of a play, as in *Timocrate*, he was guilty of violating *vraisemblance*. In *Darius* we see the curious example of a character in the play pointing out what to him is unlikely in the behavior of a fellow actor while the audience, because informed, finds nothing amiss. We refer to the second encounter of Darius and Mégabise. The former, having led Mégabise to believe in his support through his statements in the third person, suddenly appears unduly suspicious and asks Mégabise to give proof of his claim to be Darius. When Mégabise refuses, Codoman becomes adamant and insists that he (Mégabise) will not marry Statira as long as he is alive to prevent it. Mégabise understandably registers surprise at Codoman's apparent betrayal:

> Quoi? Quand je vous le dis, vous ne m'en croyez pas?
> Vos sentiments pour moi sont assez inégaux.

> Mais tantôt votre amour s'est montré plus crédule
> Me croyant Darius vous étiez sans scrupule.
>
> (III, 5)

Only moments before Codoman had seemed to make the most generous surrender to Mégabise's wishes:

> C'est trop; et mon amour avec vous s'intéresse
> Quand Darius au trône appelle la princesse.
> Pour cet illustre hymen qui lui donne ce droit
> Peut-être mon aveu peut plus qu'on ne croit;
> Mais quoiqu'il faille alors que Codoman expire,
> En vous le promettant à peine il en soupire
> Sa flamme à Darius fait gloire de céder.
>
> (III, 5)

By having Mégabise call attention to Codoman's strange behavior,
Thomas Corneille is only bringing out the reasonable doubts that
anyone would have in such circumstances. Unfortunately, however,
the irony of situation is diminished, or at best made less subtle by the
emphasis placed on Codoman's inconsistency. One might have expected him to play the scene straight, that is, to agree temporarily to
Mégabise's plans. Instead he appears to want to proclaim himself
Darius as soon as possible and preëmpt Mégabise's scheme. Had this
scene occurred just before the denouement, it would have been better
placed, but Thomas Corneille was to use ignorance of identity as the
basis of six more major scenes and could not afford to expose Darius
to the other characters.

The dramaturgical skill with which he saw this problem and his
manner of circumventing it are worth noting. We saw that Darius has
no plausible reason to hide his true identity from the king and is on the
point of confessing when he learns that Mégabise who, it should be
remembered, has been posing as Darius, has been made a prisoner.
Although Darius tries to clear matters up, he is three times interrupted
and prevented from revealing his true identity. This crucial scene (Act
IV, scene 6) is laden with suspense, for it is essential to Darius'
success that he not be made captive just yet. Ochus temporarily holds
over Darius the power of life and death. As long as Mégabise is
thought to be Darius, Codoman (the real Darius) is out of danger. A
further step is needed to prepare the recognition. It comes between
Acts IV and V during which time the people, having been aroused

to support Mégabise as Darius, imperiously demand that their long
lost prince be liberated. This is the point at which Codoman reveals
himself to Ochus as Darius. The political sagacity of this maneuver is
not allowed to overshadow the purity of Darius' motives, however,
for, far from taking advantage of the popular uprising in his behalf,
he humbly offers his life to Ochus. Moreover, he has difficulty
wresting from the proud Mégabise a renouncement of the latter's false
claim on his name. Since the king is infuriated more by the treason of
Mégabise than by the discovery of the real Darius, the "tragedy" is
allowed to draw to a happy conclusion. Ochus' daughter, Statira, will
marry Darius.

Along with the use of false identity as a spring for plot development, Thomas Corneille sought to enrich his play with the usual
accessories which by that time had become characteristic of his style
and a delight to Parisian audiences. Foremost among these *trucs* was
the voice of consanguinity, which, though insufficient to bring about
the definitive recognition of Darius by his aunt or uncle, was nevertheless a useful pretext to plant information earlier in the play than
it otherwise could have been. We are given encouragement to believe
that, despite Ochus' doubts of Darius' survival, he is indeed alive, for
Amestris, speaking to Mégabise, counters Ochus' skepticism:

> Il [Ochus] croit tout ce qu'on dit une vaine imposture,
> Et que ce Darius qu'on tire du tombeau
> N'est pour les factieux qu'un prétexte nouveau.
> Mais pour moi qu'en secret le sang tâche d'instruire
> Je crains à son erreur de me laisser séduire.
>
> (I, 1)

Thereafter references to "un secret instinct", "le suffrage du sang",
"mouvements du sang", etc. are numerous, each one intended to
titillate the imaginations of spectators without disclosing enough information to spoil the forthcoming revelations.

The contest of generosity, usually brought on by the necessity of
renouncing one's claim for affection in the interest of the beloved,
appears in typical fashion, as does the discussion of the valorous
inconnu as opposed to the titular noble. Nor should the hymn to self-
mastery (I, 4) be omitted from a list of the components of *Darius*.
Whatever other moral trivialities may pervade his identity plays,

Thomas Corneille showed his characters to have their full share of self-control. In this respect, as in some others that we shall see, he preserved the Cornelian heritage of stoic ethics.

Although *Darius* is, on the whole, a better constructed play than *Bérénice*, it is not free of blemishes. As Lancaster has pointed out, the unity of action is violated insofar as Mégabise's conspiracy is exposed by two characters who do not appear in the play (*History*, III, p. 190). Far more serious than this technical slip, however, is the magnanimous attitude of Darius toward his uncle Ochus. The latter had killed Darius' father in a treacherous and successful plot to usurp the Persian throne. To secure his position he had then proceeded to kill the legitimate heirs including, he thought, Darius. It is therefore strange that Darius should treat Ochus with such resignation, indeed reverence, in view of his knowledge of Ochus' crimes.

In the next four years, Thomas concentrated on serious political tragedy. Beginning with *Stilicon* (1660) and in *Camma* (1661), *Maximian* (1662), and *Persée et Démétrius* (1662) he made a definite break away from romanesque identity plays. From time to time he was to return to them but without producing notable innovations. He composed later identity plays, it seems, in order to capitalize on the public image of him as the author of *Timocrate*. Of these *Pyrrhus* stands out as the extreme example of the genre.

PYRRHUS

About four years elapsed between the first performance of *Darius* and that of *Pyrrhus*, which probably appeared in 1663.[7] The historical source was Plutarch but, as one might expect, Thomas had by now a backlog of dramatic techniques which with a few changes could readily serve in a new identity play. *Pyrrhus* partakes of his own *Darius* and *Bérénice* as well as Pierre Corneille's *Héraclius* and Boyer's *Tyridate* (1647). For sheer complexity it has no peer. Even if one succeeds in keeping the identities of characters well in mind, one is not always certain from what point of view a speech is being made.

---

[7]   See Lancaster, *History*, III, p. 445. The date of first performance is conjectural.

In order to have a framework of reference for our remarks, it will be useful to present the plot in summary form. Pyrrhus, thought to be Hippias but actually son and heir of the late King Aeacides, is living at the court of Néoptolemus, the present king of Epirus, with whose daughter, Antigone, he has fallen in love. For political reasons the marriage of Pyrrhus and Antigone is deemed advisable, but since Hippias, thought to be Pyrrhus, is in love, incestuously he believes, with Pyrrhus' sister Déidamie, neither he, Antigone, Pyrrhus, nor Déidamie wants this marriage. Moreover Néoptolemus, also in love with Déidamie, threatens that, unless she marries him, he will kill the supposed Pyrrhus. Androclide, father of Hippias, is reluctant to dispel the error of identities, hoping to place his son on the throne by imposture; but Déidamie, who is also aware of the exchange of names, expects that Androclide will confess in order to save his son. Instead he denounces his supposed son for having dared love Déidamie. This ruse backfires, however, for Déidamie, supposing that Néoptolemus has been told the true identities, begs him to spare her brother. He does, believing however that he is releasing Hippias, and the real Hippias becomes suspect. Androclide then incites a rebellion to gain the release of his son, who is still supposed by the people to be Pyrrhus (Act V is closely patterned after the final act of *Darius*). The real Pyrrhus puts down the revolt, Androclide is fatally wounded, Pyrrhus is recognized and will marry Antigone. Together they will share the throne with Néoptolemus. In the meanwhile the latter has renounced his pursuit of Déidamie, who has constantly resisted his advances, and permits her to marry Hippias.

A summary as brief as the foregoing can scarcely do justice to the complexities of this play. Thomas Corneille was determined, it would seem, to push the theme of false identity to its furthest potentialities. This he managed to do so successfully that he reached a point of diminishing returns, for by Act IV, the revelation of Hippias has been thrown into such confusion that it has virtually no effect on the important decision of Néoptolemus. This king finds himself in the same position as Phocas (*Héraclius*) trying to determine who is his proper enemy, except that because neither young man is his own son, he is even more arbitrary than Phocas in choosing a victim to his jealousy. He loses all sense of political wisdom, willing to sacrifice state welfare to his desire for revenge. It is difficult to avoid the impression that there are two streams of action in Pyrrhus, one dramaturgical, a pure enigma of who's who, loosely connected to the second, more dramatic, involving the interference of a king in the amorous projects of his subjects.

In view of the preceding discussions of *Timocrate*, *Bérénice*, and *Darius* we feel that little would be gained by an enumeration here of the dramaturgical components of *Pyrrhus*, which are in most respects identical. Two characters, however, deserve a brief analysis. Déidamie, sister of Pyrrhus, and Androclide, father of Hippias, are the effective protagonist and antagonist respectively. They are alone in knowing the true identities of Pyrrhus and Hippias and thereby control the action. Each uses the secret information as a weapon to force the hand of the other, now informing a third character, now remaining silent, now trying to convince someone else that what the other has said is false.

Déidamie first withholds her secret knowledge in order to tantalize Hippias. Thinking himself Pyrrhus, he tries unsuccessfully to suppress his supposedly incestuous love for Déidamie who delights coquettishly in his discomfort (I, 5). She feels, however, that the time has come to reveal Pyrrhus so that he may marry Antigone. When Néoptolemus threatens to put Pyrrhus to death, she hesitates, confident that Androclide, in order to save his son, will clarify the situation. But this old courtier is shrewder than she thought. Androclide is a gambler who dares to predicate his moves on what he predicts will be the reactions of his jealous sovereign and Antigone. He tells Antigone that Hippias (really Pyrrhus) has been courting her only to win the throne. Angered by the thought that Pyrrhus has betrayed her love, she informs Néoptolemus that Déidamie is conspiring with Hippias (really Pyrrhus). Androclide seconds this accusation and effects Hippias' release. Déidamie then tells Hippias who he is while Androclide unsuccessfully denies her assertions. The case is brought before Néoptolemus where Androclide, counting on his favor with the throne, ironically tells the truth in the expectation that feigned self-accusation will produce the impression of innocence. He charges his son with guilt. What he does not foresee is his son's loyalty to Pyrrhus and his willingness to die as the avowed lover of Déidamie.[8] In single combat Androclide would easily have outwitted Déidamie, but with the support of the two young princes and the truth, she wins.

The play is at the same time clever and awkward, intriguing and *invraisemblable*. Clever and intriguing for the same reasons that a modern murder mystery appeals to us; awkward and *invraisemblable* because too much explanation is required to justify situations. Witness for example the frequent use of words required to express relationship in the following few lines; i.e., *fils, fille, amant*, etc.:

Androclide: Mais quand l'amour par elle au devoir se préfère,
                Sera-ce la punir que d'immoler son frère,
                Ce frère que tantôt, le voyant condamner,
                Elle n'a point rougi de vous abandonner?
                C'est sur son amant seul qu'il faut que votre haine ...
Néoptolemus: L'amant comme le frère aura part à la peine,
                Et demain ...
Gelon: Quoi, Seigneur, vous les perdrez tous deux?
Néoptolemus: (montrant Androclide)
                Non, il faut épargner un père malheureux,
                Pyrrhus périra seul, mais de peur que l'ingrate
                De quelque espoir encore lâchement ne se flatte,
                Je veux que son amant, quand il perdra le jour,
                En épousant ma fille accable son amour.
                Cet hymen à leurs voeux par tant de droits contraire,
                En me vengeant du fils, m'acquitte vers le père,
                Et je ne vois ...
Androclide: Seigneur, Pyrrhus est condamné,
                Et mon fils ...   (IV, 4)

From the beginning of his career as writer of tragedy in 1656, Thomas Corneille seems to have been obsessed with his brother's *Héraclius*. *Timocrate* and *Bérénice* were attempts to recapture the excitement and suspense of the Cornelian thriller. *Darius* and *Pyrrhus* were even more closely patterned after it. The popular uprising in favor of a legitimate prince long thought dead or banished, the gnawing uncertainty of the usurper faced with the need to make a correct identification at the risk of killing the innocent party, the use of letters left

[8]   Thomas may have borrowed the idea of the relationship between Androclide and Hippias from his *Stilicon* in which also the son frustrates his father's plot to put him on the throne. See below page 113.

by the previous king (or queen) in the hope of establishing his son as successor, and finally the happy ending uniting hero with loved one; these are all ingredients common to *Darius*, *Héraclius* and *Pyrrhus*. In addition, the two last mentioned offer a latent incestuous relationship, and the usurpers in both plays threaten to force themselves by marriage upon the princes' sisters. Lancaster has observed the similarity of Phocas' disparaging couplet:

> Tu recouvres deux fils pour mourir après toi,
> Et je n'en puis trouver pour régner après moi.
> > (*Héraclius*, IV, 3, 1385-6)

with Déidamie's lines from *Pyrrhus*:

> Et tous deux aiment mieux afin de m'épargner,
> Etre amants pour mourir, que frères pour régner.
> > (IV, 3)

Even more striking is the resemblance between Léontine's defiance of Phocas and Mégabise's similar challenge to Ochus in *Darius*:

> Devine, si tu peux, et choisis, si tu l'oses.
> > (*Héraclius*, IV, 4, 1408)

> Doute, j'y consens, doute, et perds-moi si tu l'oses.
> > (*Darius*, V, 3)

In a sense the challenge expressed in the verbs "devine" and "doute" carry beyond the characters to whom they are adressed in the play straight to the spectator. They are the playwright's summons to his public to participate actively in a dramatic dénouement.

COMPARISON WITH QUINAULT

For their verve and excitement the four plays of Thomas Corneille just treated probably represent the most extreme point of reaction against the lamentatory tragedy of the Renaissance. Yet during these same years one of Thomas' contemporaries was producing identity plays in which the hero characteristically became paralyzed by deep feelings about which he could do little more than lament. This playwright was Philippe Quinault whose role in romanesque tragedy is too important to escape brief mention here in connection with Thomas' *Antiochus* (1666).

Quinault did not exploit false identity for its own sake to the extent Thomas did. Even in those plays where false identity constitutes a theme, such as his *Agrippa* (1662) and *Astrate* (1664), a resounding hymn to the god of love drowns out the dramatic irony and surprise normally indigenous to identity plays. *Agrippa*, for example, portrays a disguised hero nearly incapable of action. At a moment when his cooperation in a conspiracy planned in his behalf is imperative, he can only languish:

> Si vous connaissiez combien l'amour est doux.
>
> (IV, 4)

In Quinault's plays unrequited love generally has a debilitating effect on its victims. *Stratonice* (1660) offers a further example. In the mistaken belief that Stratonice scorns him, Antiochus develops a fever and, overcome by his effort to remove himself from her sight, faints at her feet before he can leave the room. But moments later when Stratonice coyly admits she does not hate him, Antiochus is immediately cured (V, 4). With figures like Antiochus populating his plays, Quinault must be credited for having represented the physiological manifestations of love several years before Racine's hot blooded heroines reached the stage.

ANTIOCHUS

Six years after *Stratonice*, Thomas Corneille produced a play on the same subject under the title of *Antiochus*. Of all his compositions this one comes the closest in tone and manner to those of Quinault. Like *Stratonice*, Thomas' play portrays the young prince Antiochus in love with his father's fiancée, his attempt to repress this love, and his father's voluntary sacrifice of Stratonice to his son. Like Quinault's hero, Thomas' Antiochus languishes under self-restraint. Nevertheless he manages to present a more credible image of the amorous martyr than Quinault's hero. Unlike the latter, he does not faint away from a fever of passion. Instead he requests permission to withdraw from the kingdom. In keeping with the self-discipline required of him to conceal his love is a corresponding reticence to speak of it. Hence he frequently appears tongue-tied unlike Quinault's lover who seems to delight in telling of his flame and who, to assure the audience of his sincerity, collapses in a chair as early as Act I, scene 6. Thomas' hero has a measure of self-respect that Quinault's lover lacks.

Thomas was fully aware that he was invading upon Quinault's specialty in *Antiochus*. That he was consciously trying to differentiate his hero from Quinault's is suggested by a statement from his "Au Lecteur" in which he observed:

Je me suis particulièrement attaché à donner à Antiochus le caractère de ce profond respect qui l'empêcha de recevoir personne dans sa confidence, et le fit résoudre à mourir plutôt de la fièvre lente qui le consumait, qu'à chercher quelque secours, en déclarant une passion qu'il voyait trop condamnable pour ne la détester pas lui-même.   (III, p. 422)

He was seeking a formula for compromise which might combine the sympathetic qualities of the impassioned lover with the luster of chivalric virtue. Antiochus turned out to be a fair solution which avoided the unctuousness of Quinault's *Stratonice* on the one hand and the complexities of the identity plays on the other.

It is clear that in the plays just discussed Thomas' heroes are closely patterned after the romanesque protagonists of La Calprenède. Their world bears close resemblance to the pastoral idyl. To sustain them as figures of the drama was in itself something of an accomplishment. Thomas Corneille shows himself not as an artist who seduces by the sheer poetic beauty of his creation, but as one who ingratiates himself with his audience by requiring an intellectual effort. He fails in these plays to reach the moral profundity that his brother and Racine achieved in many of theirs because he refused to permit his characters the ultimate necessity of a tragic experience. The problems which they face are solved largely by circumstances, not by decisions. It is difficult not to feel that the protracted *quid pro quo* takes on more importance to the dramatist than does the basic human problem. If we are led temporarily to believe that Timocrate, Philoxène, Darius, and Pyrrhus are involved in a momentous crisis, we learn as the plays unfold that the reasons for their consternation are only apparent and can easily be explained away when sufficient facts become known. There is therefore no purgation of passions, but rather an appeal to the imagination. One is not gripped by the pathos, but dazzled by the complexities.

Those contemporaries who demanded more of tragedy than a series of complex maneuvers may have been pleased to see Thomas Corneille abandon the identity play to take up more sobering themes. But something positive remained from his romanesque experience. With this group of plays he achieved a curious duality. To the heroic ethos of his brother's early masterpieces, he juxtaposed a morality based on passion. Whereas Quinault's heroes appear to celebrate the dissolution of Cornelian ethics, Thomas' characters simply apply the same steadfastness and rectitude in pursuit of an amorous objective. Love is still basically a game in *Timocrate* and *Antiochus*, but its rules are deadly serious.

In view of the fact that during these same years Pierre Corneille's heroines persist in belittling the powers of love when a crown is at stake, it is a pleasant contrast to find a heroine who, like Thomas' Bérénice, readily sacrifices ambition to have the man she loves. Pierre never allowed his characters to be caught inextricably by emotional demands whereas Thomas' romanesque heroes and heroines give priority to love over political ambition. They are possessed by a love untainted by ulterior motives. But for all their passion they do not, as Racine's characters will, succumb to love's furor. Love is noble and ennobling. If it simply must be subdued, it does not produce wrath and jealousy but quiet grief and bitter introspection as in *Antiochus*.

In the transition from comedy to tragi-comedy, Thomas learned to focus attention and interest on the gallant hero. It remained for him to supply a type of protagonist whose conflict was rooted in political realities.

Just as he had found in his brother's theater the prototypes for *Darius* and *Pyrrhus*, so did he now look again to Pierre Corneille, this time principally to his conspiracy plays, for a model on which to fashion some of his most provocative tragedies extending from 1657 (*Commode*) to 1669 (*Annibal*).

III. THE "CORNELIAN" TRAGEDIES

The question of the influence of Pierre Corneille on his younger brother is one which arose even before Thomas had completed half of his tragedies. As early as 1661 Chapelain noted the younger dramatist's emulation of Pierre: "A force de vouloir surpasser son aîné, [Thomas Corneille] tombe fort au-dessous de lui et son élévation le rend obscur sans le rendre grave." [1] Two years later d'Aubignac observed that Thomas was still "un apprentif qui travaille encore sur la besogne que le maître [Pierre] lui taille" (Mélèse, *Répertoire*, p. 45). More than twenty years later Racine pointed admiringly to the "conformité" of Thomas and Pierre.[2] And in his reception speech at the Academy, Thomas himself paid tribute to his brother for "tant de leçons que j'ai reçues de sa propre bouche," and "cette pratique continuelle que me donnait avec lui la plus parfaite union qu'on ait jamais vue entre deux frères" (V, p. 573).

In view of their known fraternal affection, their shared interest in the theater, and the intimacy of their living arrangements, it is not surprising that the name of the elder should have evoked the name of the younger among contemporaries as it has done subsequently among students of French classical theater. Almost invariably Pierre has been acknowledged the superior dramatist. Posterity has pronounced, irrevocably it would seem, in his favor. Among seventeenth century critics

---

[1] Reported in Pierre Mélèse, *Répertoire analytique des documents ... concernant le théâtre* (Paris, 1934), p. 45. Hereafter referred to as Mélèse, *Répertoire*.

[2] *Œuvres de J. Racine*, éd. Paul Mesnard (Paris, 1885), Vol. IV, p. 370.

this judgment had in fact already been generally accepted with few exceptions.[3]

In the preceding chapter we had occasion to compare Thomas' identity plays with those of Pierre and to show that in this particular form of tragedy, the author of *Timocrate* owed something quite definite to the author of *Héraclius*. In the plays about to be treated the influence of Pierre may be seen to play at least as great a role in the younger Corneille's theater. Thomas Corneille began to assimilate his brother's basic attitudes toward dramatic roles and situations.

While in the cases of *Laodice* and *Annibal* Thomas was to some extent making adaptations of *Rodogune* and *Nicomède*, far more than servile imitation was involved. *Laodice* and *Annibal* evince in their creator a desire to surpass in vividness the portrayal of those human qualities which his brother had taught him to admire. Thomas was not working from a recipe so much as from a conviction that what he had seen and appreciated in his brother's tragedies was worthy to be tried again with the hope of improving the image, intensifying the light, and putting the roles in *haut relief*. Hence, while it is clear that the Cléopatre of *Rodogune* is a spiritual ancestor of Laodice, it is also true that the latter surpassed the former as a characterization of moral turpitude. Thomas was a disciple of Pierre but remained sufficiently independent and vigorous to superimpose his own vision upon a given model. Cléopatre had been hailed as wicked, "homicide par ambition". Thomas makes his Laodice at least as evil and adds an incestuous passion into the bargain.

THE VILLAINOUS HERO

Laodice is Thomas Corneille's most striking heroine and certainly the most morally depraved. However, her role is not totally unexpected in his theater and in a sense is prepared by a series of character studies beginning with *Commode* in 1657 and including *Stilicon* in 1660 and *Maximian* in 1662. Two of these plays illustrate a type of tragedy in

---

[3]   Donneau de Visé, Thomas' close friend and collaborator and notoriously partial to the Corneille brothers, admired them both in such eulogistic terms that it is impossible to detect his preference for one or the other.

which the Aristotelian definition of the tragic hero undergoes an
ironic change. Commode and Laodice are neither essentially good
persons with some basic weakness, nor ones who have made an irrev-
ocable mistake, nor ones pursued by a relentless, overpowering fate.
On the contrary Commode and Laodice are villains first of all and
heroes incidentally, accidentally, or, to be perfectly exact, only thea-
trically. Stilicon and Maximian may also be classified as hero-villains,
but of a diffferent sort as we shall see later.

The juxtaposition of contrasting roles, those of hero and villain,
was a common device in comedy and tragedy alike. The fusion of
these two roles into one was less usual and had certain curious implications both technical and dramatic. By making a villain the hero of
a play a dramatist gave special emphasis to the struggle of good and
evil. When this figure took the form of the sovereign (Laodice and
Commode), evil appeared to enjoy a special sanction, and the power
of good had to be upheld by characters of lesser official stature. Hence
in *Commode* and *Laodice* there is a conspiracy; but unlike the standard
conspiracy, these are intended as defensive measures against the baleful
plans of a depraved monarch and as such take on a benign aspect. The
conspiracies in *Stilicon* and *Maximian* are more nearly "standard",
since the villain in both cases is instigator *and* would-be usurper.

Technically the development of an illegal scheme in a tragedy
required of the dramatist certain precautionary maneuvers to avoid
incredible situations. Plans for the conspiracy had to be made in a
room unlikely to be visited by the intended victim.[4] The chief conspirator had to combine two roles into one: the first as unscrupulous
schemer and the second as hypocritical favorite of the throne, for it
was in some respects useful to make these two roles coincide. Since
the success or failure of the conspiracy was contingent upon wavering
loyalties, secrecy, and deception, the playwright had to pay especially
close attention to the timing of exits, entrances and confrontations.

Such dramaturgical intricacies were not new for Thomas Corneille.
Not only could he draw from his own experience in romanesque
tragedy but also from examples of his brother's conspiracy plays,

---

[4] Pierre Corneille chose to violate the unity of place in Act IV of *Cinna*
rather than have Maxime reveal the conspiracy to Emilie in the same room in
which Auguste has just heard of it.

Cinna, Pompée and, later on, *Othon. Cinna* particularly seems to have haunted Thomas as we shall attempt to show in discussing *Commode.*

LA MORT DE L'EMPEREUR COMMODE

La Mort de L'Empereur Commode marked a distinct change in tone from Thomas Corneille's *Timocrate* and *Bérénice.* The latter, written the same year, contained one important feature in common with *Commode,* that is, the role of villain to which the character of Commode gave prominence. Commode himself is the villain and hero. He is the hero because the tragedy celebrates his death and because he acts positively and defiantly toward the accomplishment of his ideals. He is villainous because his means are perfidious, treacherous, and perverse.

The action of the play may be simply described as the events leading to the death of a tyrant who brings about his own destruction through ineptitude in handling his courtiers, capriciousness, and a ruthless decision to assassinate all who oppose his desires. To portray these events Thomas used two basic structural devices, the juxtaposition of characters with conflicting interests and the actual engagement of these interests in dynamic conflict. Act I is used to describe the tenuous equilibrium existing between Commode and his chief subjects, an equilibrium made possible only by the temporary stability of the contingent loyalties of these subjects. On one side of the equation stands the emperor, alone, cruel, reckless but sovereign. On the other, two couples, Helvie-Laetus and Marcia-Electus, each representing something of a quarter of a power unit in counterbalance to the unity of Commode. But as we shall see shortly, there is also a linear relationship which, beginning in the second act, comes to prevail as the structural pattern until the beginning of the fifth act when again Thomas Corneille opposed the two original forces to show the imbalance resulting from the intervening action.

After an exposition which was relatively slow for Thomas Corneille, events succeed one another at a rapid pace. Although Commode appears rarely on stage, seven scenes of the total thirty-two, his image is repeatedly brought to the attention of the audience by the other characters. He is first mentioned by Marcia and Helvie in scene 1. The latter dwells on his cruelty while the former does her best to defend him. Engaged to become his wife, Marcia is willing to overlook Commode's shortcomings in deference to her own overriding ambitions. In Act I we are given to believe that Commode's wishes will materialize; that is, Marcia, by marrying him, will attach to the throne the support of her father, Pertinax. Electus, in love with Marcia, is nevertheless willing to sacrifice his affection to see her become empress. Laetus is in love with Pertinax' other daughter, Helvie, who, like Electus, is willing to have her lover make an advantageous marriage with Commode's sister. It would seem, then, that everything is already resolved if not happily at least "convenablement".

Lancaster has observed that the exposition of Commode is slow, the action late in starting (History, III, pp. 191-192). The complex arrangement of characters into a pentagonal relationship required a relatively elaborate description. Although it was important to establish that Helvie, Marcia, Electus, and Laetus were making sacrifices to meet what they thought to be the conditions sought by Commode in the interests of state, the action could have begun earlier. It would have helped to introduce Commode, perhaps with a confidant, in order to make his motivation clear from the start. His rare appearances constitute one of the play's main weaknesses. The only defense for this slow exposition is in the greater contrast achieved as an after effect; for as one thinks back on the solicitous efforts of his subjects trying to keep peace in Act I, Commode's later reckless behavior stands out more harshly. Meanwhile as Act I concludes, no significant action has occurred; the scale is balanced.

In Act II Commode changes his mind, and the equilibrium is disturbed. He transfers his affections from Marcia to Helvie. The latter, however, does not share her sister's attitudes and refuses Commode who then (Act III) threatens to kill Pertinax if Helvie does not agree to marriage. Between Acts III and IV Helvie makes an unsuccessful attempt on Commode's life, which prompts him to draw up plans to assassinate not only Helvie, but also Marcia, Electus, Laetus, Pertinax and half of the senators. These plans, having been committed to "tablettes", are discovered between Acts IV and V by Marcia who then, retracting her hopes of a union with Commode, casts her lot with the others in a plan to kill him. The plan is executed successfully, and popular, old Pertinax accedes to the throne. His daughters will marry their respective suitors.

Structurally the play points toward Racine. Each decision of the emperor is followed by a series of responses not unlike the chain reactions which we shall find ten years later in *Andromaque*. Like Hermione, Marcia is jilted by a sovereign, treats sarcastically the woman who has replaced her, and promises herself to her suitor if he will kill the faithless sovereign.[5] A further point of similarity is the fact that in both *Andromaque* and *Commode*, the characters whose lives are threatened in order to force the hands of Andromaque and Helvie do not appear. The absence of Astyanax in Racine's play may be excused on the grounds that he was a child and that his presence was more important psychologically than physically.[6] In *Commode* Pertinax' absence is not so easily dismissed, however, since his involvement is central to the events of the play. First of all it is his popularity which accounts for the pressure on Commode to marry one of his daughters. Then the threat on his life prompts Helvie's attack on Commode; and finally, he is acclaimed emperor after Commode's death. It would not have been difficult or in any way irregular to include Pertinax in the cast, for his appearance with his daughters at some point would have been entirely natural in the circumstances.

In other regards the composition of *Commode* is conservative and respectful of the usual demands of sober tragedy. It is the first of Thomas Corneille's plays not dependent on a series of *quid pro quo*. Characters appear under their proper names, their motives are clearly drawn, and, with one exception, mutually understood. This one exception gives rise to one of the best scenes (III, 5). It involves Marcia's scornful treatment of her sister who, she believes, has purposely diverted Commode's affection from her. Nothing could be further from the truth, but Helvie, feeling that self-defense would only resemble hypocrisy, nobly withstands the onslaught of Marcia's sarcasm. The irony of the situation draws our sympathy to Helvie,

[5] For a summary rapprochement of the two plays, see Lancaster, *History*, III, p. 193.

[6] Nevertheless an engraving by Chauveau for the 1676 edition showing Astyanax being carried by Phoenix suggests that a child may have appeared briefly on stage in early performances.

for Marcia's accusations are more applicable to her own actions than to the unselfish decision of Helvie to sacrifice herself for her father's safety.

To match the sterling quality of Helvie, one of Thomas Corneille's outstanding feminine roles, the dramatist created a suitor worthy of her in the person of Laetus. He did not allow Laetus to fall simply into the standard and all too common category of the noble lover, but attempted to enrich his role to include a deeply personal conflict of loyalties. Commode asks Laetus to tell Helvie that she, and no longer Marcia, is the one he wishes to marry. In itself this mission is disagreeable enough to Laetus. But Commode goes on to stipulate that Laetus must make it appear that it is through his (Laetus') advice that Commode has made this choice.

The scene in which Laetus carries the message to Helvie and reluctantly presents Commode's proposal is a crucial one, for from it the decisive movement of the tragedy is unleashed. Helvie's refusal leads to the threat on her father's life, which in turn forces her to accept Commode's conditions. Marcia's cruelty to her sister together with Helvie's own horror of Commode lead to Helvie's attempt on his life; and this in turn, to his wild retaliatory scheme to assassinate half his entourage. Cause and effect are carefully observed throughout these various reactions. Hence we endorse Lancaster's observation that the play's structure (we would add also its psychology) bears a resemblance to the form later to be used by Racine.

CINNA AND COMMODE COMPARED

Similarities far more striking can be shown, however, if we compare Commode with Cinna. Not that the plots of these plays resemble each other closely in total effect nor that Auguste and Commode have much in common as personalities, but that several details of the later play echo familiar situations from the earlier masterpiece. Where Thomas' lines do not suggest a close imitation of Pierre's, they do express the same idea and are frequently motivated by the same kind of emotional or circumstantial demands.

The following comparative analysis is offered as evidence of

Thomas' indebtedness to his brother's *Cinna*. The comparison does not yield an irrefutable conclusion, but the similarities are too numerous for coincidence to explain them. On the whole, this comparison reveals as strong a case of influence as can be found between the brothers. It is all the more striking because of the underlying thematic differences.

In Act I, scene 4 of *Commode*, Laetus and Electus are seen advising Commode on the manner in which it befits him to be escorted to the Temple of Janus for the festal celebration. This is Commode's first appearance in the play. Likewise did Auguste first appear in *Cinna*, Act II, scene 1, soliciting counsel from his favorite courtiers. Cinna and Electus have corresponding roles, a fact brought out by their respective emperors as follows:

Auguste: Voilà, mes chers amis, ce qui me met en peine.
　　　　　Vous qui me tenez lieu d'Agrippe et de Mécène,
　　　　　Pour résoudre ce point avec eux débattu,
　　　　　Prenez sur mon esprit le pouvoir qu'ils ont eu.
　　　　　　　　　　　　　　　　　(Cinna, II, 1, 393-6)
Commode: J'ai toujours avec joie écouté vos avis,
　　　　　Et ce sont presque en tout les seuls que j'ai suivis.
　　　　　　　　　　　　　　　　　(Commode, I, 4)

Both young men are trying to dissuade their sovereigns from taking an unworthy course of action (Commode from being escorted by gladiators instead of senators; Auguste from abjuring his sovereignty). Their persuasiveness, based on an appeal to Roman welfare, prevails in both cases and brings from each emperor the concessions sought:

Auguste:　N'en délibérons plus, cette pitié l'emporte.
　　　　　Mon repos m'est bien cher, mais Rome est la plus forte.
　　　　　　　　　　　　　　　　　(Cinna, II, 1, 621-2)
Commode: Eh bien, il faut céder aux avis qu'on m'en donne,
　　　　　Electus le croit juste, et Rome nous l'ordonne.
　　　　　　　　　　　　　　　　　(Commode, I, 4)

Like Cinna, Electus is solicited by the woman he loves to kill the emperor in return for her affection. Marcia proposes:

　　　　　Pour te justifier, apporte-moi sa tête,
　　　　　Et d'un noble courroux te laissant enflammer
　　　　　Parais digne aujourd'hui d'avoir osé m'aimer.
　　　　　　　　　　　　　　　　　(Commode, III, 6)

Emilie's conditions to Cinna were essentially the same. Speaking to
her confidant she stipulated:

> Je l'ai juré, Fulvie, et je le jure encore,
> Quoique j'aime Cinna, quoique mon cœur l'adore,
> S'il veut me posséder, Auguste doit périr:
> Sa tête est le seul prix dont il peut m'acquérir.
>
> (*Cinna*, I, 2, 53-6)

For Electus as for Cinna this urgent plea from the woman he loves
to betray the man to whom he owes so much creates a serious conflict.
Describing his state of mind in terms of the struggle between "vertu"
and "amour", Electus observes:

> L'une et l'autre a sur moi toujours le même empire.
> Mais leurs droits sont divers, et c'est dont je soupire,
> Puisque des deux côtés mon cœur trop combattu,
> Voulant tout par amour, n'ose rien par vertu.
>
> (*Commode*, III, 6)

And Cinna in the same vein:

> Emilie et César l'un et l'autre me gêne
> L'un me semble trop bon, l'autre trop inhumaine ...
> Des deux côtés j'offense et ma gloire et les Dieux;
> Je deviens sacrilège ou je suis parricide,
> Et vers l'un ou vers l'autre il faut être perfide.
>
> (*Cinna*, III, 2; 797-8, 816-8)

Cinna's situation may be fairly described as a dilemma since he is
bound by oath to implement Emilie's will and by gratitude to acknowledge Auguste's generosity. Electus makes no such commitment to
Marcia, but her prodding incites him to defend his benefactor in no
less grateful terms. Electus' speech:

> Et lorsqu'en ma faveur chaque jour il s'explique
> Pourrais-je prendre part à la haine publique?
>
> (III, 6)

is a recasting in a different style of Cinna's

> Plût aux Dieux que César employât mieux ses soins
> Et s'en fît plus aimer, ou m'aimât un peu moins.
>
> (III, 2, 799-800)

Both young men recoil at the idea of dealing the death blow:

Cinna: Et je puis dans son sein enfoncer un poignard!
                                (*Cinna*, III, 2, 812)
Electus: Et portant un poignard dans le sein de mon maître
          [Jugez si je pouvais]
          Joindre au titre d'ingrat l'infâme nom de traître.
                            (*Commode*, III, 6)

Having made no oath Electus is in a better position to honor the fact that his entire career is the work of Commode:

Electus: De tout ce que je suis son bras est le soutien,
         Pour élever mon sort il ne réserve rien.
                         (*Commode*, III, 6)

Cinna makes a similar acknowledgment but, feeling powerless to break his oath, he has to be reminded of it humiliatingly by Auguste:

Auguste: Ma faveur fait ta gloire, et ton pouvoir en vient:
         Elle seule t'élève, et seule te soutient.
                  (*Cinna*, V, 1, 1527-8)

It must be conceded that the roles of Cinna and Electus do not remain parallel throughout the plays. Indeed by the end of Act III of *Commode*, Electus has cast his lot, at least temporarily, with the emperor. Upon learning later that Commode plots his death along with the death of his fellow courtiers, Electus finds himself confronted with a problem quite different from Cinna's. As a matter of self-defense and public welfare, he must finally conspire with the others to destroy the tyrant. Cinna had no such excuse. He could not justify his attitude toward Auguste on personal or political grounds, for the emperor had lavished favors upon him and expressed willingness to concede to Cinna's political maxims as well.

The parallel may be resumed, however, if instead of to Electus we look to the roles of Laetus and Helvie. Between Acts III and IV Helvie makes an unsuccessful attempt to kill Commode, whose immediate reaction is not unlike that of Auguste when the latter discovers Cinna's treason. Commode laments:

> Ô crime, ô trahison trop lâche pour Helvie!
> Quand je lui donne un trône, attenter sur ma vie!
>   (*Commode*, IV, 1)

Auguste had apostrophized similarly:

> Ô trahison conçue au sein d'une furie!
> Ô trop sensible coup d'une main si chérie!
> Cinna, tu me trahis!
>   (*Cinna*, IV, 1, 1097-9)

Both emperors are advised to exercise clemency:

Flavian: Ce crime veut sans doute une pleine vengeance,
         Mais on la peut, Seigneur, trouver dans la clémence,
         Et l'âme abandonnée à ses remords secrets
         A toujours son supplice et ses bourreaux tout prêts.
                                        (*Commode*, IV, 1)
Livie: Essayez sur Cinna ce que peut la clémence;
         Faites son châtiment de sa confusion.
                                  (*Cinna*, IV, 3, 1210-1)

Both emperors have pangs of conscience as they reflect that their own past actions have perhaps been responsible for the treacherous acts made against them. Commode cuts short his rage to ask himself:

> Mais d'un transport aveugle où va la promptitude?
> Quoique ce couple ingrat ait fait, ait projeté,
> J'en suis le seul coupable, et j'ai tout mérité.
>   (*Commode*, IV, 4)

In his speech beginning "Rentre en toi-même, Octave, et cesse de te plaindre" (*Cinna*, IV, 2, 1130), Auguste expresses a similar if more heartfelt acknowledgment of his own shortcomings.

A further comparison may be drawn between the situations of Emilie and Cinna on the one hand and Helvie and Laetus on the other. Like Emilie, Helvie refuses to plead in her own defense. Their lovers try to divert the blame by claiming themselves to be guilty. But Helvie and Emilie are proud of having sought to destroy their respective emperors:

Helvie: Quoi, Laetus, s'il est vrai qu'un pur amour t'inspire,
        Est-ce là m'en prouver le vertueux empire,
        Et quand ma gloire avoue un illustre attentat
        La tienne a-t-elle droit d'en affaiblir l'éclat?
                                        (*Commode*, IV, 3)
Emilie: Cinna, qu'oses-tu dire? est-ce là me chérir
        Que de m'ôter l'honneur quand il me faut mourir?
                                  (*Cinna*, V, 2, 1639-40)

The defiance of these heroines might be expected to produce a reaction unfavorable to their welfare. This is indeed the case with Helvie, for Commode proceeds to a general purge of his court. Before leaving stage to make preparations, however, he speaks ironically of administering justice to Laetus and Helvie by uniting them:

> Ils veulent être unis, il faut y consentir.
> (*Commode*, IV, 4)

Auguste had offered the same strange promise to Cinna and Emilie:

> Oui je vous unirai, puisque vous le voulez.
> (*Cinna*, V, 2, 1659)

The foregoing examples of resemblance show that Thomas had assimilated much more of his brother's dramatic method than is usually realized.[7] A review of the preceding rapprochements will further reveal that the relative position in each play of the passages here quoted corresponds closely.[8]

In writing his tragedy Thomas Corneille may have been unaware of the degree to which he was dependent on *Cinna*. Certainly his choice of subject and his characterization of Commode do not suggest a deliberate attempt to recreate a version of Auguste. Thomas' play is something of a counterpart to Pierre's since, in contrast to *Cinna*, it shows conspiracy bringing out the noble aspects of the conspirators. And conversely, as Thomas portrays him, Commode is the antithesis of his illustrious predecessor, Auguste. He is shown to embody not only the lowest standards of human conduct but also to defy the deities. Just before dying he blasphemes:

> Dieux, dont l'être n'est dû qu'à notre folle erreur,
> Vains dieux, aveugles dieux, dont la jalouse envie
> Destinait le poison pour la fin de ma vie,
> Malgré vous jusqu'au bout je réglerai mon sort

---

[7] Other random lines from *Commode* in which snatches of Pierre's verses recur are to be found as, for example, Helvie's pairing of the terms *vaincre* and *triompher* in her lines to Laetus:
Et ma vertu qu'alarme un tumulte secret,
Ne vainc qu'en soupirant, et triomphe à regret. (I, 3)
Commode refers to Helvie in the same manner that Cinna announces Emilie:
Mais voici de retour cette aimable inhumaine (*Cinna*, III, 3, 905)
Vient-elle cette aimable et fière criminelle? (*Commode*, IV, 1)

[8] Even the "tête" motif (*Cinna*, I, 2; *Commode*, III, 6) is brought up again in *Cinna* at the end of Act III.

Et vous démentirai jusqu'au choix de ma mort.

(*Commode*, V, 7)

Yet this final, proud defiance helps to restore his stature as the play's villainous hero.[9]

Commode is a significant play in Thomas Corneille's career, for it is a veritable amalgam which combines an earlier conception of tragedy with a later one. If on the one hand it derives important elements from *Cinna*, it could well have served in turn as a source for one of Pierre Corneille's later plays, *Attila*. The structure of *Attila* (1667), its disposition of characters and theme are parallel with those of *Commode*. Both plays portray a ruthless sovereign pitted against a double pair of lovers. For each character in Thomas' play there is a corresponding role in *Attila* with a similar function. Like Commode, Attila shifts his attentions from one woman to the other and creates dissension among the lovers. He is guided exclusively by Machiavellian considerations. The death of Commode and of Attila is joyously received by a populace grown tired of their tyranny. The description of Commode's rage and blasphemy at the approach of death bears a particular resemblance to the manner of Attila's death. In short, Pierre could find in his brother's play a ready made blueprint after which to fashion *Attila*.

In the gallery of tyrants and villainous heroes that appeared on the French stage in this period, Commode figures as a curiously appropriate transitional character. He bears the early signs of a psychology of emotions which will come to characterize tragedy in the decade of Racine's greatest popularity. Preceding Racine's first tragedy by seven years, *Commode* may be said to illustrate the effect that a new morality was beginning to have in a general way on the characterization of tragic figures. The most direct manifestation of the change is a shift of emphasis in the role of love, which was becoming increasingly important as the foundation of moral authority. In the identity plays where love's preëminence was never seriously threatened by opposition of principles inimical to it, love could easily be shown as the ennobling virtue. But in sober tragedy it was more likely to produce moral

[9] This speech rings a powerful note of modern existentialism. One can readily conceive of these words appearing in a play by Sartre.

degeneration through the surrender of principles. Commode claims to renounce his sovereignty as a token of his love for Helvie:

> Et la gloire d'un être approchant du divin
> Permettait à mes voeux le choix de mon destin.
> Il n'en est plus ainsi, vous en êtes l'arbitre.
> Par vous de souverain je n'ai plus que le titre,
> Et je fais vanité d'abaisser à vos pieds
> La fière majesté du trône où je m'assieds.
>
> (III, 2)

The speech is in the conventional idiom of amorous parlance and therefore should not be construed as a genuine abdication of power. Nevertheless it is a symptomatic expression of the ascendency of love over political considerations appearing several years before Racine was to make this theme his stock in trade.

The phenomenon is all the more significant in a play whose kinship with Pierre Corneille's tragedies is so close. Commode is the first of Thomas Corneille's characters to embody the contrast of sensibilities resulting from the rational rigorism of Pierre's generation in conflict with what might be called Racinian *mollesse*. Among dramatists Quinault was primarily responsible for the cult of love as morality. Thomas Corneille was clearly affected by a similar predilection. But unlike Quinault's characters who surrender to the beatific charms of love or Racine's, who succumb to love's fury, Thomas' heroes valiantly struggle against surrender. For this reason Commode and Sinorix of *Camma* even more stand out as witnesses to a changing mood. The former remains true to the older tradition, for he vanquishes amorous inclinations to espouse political ambition. We shall see in discussing *Camma* how Sinorix gropes in vain to reconstruct his morals on the older pattern but is defeated by love. Even Thomas' most "Cornelian" character, Laodice, will be seen making a momentary concession to the god of love.

In quite a different aspect *Commode* anticipates Racine's *Britannicus*. In his reluctance to follow a dictated policy, his eagerness to be rid of the shackles imposed by advisors and his unscrupulousness in demanding the affection of a woman loved by an important courtier, Thomas' brooding and secretive emperor prefigures Néron. Junie, forced to affect an attitude of indifference toward Britannicus, recalls

Laetus' predicament in which, by Commode's order, he is forced to advise Helvie to marry the emperor. Just as Commode feigns acquiescence in Electus' advice, so does Néron pretend to accede to his mother's wishes. Beyond these definite points of similarity, one can observe in Commode the somberness and horror of the moral monster which Racine strove to portray in Néron.

In *Commode* Thomas created a potentially great characterization. Yet the play's weaknesses derive largely from the lack of a dominating and decisive trait in the hero. Thomas seems to have lacked a firm conception of him. Torn between good and evil instincts, Commode is now a monster, now a sensitive ruler, resolute when left alone but easily swayed by advice, benevolent and cruel by turns, amorous and vindictive, cunning as a political schemer but awkward and reckless in executing his policies. He embodies diffuse qualities but none uniquely. Thomas Corneille was striving for a synthesis too inclusive for the confines of a single tragedy. As if recognizing the limitations of *Commode*, he may have projected his subsequent tragedies as corrective sequels to it. Each of the five plays to be discussed in this chapter illustrates in detail some facet of *Commode* that had been left in a stage of partial development.

Stilicon and *Maximian* enlarge upon the theme of conspiracy which in *Commode* had occurred late and only as the solution to a problem. As a character Commode prefigures Sinorix of *Camma* and Laodice. The latter shares Commode's moral depravity, for they both would resort to wholesale murder without the slightest misgivings. In his irresoluteness and his sense of guilt, Commode prepares us for the incipient madness of Sinorix. Finally in his efforts to play off one character against another, Commode anticipates Prusias' unsuccessful attempts to steer a precarious course of unscrupulous political expediency in *Annibal*.

STILICON

Three years after *Commode*, Thomas Corneille offered his *Stilicon* to the Hôtel de Bourgogne. Its success, which has been attested by Somaize and especially by Jean Loret (*Muze historique*, letter of 31 January 1660), was due to the felicitous combination of a forceful hero and the suspense of a fast moving plot. As is so often the case in Thomas Corneille's dramas, one may divide the play into two principal series of events: one, purely dramatic, involving the hero's conspiracy to place his son on the throne; and the other, primarily dramaturgical, dealing with the love affair between Euchérius and Placidie. Normally one would not expect the latter aspect to be thought of as a dramaturgical device. However, when an amorous relationship can be shown to function largely as a support to further action, it may be properly labeled a device as well as a theme. It was probably inevitable that Thomas Corneille's typical urge to achieve a unity of action through eclectic means should have compelled him to subordinate one theme to another rather than to eliminate one theme altogether. The main action could have sprung from purely psychological motivations without the aid of a subplot, but it was not Thomas' nature to reduce action to its simplest, most intense form. Like his brother he preferred to enrich the tragedy with as much activity as it could suitably contain. Nor is the love interest, provided by Euchérius and Placidie, without a curious appeal in its own right. Through his portrayal of the proud, haughty heroine and the respectful, resigned lover, Thomas Corneille pushed to its ultimate point the *précieux* ideal of courtly love. The fact remains that the relationship also provided a suitable motivation for Stilicon's indignation and subsequent actions. The episode involving Placidie and Euchérius is well justified technically but is given undue prominence after having served its purely dramaturgical function in the first Act. Thomas Corneille never purged himself of an infatuation for gallant badinage in the *précieux* manner. *Stilicon* is first of all a conspiracy play into which a love affair has been integrated.

It is ironic that in a conspiracy play virtually all the action of the conspirators should be relegated to the wings. It is the peculiar nature of this type of play to conceal many of the incidents simply as a means of protecting *vraisemblance*. Yet other conspiracy plays of the time, among them *Cinna, Pompée*, Tristan's *Mort de Sénèque* and Racine's *Bajazet*, gave considerable prominence to the subterfuge of the conspirators.[10] Thomas Corneille chose on the contrary to treat the

---

[10] Racine's play is singular in making the conspiracy the framework of all the action — an approach made possible by the total absence of Amurat.

conspiracy primarily as an off-stage event. The effect of this manner of handling the situation is worth a brief appraisal.

We saw that in *Commode* the conspiracy against the emperor resulted spontaneously as a counter-measure to Commode's plan of mass assassination. It was one of several available means that the dramatist might have chosen by which to conclude his play. In *Stilicon*, however, the conspiracy dominates the mode of action beginning very early. In Act I, scene 7, Stilicon exposes his motives for wanting to kill Honorius and resolutely defends his position on the grounds that a crime of such magnitude, successfully executed, is its own justification. He has served Honorius devotedly through the years and has come to admire him. But Honorius' sister, Placidie, scorns his lowly birth and refuses to marry his son, Euchérius. Stilicon becomes vindictive. Without enlisting the support of Euchérius, he plots the emperor's demise, intending that Euchérius should then accede to the throne. Act I concludes as Stilicon exits to make concrete plans for the assassination.

In the third scene of Act II an apparent peripetia occurs when Honorius receives a letter from the conspirator Zénon divulging the plot without, however, revealing the names of those concerned. This information gives the play a new direction; for now, in addition to showing the progressive stages of the development of the conspiracy, the dramatist had to give equal attention to the counter offensive intended to thwart it. Corneille managed both simultaneously through the simple but effective expedient of using Stilicon as champion of both sides. One can see here Stilicon's close affinity to Timocrate. Ostensibly Stilicon is working on behalf of Honorius. Indeed for a time his efforts to apprehend the guilty party are so convincing that one begins to wonder if he has renounced his treacherous plans altogether. Just as Cinna's eloquent plea that Auguste remain politically absolute had prompted Maxime to question Cinna's loyalty to the conspiracy (*Cinna*, II, 2, 647), so Stilicon's persistent effort to inculpate his own son perplexes Mutian. The latter is deceived by his master's ruse and seeks assurance of his steadfastness:

Mutian: Seigneur, contre ce fils témoigner tant de haine?
Stilicon: Je sais ce que je fais, ne t'en mets point en peine,
         Et demain tiens-toi sûr de voir selon tes voeux

Euchérius au trône et Stilicon heureux.

(III, 6)

Yet Stilicon's presence on stage suffices to remind us that the conspiracy is still alive. Since none of the plotting occurs on stage and no other conspirator save Stilicon himself figures in the cast, we are forced to interpret his every action as the inverse of what it appears. He has to symbolize the conspiracy and reflect its progress.[11] We must assume, for example, that when Honorius tells Stilicon of Zénon's letter, Stilicon suffers a crushing setback. His reaction of feigned indignation over the conspiracy, however, leads us to assume that he will maneuver defensively, change tactics perhaps but not abandon the plot. Thomas Corneille enables his audience to deduce the progress of the conspiracy by observing the results it produces in the entourage of the intended victim.

As off-stage action becomes more intense its visible repercussions are represented more forcefully on stage. Thomas used eight *récits*, a rather excessive number for a tragedy (III, 3; IV, 1, 2; V, 2, 3, 4, 6, 9). Since each *récit* involved the entrance of a character bearing new information and each entrance implied a new scene, a rapid succession of scenes reflects a corresponding acceleration of activity behind the scenes. The result is a crescendo of action culminating in three quick, decisive strokes: the death of Euchérius, Stilicon's grief and confession, and finally his suicide.

Meanwhile the effective action consists of the efforts of Honorius, ostensibly aided by Stilicon, to break the conspiracy. This effort is primarily an exercise in courtroom logic and is presented in a series of movements each having three sequential steps. First a piece of evidence is introduced and evaluated (Zénon's letter revealing conspiracy by persons anonymous); then a tentative supposition is made

[11]   Thomas could find formal justification for his manner of presenting the action of *Stilicon* in Pierre Corneille's *Discours des trois unités* in which Pierre contended that:

Le poète n'est pas tenu d'exposer à la vue toutes les actions particulières qui amènent à la principale: il doit choisir celles qui lui sont les plus avantageuses à faire voir, soit par la beauté du spectacle, soit par l'éclat et la véhémence des passions qu'elles produisent, soit par quelque autre agrément qui leur soit attaché, et cacher les autres derrière la scène pour les faire connaître au spectateur ou par une narration, ou par quelque autre adresse de l'art. (*Œuvres*, I, 100).

(Euchérius suspects Zénon); finally action is taken (Euchérius is dispatched to interview Zénon). Waiting for Euchérius' return, Honorius informs Stilicon of the conspiracy. Euchérius returns to report that Zénon wants a secret meeting with the emperor. His secrecy is suspect and serves as a new evidence of his supposed guilt and the beginning of a new series of actions. Stilicon suggests remedial action. He will arrest Zénon and change the guard. Shortly after, the third movement begins with the report of fresh information: Zénon has been stabbed. Honorius now turns his suspicions on Euchérius and Stilicon, settling on the former whom he has arrested.

Having established something of a legalistic framework for the action, Thomas Corneille proceeds in Act IV to a full scale trial. Euchérius as defendant must prove his innocence since circumstantial evidence weighs heavily toward his guilt. His only defense, however, consists in a denial of guilt. At first his cause is bolstered by Placidie who feels that anyone who loves her is incapable of a misdeed. Word arrives that Félix, a conspirator, was the assassin of Zénon. Temporarily the evidence points to Euchérius' innocence since it has been supposed that he had killed Zénon.

Meanwhile a series of depositions against Euchérius has been trickling in as suspects have been apprehended and forced to confess. Under previous orders from Stilicon they have consistently named Euchérius as head conspirator. The latter can do nothing but give verbal assurance to the contrary. After both Placidie and Stilicon finally denounce him, Honorius judges him guilty but, like Auguste, is disposed to pardon him in return for a display of repentance. Euchérius refuses to repent of a crime he did not commit.

Throughout Acts III and IV the characters indulge in logical gymnastics worthy of the sleuths in modern detective fiction. A motive is sought, suspects are submitted to rigorous rational diagnosis. All this is done with considerable legal perceptiveness the more impressive because, although we know Euchérius to be innocent, we have to acknowledge the validity of the steps leading to his indictment. Thomas Corneille casts his audience as a kind of omniscient jury possessing all the essential facts necessary for a judgment but willing to defer to an orderly and formal presentation of the case in the interests of due process. Hence the individual spectator of *Stilicon* might be compared to a juror who is personally convinced of the defendant's innocence but feels constrained by duty to observe a procedural objectivity. The result is that dramatic interest in the play is made to depend not so much on the "curiosité émotive" but rather more on the "curiosité intellectuelle" of the spectator. We are treated as accomplices of the author rather than as sympathizers to the characters.

With this view in mind it is fair to observe that Lockert's criticism of Thomas' dramaturgy for leaving too many actions off-stage, while ostensibly applicable to *Stilicon*, must nevertheless be qualified to allow for the kind of dramatic experience that this dramatist intended his audience to enjoy. Much action does indeed occur off-stage and between acts: between Acts I and II an important meeting of the conspirators takes place as well as Zénon's defection; between Acts II and III Zénon's murder is carried out and the guard is changed; between Acts III and IV a roundup of conspirators takes place; between the fourth and final acts the remaining conspirators make final preparations to strike at Honorius. Now with a little manipulation Thomas Corneille could have presented some of this action directly to the audience. However, since he revealed Stilicon's basic plans in Act I, he may have felt that the details involved in the implementation of this plan would be anti-climatic. Moreover, except for Zénon's defection, the off-stage action is not inconsistent with what the spectator could readily deduce from visible circumstances. It may be argued that a certain amount of concealed action is not only necessary but desirable in a conspiracy play to enhance the sense of mystery and intrigue. One might plead in the name of realism that the background representation of the conspiracy is, considering the prominence of the role of the victim, quite exact. The numerous *récits* are so many rumors contributing to the emperor's discomfiture. Knowing that Honorius' life is in danger, we find it entirely natural that he be the center of attention, a central agency, as it were, for receiving information and giving commands.

Of the two roles which deserve special notice as characterizations, those of Stilicon and Placidie, the latter is of particular interest for the position she holds among Thomas Corneille's heroines. She epitomizes those romanesque concepts of complacent self-righteousness according to which even the unassuming and valorous Euchérius is judged a groveling *arriviste*. She illustrates in a much exaggerated version those qualities of soul and temperament frequently imputed to the heroines of Pierre Corneille. Placidie is a woman of iron will and intransigent faith in her own sense of propriety. Chimène and Emilie, both zealots of inexorability, pale by comparison, for Placidie nurtures along with a dogged willfulness an unconscionable pride. Her pride is more than the haughtiness resulting from a sense of social superiority, more than a conviction of personal dignity. She is egotistical to the point of posing her own sentiments as an objective standard by which to authenticate the feelings of others. For example she is sure that anyone capable of loving her is by definition a paragon of virtue. She *knows* that, because Euchérius loves her, he is innocent of the crime attributed to him. How can she be sure he is not feigning love? She loves him, *ipso facto*. There is a naïve astonishment in Placidie's tone of voice that is ludicrous. To think that anyone should ask how she knows! In the following scene Lucile, a confidant, has just reported the accusation of Euchérius and concludes:

Lucile: Tout le rend criminel.
Placidie: Mais il est innocent;
           Et de quoi que son cœur pour régner fût capable,
           Quiconque ose m'aimer ne peut être coupable.
Lucile: Un si beau sentiment ferait tout présumer,
           Si l'on aimait toujours quand on jure d'aimer.
           Il peut feindre avec vous.
Placidie: *Mais Lucile je l'aime,*
           S'il peut feindre avec moi, puis-je feindre de même
           Et crois-tu que mon cœur pût trahir ma fierté,
           Jusqu'à vouloir s'entendre avec sa lâchete?
           Non, non, ces vains dehors d'une fausse tendresse
           N'éblouissent jamais les yeux d'une princesse.
           Elle prend dans son sang l'infaillible pouvoir
           De donner de l'amour avant qu'en recevoir
           Incapable d'erreur dans les feux qu'elle excite
           Elle y voit la vertu soutenir le mérite,
           Et sur ces seuls garants se laissant enflammer,
           Elle est sûre en aimant de s'être fait aimer.
                    (*Stilicon*, IV, 1; emphasis supplied)

Later Placidie is forced by the evidence to admit that Euchérius may indeed be guilty but feels that the crime of lèse-majesté is less serious than his having caused her to love him:

Placidie: Je t'en vois convaincu vers l'état, vers ton maître,
Mais je n'y puis penser que surprise d'effroi
Je n'en trouve un second qui ne touche que moi.
Ne dis plus qu'à tes voeux mon cœur fut inflexible,
Tout superbe qu'il est, tu l'as rendu sensible,
Et son plus vaste orgueil n'a pu le garantir
D'admirer ce qu'enfin je te vois démentir.
C'est là ce crime ingrat . . .

(IV, 3)

Then she bids him prove his innocence not to exculpate himself so much as to prove that her original sentiments had been correct after all. It would be difficult to find in French classical theater another heroine who embodies a more monumental conviction of self-righteousness.[12]

Yet Placidie has her antecedents within Thomas Corneille's own drama. Jacinte of *Les Illustres ennemis* displayed a similar temperament, but her principles were founded on a sense of honor and personal integrity relatively devoid of egotism. In *Timocrate* Eriphile flares up when Cléomène encourages her alliance with Timocrate. She feels, along with Statira of *Darius*, that a suitor, though disqualified by birth, must nevertheless remain in a state of hopeful resignation. For the suitor to suggest that his beloved princess seek the match which she avowedly must make in order to fulfill her destiny borders on infidelity if not treason. Even modest Bérénice commands Philoxène: "Ose m'aimer encore pour vivre malheureux" (*Bérénice*, IV, 3).

No one is likely to defend these heroines for their psychological acumen. And yet oddly enough their Platonic mandates were astonishingly well received by a species of hero begotten of romanesque

---

[12] For a caustic analysis of Placidie, see Lockert, *Studies*, p. 225. In fairness it should be noted that Placidie did have a brief moment of uncertainty about Euchérius' feelings toward her. In Act II, scene 1, she expressed misgivings about his love:

Mais que dis-je! Sur lui si j'obtiens quelque empire,
Par son lâche conseil il cherche à s'en dédire;
Et j'ai cru bien en vain qu'il avait mérité
Des dédains où pour lui j'excitais ma fierté.

etiquette. If on the one hand the heroine's plea for fidelity without requital strikes us as naïve psychological advice, it nevertheless reflects an emotional reaction which is quite genuine. These princesses feel they are making a sacrifice in renouncing their lovers. Although the choice to do so is entirely their own, they are unable to palliate a deep-rooted affection or to adjust abruptly to an attitude of indifference. As an indication of their inability to make this adjustment the "Ose m'aimer encore" is a natural emotional response.

We have already quoted examples of the contest of generosity between two lovers. The relationship of Placidie and Euchérius provided the essential ingredients for another. However, Thomas Corneille may not have wished to repeat himself. In Placidie he sought to create a character of extreme proportions based on some of his own models but different by virtue of excess. On the whole Placidie remains unconvincing, but Thomas did not abondon the hope of portraying a female of indomitable will and pride just as Pierre had done. His mistake was in attempting to cast such a personality as a heroine — a mistake which he must have realized when he decided to fuse heroine with villain in the successful role of Laodice. Interesting as a study in character, Placidie and her relationship with Euchérius demanded an inordinate amount of treatment. As a result the major subject, which is to us more original and constitutes the only tragic dimension, could not be adequately developed. Stilicon's great speech at the moment of defeat would have been more effective if, instead of Placidie, the father-son relationship had been kept before us throughout the play.

Stilicon himself provides the second main character interest and holds an interesting position in Thomas' gallery of villainous heroes. He evinces a consistent duality owing to the conflict of his natural greatness and the role he forces himself to play as villain. Ostensibly cunning, hypocritical and cruel, he is nevertheless endowed with a capacity for sympathy toward the man he intends to kill and a deep affection for his own son. Despite his efforts to glorify the crime he contemplates, it holds no real appeal for him. One feels that his maxim "Et pour faire un grand crime il faut de la vertu" is uttered more in the nature of a rationalization intended to strengthen his resolve than as a heartfelt moral truth. Even in his relentless prosecution of

Euchérius, Stilicon is, paradoxically, expressing the utmost respect and affection for his son.

The dual nature of his role produces irony at every turn, sometimes conspicuous as when he says to Honorius: "Souvent pour mieux trahir le plus zélé peut feindre" (II, 5), sometimes tragic as in his confession:

Je vous aimai, Seigneur, et l'on ne vit jamais
Plus de zèle répondre à de rares bienfaits.
Ce zèle dans mon cœur n'en souffrant aucun autre,
M'eût fait cent fois donner tout mon sang pour le vôtre,
Et dans vos intérêts ma tendresse et mes soins
En ont peut-être été de fidèles témoins.
La vertu m'inspirant par de secrètes flammes,
J'eus tous les sentiments qui font les grandes âmes,
La gloire me fut chère, et cent nobles exploits
Pour en marquer l'ardeur ne manquent point de voix,
Heureux, si du destin la jalouse puissance
M'eût épargné d'un fils la fatale naissance.
Par là de ma vertu sa rigueur vint à bout,
Ce fils fut une idole à qui j'immolai tout.
Mon amour dans ce fils, ou bien plutôt ma rage,
Du titre de sujet ne put souffrir l'outrage,
Et sans l'en consulter, mon ingrate fureur
Voulut par votre perte en faire un empereur.
J'en prononçai l'arrêt, et je la crus certaine.
Jugez par cet aveu de l'excès de ma peine.
Pour élever mon fils au rang où je vous vois
J'ai trahi vos bienfaits, j'ai violé ma foi,
J'ai démenti mon sang, j'ai pris le nom de traître,
J'ai porté le poignard dans le sein de mon maître,
J'ai souillé lâchement la gloire de mon sort,
Cependant, cependant, Seigneur, mon fils est mort. (V, 7)

Paternal affection, which was not a dominant theme in seventeenth century French theater, is painted here with masterful strokes. This speech reaches the level of Racine's poetry, for we are made to feel Stilicon's grief on losing his son at least as forcefully as we are in Racine's portrayal of Thésée's remorse on the death of Hippolyte. This is as close as Thomas Corneille ever came to high tragedy.

Stilicon's plot failed not from lack of ingenuity on his part, but from his failure to appraise accurately his son and Honorius' unforeseen precaution of surrounding himself with a personal guard. He intended to keep Euchérius clear of reproach by excluding him from the conspiracy altogether in the hope that, once Honorius was dead, Euchérius could not refuse the throne. It is questionable whether Euchérius, so submissive and loyal to Honorius, could have been counted on to fulfill his father's ambitions.

By common consent *Stilicon* is labeled as one of the Cornelian plays. Yet none of Pierre's tragedies dealt with the theme of the father ambitious for his son. Pierre never portrayed a heroine quite like Placidie nor a noble as submissive as Euchérius. There is some parallel between Honorius' dilemma in choosing a guilty party from two cherished persons and Antiochus' consternation in Act V of *Rodogune* where he is faced with a similar choice. Phocas of *Héraclius* struggled with the problem also. Still the situation was fairly standard. Where, then is the resemblance? It must be acknowledged that a comparison such as the one undertaken above of *Commode* and *Cinna* is not to be found between *Stilicon* and a play by Pierre Corneille. The reason for labeling *Stilicon* a Cornelian play lies in the fact that this tragedy, like most of Pierre's, emphasizes a forceful hero in pursuit of a definite goal — in general terms probably the most characteristic trait of the elder Corneille's theater. Stilicon falls in the lineage of Médée, Horace, Polyeucte, Cléopatre, Phocas, Nicomède, and later Viriate, Sophonisbe, and Attila, to mention some of Pierre's outstanding theatrical portraits. Placidie, too, grotesquely portrayed though she is, conforms ironically to Pierre's notion of "élévation de caractère". We say ironically because Pierre, in that part of the *Discours du poème dramatique* in which he speaks of *bonnes mœurs*, had reference to vicious characters possessed of "grandeur d'âme qui a quelque chose de si haut, qu'en même temps qu'on déteste ses actions, on admire la source dont elles partent" (*Œuvres*, I, p. 32). Now Placidie is not vicious in the usual sense, but she nearly becomes so by excess of "Vertu". Pierre Corneille did not dramatize the story of *Stilicon*, but how like him it would have been to do so. It is strange that he did not. Fouquet is said to have suggested three subjects: Oedipe, Camma and Stilicon, of which Pierre chose the first, Thomas the other two (Lancaster in claiming that the third subject "remains unknown" overlooked a reference to the three plays in Loret's *Muze Historique* of January 29, 1661). In view of his predilection for characters who shape their own destinies, it would seem that Pierre might have preferred to treat Stilicon or Camma. He could not resist having Thésée cry out against the fatalism of Oedipe's predicament (*Oedipe*, 1149 ff). In *Stilicon* he had a figure and a situation which must have tempted him. He may have felt that Fouquet's first choice was Oedipe. In his "Au Lecteur" of this play he said: "Sans ses commandements je n'aurais jamais fait l'Oedipe" (*Œuvres*, VI, p. 126).

MAXIMIAN

We shall postpone discussion of Thomas Corneille's next tragedy, *Camma*, in order to treat first *Maximian* (1662) whose affinity with *Stilicon* makes a comparison of these plays desirable. In Chapter II we showed how Thomas in treating a single basic theme, the *héros méconnu* or *inconnu*, managed to introduce significant variations in the manner of handling plots. *Darius* and *Pyrrhus* were seen to be essentially the same as subject matter and in the overall effect they produce. Yet these plays differ in important details and technical aspects. Thomas Corneille did not hesitate to imitate himself. He probably did so very consciously, however, for where the similarity of subjects might have tempted him to let a previous dramaturgical pattern serve unmodified in a later play, he always sought innovations in developing a plot. Such is the case with *Maximian*.

Both *Stilicon* and *Maximian* portray events which took place toward the end of Roman imperial rule. A brief glance will show that the situations are very similar. A trusted and powerful adviser conspires to usurp the throne by assassinating the emperor. Both Stilicon and Maximian direct the conspiracy while remaining in the confidence of their respective sovereigns. Each has recourse to feigned self-accusation as a means of producing an impression of innocence, and each accuses his own child of the crime. Having failed, both Stilicon and Maximian commit suicide. The relative position in the plays of corresponding events can be shown to be parallel. There are, however, differences.

Of the two, Maximian is shown to be the more ingenious manipulator, for he plays one character against another with admirable psychological dexterity, taking advantage of the moral integrity and emotional inclinations of others to implicate them or render them harmless to his cause. Lockert has admired him as "one of the most impressive figures to be found anywhere in French-classical drama" (*Studies*, p. 228). As a personality he is less sympathetic than Stilicon, who was motivated by a sense of family pride and paternal concern. Maximian is inspired by purely selfish ambition.

One basic difference between Stilicon and Maximian is reflected in the very dramaturgical evolution of events in the respective plays. Stilicon is stealthy; hence his conspiracy is implemented with utmost secrecy. Plans are made off-stage. He trusts no one, especially his son. Maximian on the contrary is an extrovert. He invites participation, carries out his plans openly and flaunts his opponents with impunity. He is seen and heard not only talking about his schemes but carrying them out. The progress of the play can be best traced through the hero's changes of fortune, for Maximian dominates the action.

In scene 3 of Act I he tells of his intentions to regain the throne which he had been persuaded to renounce along with Diocletian a few years earlier. His first step will be to gain the support of Sévère who has just returned from a successful military campaign to discover that Maximian's daughter, Fauste, has married the emperor Constantine. Sévère is stupefied because Fauste had been engaged to him. Maximian will appeal to Sévère's jealousy, enlist his sympathy, and offer Fauste as a reward for helping him to kill Constantine. In the final scene of Act II, Maximian makes his proposal to Sévère who pretends to accept it.

Maximian's second maneuver, which never quite materializes, involves changing the imperial guard headed by Licine, a noble in love with Constantine's sister Constance. Knowing that the emperor intends to give Constance to Sévère as a consolation for losing Fauste, Maximian succeeds in casting suspicion on Licine whose natural displeasure at losing Constance makes him an eligible suspect for revenge against Constantine. Martian and a few conspirators are arrested owing to the defection of one of their members, Straton. Martian names Licine as the author of the conspiracy. In feigned magnanimity Maximian defends Licine whom the emperor puts under arrest. Meanwhile Fauste, through Sévère, has discovered to her horror that her father is the traitor. Thus when he offers to supervise the changing of the guards, she intervenes and prevents this key maneuver in order to keep Constantine from peril. The third act ends with Maximian momentarily checked. But his recuperation is quick.

In Act IV he tells of having secretly armed the arrested conspirators. His plan is that they shall kill Constantine when the latter comes to hear their confessions. To prevent this, Sévère has sent a note to Fauste warning her to keep Constantine away from the imprisoned conspirators. The emperor intercepts the note, which is worded ambiguously, and is convinced that Sévère and Fauste are guilty. Maximian successfully encourages this error, prevailing over the protests of Sévère who finally tells the truth about the entire situation and accuses Maximian. This cunning traitor has so thoroughly ingratiated himself with Constantine that he doesn't fear Fauste's threat to confirm the charge which Sévère had already made without effect. With the end of Act IV then, Maximian's plans appear to be on the point of materializing.

To this point Thomas Corneille maintained a high degree of suspense with a wavering conflict. Unfortunately the unity of action is broken by a fortuitous but decisive episode occurring between the fourth and final acts. Valère, a conspirator heretofore unmentioned, is sent by Maximian to free Martian but instead reveals the entire plot to Constantine. On the basis of this information, the emperor is finally convinced of Maximian's guilt.[13]

Act V portrays the progressive breakdown of Maximian's scheme as he shifts from offensive to defensive strategy and finally, in desperation, commits suicide. Even in defeat he maintains his composure, ingeniously explaining away successive bits of incriminating evidence until all his embattlements fall away. First Sévère is reported dying from a wound inflicted at Maximian's command. "Seigneur, quelle surprise!" exclaims the wily courtier. His astonishment is, of course,

---

[13] Lockert is perfectly correct in criticizing Thomas Corneille's dramaturgy on this point (*Studies*, pp. 230-231). Valère's sudden involvement does not issue from necessary causes. The only defense that may be made is the fact that Thomas Corneille had introduced earlier a conspirator whose defection might serve as a model for Valère's action. When Valère is introduced, one recalls the parallel with Straton, a character who had also denounced the conspiracy and exposed many of the participants without, however, being able to name the chief.

not that Sévère has been stabbed but that he is not already dead. His next breath shows, however, with what resourcefulness he is capable of meeting the situation:

> Seigneur, quelle surprise!
> Mais s'il n'est que mourant le ciel me favorise.
> Comme il a sur moi seul jeté la trahison,
> Il parlera sans doute et voudra se dédire.
>
> (V, 4)

A moment later Sévère is brought on stage and accuses Maximian of assassinating him, to which the schemer replies with condescending pity:

> J'ai voulu jusqu'au bout lui voir pousser son crime,
> Il meurt en m'accusant, laissez couler vos pleurs,
> Vous les devez, Madame, à ses tristes malheurs.
>
> (V, 6)

Asked to acquit himself of Sévère's charge, Maximian, as if indignant at the naïveté of such a request, accuses Licine. The latter, reasons Maximian, wanted to rid himself of his collaborator, Sévère. Licine now appears and, to prove his innocence, surrenders. Maximian belittles Licine's gesture as empty bravado, claiming that Licine knows the people will not permit him to be harmed. Licine defends himself convincingly. Maximian objects that, Martian having been set free (so he mistakenly believes), there is no witness to counter Licine. At this, Constantine drops the pretense, tells of Valère's deposition and Martian's pretended escape. Maximian, defenseless, has to acknowledge his guilt but in proud defiance prefers death to the clemency which Fauste asks her husband to grant him.

The fact of giving prominence to the head conspirator (twenty of the thirty scenes), and the acts of conspiracy had the correlative effect of reducing the role of the emperor, who nevertheless appears in fourteen of the thirty scenes including all seven of the last act. Dramaturgically Thomas Corneille treated the story as a problem in successive enlightenment beginning with the audience and proceeding to Sévère, Fauste, Constantine, and Licine in that order. Once all these persons know who is guilty, there remains one final revelation and that, ironically, is to tell Maximian that everyone else is now aware of his treason. The poignancy of the last act is heightened by the sudden reversal in roles, the intended victim having become prosecutor. All of Maximian's feigned indignation, hypocritical praise, and coy magnanimity are accentuated by the spectator's knowledge that at least one other character on stage penetrates the imposture.

A further effect of emphasizing the conspiracy as visible action is the consequent reduction of amorous apologetics. While it is true that Sévère is genuinely heartbroken at losing Fauste, he spends a relatively brief time saying so. Nor do Fauste, Licine and Constance bewail their misfortunes at any length. All four are so solicitous of Constantine that their efforts are given almost wholly to protecting him. The love relationships are important for establishing motivations which Maximian mercilessly exploits, but the lovers themselves contribute more to the active campaign against the conspiracy than to a display of their passions. Pierre Corneille doubtless approved.

Fauste, whose situation is patterned closely after that of Pauline in *Polyeucte* is a thoroughly Cornelian character as is her suitor, Sévère. They refuse to yield to their now illegitimate passion, although Maximian offers them a means of restoring their former relationship through the murder of Constantine. Sévère's return after a successful campaign, his controlled respect and unwillingness to harm Constantine are reminiscent of the magninimity of the Sévère in *Polyeucte*.

Maximian did not match *Stilicon* in popularity during Thomas Corneille's lifetime. Lancaster has suggested that because of their resemblance they could not both remain in the repertory. On the whole *Maximian* gives evidence of technical improvement particularly in the dramatist's handling of the conspiracy. He let the audience know in advance what was happening and substituted for the sudden *coup de théâtre* of *Stilicon* a series of revelations to other characters of the play. The lovers of Maximian elicit genuine sympathy and play an integral role throughout the tragedy rather than exclusively at the beginning as in *Stilicon*. Sévère and Fauste share a simple love free of the inflated decorum which accompanied Placidie's sentiments toward Euchérius.

As a hero Stilicon possesses greater depth than Maximian. His downfall is more tragic because his motivations are less purely selfish than Maximian's. He is an essentially good man come to grief. Despite the cleverness with which Maximian is portrayed, he inspires no pathos since we are not made aware of the humiliation and suffering he may have endured in his status as abdicated emperor. If one of these plays were to be revived today, the choice of the better one would by no means be a foregone conclusion.

CAMMA

Considered purely from the standpoint of plot, *Camma* (1661) is a logical sequel to *Stilicon* and *Maximian*. These two plays portrayed events leading to an unsuccessful attempt on the life of a sovereign. *Camma* shows what might happen afterwards if such a conspiracy succeeded. Using historical material from Plutarch, Thomas composed his tragedy around the theme of revenge. As others have observed, the events in *Camma* are similar in many respects both to Pierre Corneille's *Pertharite* and to Racine's *Andromaque* (Lancaster, *History*, III, p. 441 and Lockert, *Studies*, p. 226). As in the latter play, *Camma* portrays a sovereign who coerces a widow to marry him by threatening the life of her child. Hésione's request to Sostrate to gain her love by embracing her vengeance is similar to Hermione's mandate to Oreste. Finally Camma's plan to kill herself after the marriage ceremony is also adopted by Andromaque.

Sinorix, usurper of the throne of Galatia, wishes to marry Queen Camma, widow of Sinatus. Having discovered that Sinorix had poisoned her late husband, she seeks revenge. To discourage his suit she reminds him of his engagement to her step-daughter, Hésione. Meanwhile both mother and step-daughter urge Sostrate to kill Sinorix. When this loyal lieutenant refuses, Camma takes it upon herself to do so. Just as she is about to plunge a dagger into Sinorix, Sostrate enters and knocks it from her hand. Sinorix turns around but is unable to determine which of the two was his intended murderer.[14] Sostrate claims guilt, and Camma, wishing to remain free for a second attempt, fails to exculpate him. Hoping to get rid of his obligation to marry Hésione, Sinorix offers to pardon Sostrate if the princess will marry him (Sostrate). She refuses. As a last resort Camma then agrees

[14] Thomas Corneille may have been inspired by a similar scene from Quinault's *Amalasonte* (IV, 6).

to marry Sinorix provided that the latter free Sostrate. The marriage takes place between Acts IV and V. The last act is one of confusion. Sostrate admits his love for Camma. She in turn tells Sinorix how she knew he had poisoned her husband, how she had tried to kill him (Sinorix) but had been prevented by Sostrate, and finally how she had married him only to save Sostrate. Sinorix offers his life to Camma who, however, has already given him poison in the "coupe nuptiale" and has taken some herself. They both die. Hésione presumably will succeed her step-mother on the throne.

Camma has been called a well made play (Lancaster, *History*, III, p. 442). This judgment is particularly valid if the play is viewed as a series of situations producing conflicts of interest. There is, however, an unsatisfying quality which results from the lack of forcefulness on the part of Sinorix. His decisions have little impact since the reactions they provoke in the other characters are the same ones these characters had shown *before* Sinorix entered the picture. In addition, Thomas' excessive reliance on ambiguity obscures the interrelationships of characters.

Pervading much of the dialogue there is a quality of irritability and dissonance more appropriate to comedy than to tragedy. This is particularly notable in the role of Hésione. Although the main problem is Camma's revenge, the means by which Thomas Corneille chose to bring about Sinorix' death involves the principal figures in a series of sarcastic verbal exchanges which, despite the refined vocabulary and the stature of those involved, suggest a snarling domestic *brouillerie*. Mutual scorn reigns supreme: Camma despises Sinorix who in turn cares nothing for Hésione. The latter hates Sinorix, distrusts her step-mother and rejects the only decent suitor she could hope for, Sostrate. In brief, the usual premises on which character relationships are founded are almost entirely lacking. Camma and Hésione are not endowed with the least maternal or filial affection, a state easily enough explained by the fact that Hésione is Sinatus' daughter by his first wife. But neither do they evince genuine hatred of each other. Their relationship is rather one of indifference. Sinorix is like a stranger in a household of which he is the nominal head but disrespected, even scorned. The impact of his decisions is rendered virtually ineffectual by the jeering manner in which they are received.

Witness, for example, Hésione's peremptory retort as Sinorix abjures his obligation to marry her:

Sinorix: J'osai me consulter sur le choix d'une reine
Et sans amour pour vous, je crus honteux pour moi
De sembler vous devoir la qualité de roi.
Hésione: Moi que par une lâche et honteuse faiblesse
Je cherche de ton cœur à me rendre maîtresse? ...
Qui tient pour y monter [au trône] le chemin que tu prends,
Mérite d'y périr comme font les tyrans.

(II, 1)

She consistently uses the familiar form of address with Sinorix, braving his threats with defiance. After a mild threat (C'est à vous de songer à vous mieux secourir), Hésione replies:

A quelle indignité je te vois recourir!
Quoi, sur ce vain courroux tu crois que je me rende?
Eclate, ordonne, agis, c'est ce que je demande.
Mais ne t'arrête pas, quand tu peux m'accabler,
A l'inutile effort de me faire trembler.

(III, 6)

Nor is she much more civil with Camma whose self-immolation she interprets as coquetry. A thoroughgoing rebel, Hésione at no time concedes to the wishes of another even when to do so would save her from exile and Sostrate from death. It is questionable whether her role as Thomas Corneille conceived it contributes to the unity of the play. The fact that she had been engaged to Sinorix serves as a pretext for Camma to remind Sinorix of his bad faith, but since Hésione holds him in such contempt, one is inclined to feel that he is justified in renouncing her. She is ineffectual as a victim of Sinorix' threat of exile because she defies him with such vigor as to suggest she would like nothing better.

If Hésione is acrimony personified, Sostrate is a model of respectfulness and self-control. He has the delicate role of trying to serve two masters. Bound by affection to Camma and by loyalty to Sinorix, he is the pawn of both. Only Camma is aware of his love for her. Sinorix and Hésione believe him to be in love with Hésione. The most sympathetic character in the play, he is treated the worst, by Camma who lets him take the blame for her attempt on Sinorix' life, by Hésione who, though believing she has caused his guilt, refuses to save him, and finally by Sinorix who mistakenly suspects him of treason.

Lancaster and Reynier, while admitting that *Camma* is one of the best constructed of Thomas Corneille's plays, devote little attention to internal details or characterization. Lockert makes a closer analysis (*Studies*, pp. 225-228), but all three overlooked a significant aspect of characterization to be found in the role of Sinorix. This usurper is probably the most sensitive of all who appeared in seventeenth-century French tragedy. He is endowed with a conscience which gives him a sense of frustration, guilt, and repentance finally bordering on insanity. Tristan l'Hermite's Hérode of *Mariane* and Rotrou's Cosroès had been victims of some degree of psychological disorder as Racine's Oreste was to be a few years later. But Thomas Corneille in Sinorix made a rather well developed study of incipient madness unmatched, so far as we know, by anything of the times.[15]

We first see Sinorix struggling with his conscience in Act I, scene 1. Having made a successful *coup*, he is yet unable to reconcile himself to exercising the autocratic power which his throne bestows. In vain does his confidant exhort him to take a forceful stand, he is already afflicted with gnawing pangs of guilt:

Sinorix: Ce sont là des tyrans les damnables maximes,
          En qui l'impunité fait le pardon des crimes;
          Et qui d'un noir forfait espérant quelque bien,
          Après l'avoir commis ne se reprochent rien;
          Mais las! tu me plaindrais si tu pouvais connaître
          Ce que dans un grand cœur le repentir fait naître.
          Quand après un effort mille fois combattu,
          Le crime par contrainte échappe à la vertu,
          De son indigne objet sans cesse possédée,
          L'âme entraîne partout l'épouvantable idée;
          Un vif et dur remords n'en est jamais banni,
          Et coupable un moment on est toujours puni.
                                                                (I, 1)

Nevertheless he is determined to win Camma's hand. To do so he has recourse to coercive measures, but to avoid further self-incrimination he tries to place the responsibility for these measures on other

---

[15]   On the theme of madness in the theater of an earlier part of the century, see Gustave Van Roosbroeck, "A Commonplace in *Mélite*: the madness of Eraste", *Modern Philology*, XVII (1919-20), 141-149.

shoulders. In threatening to banish Hésione if she refuses to marry Sostrate, he makes it clear that she is forcing her own punishment:

> Je vous le dis encore, c'est à vous de résoudre,
> Il est en votre choix de repousser la foudre,
> Je la tiens suspendue, et malgré mon courroux,
> J'ai peine à consentir qu'elle éclate sur vous;
> Mais votre orgueil m'y force ...
>
> (II, 1)

She answers with defiance, and he weakens at the prospect of carrying out his threat:

> Ah! Laisse-moi trembler du dessein que je fais,
> Et souffre à ma vertu, que mon amour opprime,
> De faire quelque effort pour m'épargner un crime.
> Cet exil qu'elle presse a droit de m'effrayer,
> Avant ce dur remède il faut tout essayer.
>
> (II, 2)

Shortly afterwards, Camma attributes his threat not to his love for her, but to his "fureur":

> Vous appelez amour ce qui n'est que fureur.
> Quoi! Si je me défends de faire une bassesse,
> Il faut soudain d'exil menacer la princesse ...
>
> (II, 4)

Having been scoffed at by Hésione and incited by Camma, he brings pressure to bear on the latter to marry him. If she agrees, he will withdraw his threat to exile Hésione. In the process of dealing with the two women, Sinorix' conditions change. To Hésione he had said: marry Sostrate or else! to Camma, marry me or else! His inconsistency may be explained by acknowledging Sinorix' wavering faculties. He is at least consistent in wanting and seeking Camma's affection; joining Hésione with Sostrate would, he feels, facilitate this quest. The fact remains that no premeditated strategy figures in the various steps he takes to win Camma. He acts impulsively, always grasping for the most immediate solution. Unable to accept the contradiction between his gallant principles (he wants Camma to love him, not merely acquiesce in marriage), and the coercive measures he finds necessary, he seeks to dissociate himself from these measures. Doggedly he tries to blame Camma:

C'est un mal qu'à vous seule il faudra qu'on impute.
Et ce sera pour vous un genre de forfait,
D'avoir pu l'empêcher, et ne l'avoir pas fait.

(II, 4)

But Camma, astute enough to capitalize on Sinorix' sensitivity, has no difficulty exposing to him his irreconcilable attitudes. Sinorix is thoroughly frustrated. A clear suggestion that his frustration is developing toward insanity is made a few scenes later as, alone with his confidant, Sinorix reports his hallucinatory experience:

Oui, Phédime, et mon âme étonnée, interdite,
Se veut en vain soustraire à l'horreur qui l'agite.
Plus j'ai lieu de tenir mon bonheur assuré
Plus par de vifs remords je me sens déchiré.
Une secrète voix que leur rigueur anime,
De moment en moment, me reproche mon crime;
Et lorsque j'en frémis, pour me confondre mieux,
L'ombre de Sinatus se présente à mes yeux...
Ses yeux quoiqu'égarés, fixés sur le coupable,
Me lancent un regard affreux, épouvantable;
Et comme si c'était me faire peu souffrir,
Je l'entends s'écrier, *Tyran, il faut mourir* ...

(III, 1)

Follows the report of Sinatus' threatening words to Sinorix, who then concludes:

Là, j'ai beau repousser cette funeste image,
L'horreur qu'elle me laisse accable mon courage,
Et, sans cesse, agitant mon esprit incertain,
Me montre un bras levé pour me percer le sein.

(III, 1)

In despair Sinorix apostrophizes on his misfortune and is about to relapse into another hallucination when he is called back to reality by Camma's attempt on his life. His guilt complex magnifies his suspicions to such a point that he imagines a general conspiracy has been planned. Still unable to make a solid decision, he tries once more unsuccessfully to make Hésione his scapegoat. Marry Sostrate, and all will be pardoned:

Voyez que sous vos pas s'ouvre le précipice
Si je veux consentir à me faire justice,

> C'est à vous de songer à vous mieux secourir.[16]
>
> (III, 6)

Phénice aptly describes his state of mind in the following terms:

> Jamais tant de fureur ne se peut concevoir
> Qu'en tous ses sentiments Sinorix en fait voir.
> Indigné de l'orgueil que montre la princesse
> Il éclate, il foudroie, il s'emporte sans cesse.
>
> (IV, 1)

When at last he achieves his goal by marrying Camma, his happiness is shattered by Sostrate's confession and by Camma's disclosure that she has always known that Sinorix poisoned her late husband. In a final desperate effort of self-delusion, Sinorix invokes the actions of Camma herself as proof of his innocence. "Your willingness to marry me was a tacit admission of my innocence", he insists:

> Non, vous cherchez en vain à me faire douter.
> Les soupçons qu'en votre âme on aime à faire naître
> Font périr Sinatus par le crime d'un traître,
> Sa mort rend de courroux votre cœur embrasé,
> Et m'en croyant l'auteur, vous m'auriez épousé?
>
> (V, 3)

It is unfair to say that Sinorix is insane, for his reasoning has an accountable logic. But his persistent attempts to dispense with the realities of his situation, to erase his past crime by ignoring it, to avoid responsibility by transferring it undeniably forebode a psychopathic condition.

Sinorix is unique among Thomas Corneille's heroes for yet another reason; he labors under the onus of fate.[17] His downfall is announced by references to "quelque ombre", that he feels is opposed to his

---

[16] This threat, always accompanied by a choice, is repeated twice, to Hésione:

> Au moins, ce lui [à Sostrate] doit être un supplice assez rude
> De n'en devoir l'arrêt qu'à votre ingratitude;
> Et de voir qu'en effet, qui doit le secourir,
> Quand je veux le sauver, le condamne à périr. (III, 6)

and to Camma:

> Et vous pouvez choisir, si ce prix est trop haut,
> De monter sur le trône, ou lui [Sostrate] sur l'échafaud. (IV, 3)

[17] As we shall see shortly, Annibal, too, is a fated hero but in a different sense.

happiness, to "le sort" which "fait en vain tant de miracles" in his behalf. His death is prefigured in Camma's account of Sinatus' death, for Sinorix, like his predecessor, was to die by poison:

Camma: Le vase nuptial tout-à-coup s'épandit.
          De ce triste accident l'infortuné présage
          D'une secrète horreur saisit tout mon courage;
          Et m'annonça dès lors les funestes malheurs
          Qui pressent ma vengeance et font couler mes pleurs.
                                                    (I, 3)

Sinorix is aware that his actions may be precisely those ordained by fate but is powerless to do anything about them. He asks himself:

          Est-ce un avis du ciel, qui cherche à m'annoncer
          L'arrêt que son courroux s'apprête à prononcer?
                                                    (III, 2)

He accounts for the attempt on his life not so much as the work of a traitor as the inevitable decree of fate:

          Mais j'ai tort d'accuser mon ingrat ennemi,
          Il n'est dans son forfait coupable qu'à demi,
          Il suit l'ordre du ciel, dont l'arrêt trop sévère
          Trouve pour moi la mort une peine légère.
                                                    (III, 4)

In his unsuccessful attempts at clemency, Sinorix may be seen as an Auguste *manqué*; in his submission to a fatal passion, a Pyrrhus *avant la lettre*.

PERSÉE ET DÉMÉTRIUS

In the theatrical season following *Camma*, Thomas Corneille produced one of his least successful tragedies, *Persée et Démétrius* (1662), which we shall mention only briefly. From Books XXXIX and XL of Livy he derived a story of rival brothers reminiscent of *Nicomède*. The younger brother, Démétrius, like Attale, is seen back in his father's kingdom having spent most of his life in Rome. He loves a Thracian princess, Erixène, who is also loved by his older brother, Persée. After King Philippe makes an unsuccessful attempt to reconcile his sons, Persée appeals to him to resist Roman interference and, with the aid of a forged letter, convinces him that Démétrius is a traitor. Démétrius is imprisoned and sentenced to death but commits suicide first in the mistaken belief that Erixène now scorns him.

The action is motivated by an infelicitous mixture of amorous and political reasons, none of which are reinforced by a sense of deep conviction in the characters. Misunderstandings or ruses constitute the source of dramatic conflict. Contrary to what is thought to be true by the other characters, Démétrius, as portrayed, is not a zealot of Roman expansionism and does not lead a movement against his father. This critical issue is in fact a pretext for Persée to pursue selfish aims. The play has an unsatisfactory ending since the fate of Erixène is left unresolved and Persée is left at the edge of disaster awaiting Roman vengeance.

The play contributes little toward a total view of Thomas Corneille's theater. The devices he used had been implemented more effectively elsewhere, and the historical background of conflict between Rome and outlying kingdoms was to be the subject a few years later of a far more significant play, *Annibal*. *Persée et Démétrius* is the only play in which Thomas portrayed feuding brothers. He failed to describe either a sense of former intimacy or of long brooding hatred between them which might have been worked into a climax of tension as in Racine's *Thébaïde* the following year. Their relations are official rather than personal as one can see in the long scene of deliberation with their father whose role resembles that of a judge (II, 3). By contrast Thomas' next play, which also exploited a family relationship, was to be one of his best.

LAODICE

Laodice (1668) was first given at the Hôtel de Bourgogne and enjoyed initial success, although it did not long remain in the repertory of Parisian theaters. In his "Au lecteur" Thomas tells us that he drew his subject from the thirty-seventh book of Justin where it is recounted how Laodice killed five of her six sons and how the sixth, reared away from her, succeeded to the throne after the people had killed Laodice for her crimes. To this historical background, Thomas added details that could have been suggested to him by his brother's *Pertharite*, *Héraclius*, *Don Sanche* and especially *Rodogune* as well as his own identity plays.

In no other play did Thomas Corneille portray more successfully a striking central character in a series of ironic situations. For the first time in his career as author of tragedies he managed to subordinate his flair for dramaturgical *éclat* to the close psychological analysis of a moral monster. We have witnessed in *Commode*, *Stilicon*, *Maximian* and *Camma* the gradual awakening of the playwright to the possibilities of serious character portrayal. It is as if he were striving to give examples of what Pierre described as that "grandeur d'âme qui a quelque chose de si haut, qu'en même temps qu'on déteste ses actions, on admire la source dont elles partent". Laodice represents the culmination of Thomas Corneille's hero-villains.

It is quite clear that he had Pierre's Cléopatre very much in mind when he created Laodice. Yet no comparative analysis of these plays has been made to show the extent of their similarity. There is indeed a resemblance but also important differences. That Laodice and Cléopatre are spiritual cousins is obvious enough. Both are obsessed with their regal power and are willing to use any means to retain it. Like Cléopatre, Laodice is a ruthless politician experienced in the diplomacy of despotism, inured to the use of deception and criminal expediency to achieve her ends. Reduced to the necessity of choosing a male successor, she seeks one who will leave her the effective power:

> Qu'elle [Rome] en murmure ou non, je saurai faire un roi,
> Qui, dédaignant ses lois, n'en prenne que de moi.
> (Laodice, II, 1)

Similarly Cléopatre had insisted that her successor must be a pawn:

> Ce n'est qu'en me vengeant qu'on me le [rang] peut ravir,
> Et je ferai régner qui me voudra servir.
> (Rodogune, II, 2, 501-2)

No tie is sacred to them. Frustrated in her attempt to create dissension between her sons, Cléopatre has one of them put to death and barely misses the other. Laodice, endowed with greater foresight, had killed five of her six sons while they were still children. She is clever enough to keep alive the rumor that the sixth still lives in order to prolong her own reign. But when his appearance becomes imminent she immediately lays plans to assassinate him.

A striking trait that these "heroines" hold in common is the complete awareness each has of her own criminal temperament and the ease with which each justifies her maneuvers on the basis of this temperament. Laodice goes so far as to assume that any son of hers would naturally inherit her perversions. Speaking of her son, Ariarate, she observes:

> Si j'immolai sa vie à l'ardeur de régner,
> Pour régner à son tour voudra-t-il m'épargner?
> C'est mon sang, et ce sang du trône est trop avide
> Pour trembler à l'aspect d'un simple parricide.
>
> (III, 3)

The attribution to her son of her own depravity, an ironic hypothesis in this case since Ariarate is a paragon of virtue, is her demonstration of the need to be rid of him. She is willing to envisage momentarily the possibility that Ariarate, if named king, might be generous and guarantee her effective sovereignty. But even if he were to do so she would seek his death, for he would thereby be repudiating the only inheritance she can leave him — one of criminal ambition. She reasons:

> Je dis plus. Quand j'aurais une entière assurance
> Qu'il dût laisser toujours le trône en ma puissance,
> Toujours comme sujet me soumettre son sort,
> J'aurais la même ardeur à poursuivre sa mort.
> Pour en tenir l'arrêt et juste et légitime,
> Il suffirait de voir qu'il fit grâce à mon crime,
> Et que je périrais si, par un noble effroi,
> Il ne refusait d'être aussi méchant que moi.
>
> (III, 3)

This fatalistic resignation to one's depravity, a Jansenist attitude frequently attributed to Racine's heroines, is, in the hands of the Corneilles, converted into an active defiance of any effort toward moral recuperation.

Phèdre's recognition of her evil nature involves a sentiment of alienation and self-pity: "Et moi, triste rebut de la nature entière" (Phèdre, IV, 6). With Laodice and Cléopatre it is merely one of the facts in the case which needs to be met realistically in choosing a course of action. There is no sigh of remorse. Laodice and Cléopatre,

having found in themselves the potentiality for crime, willfully cultivate it and, to remain true to themselves, seek to perpetuate it. Witness
Cléopatre's parting malediction to her son, Antiochus, and Rodogune:

> Puissiez-vous ne trouver dedans votre union
> Qu'horreur que jalousie, et que confusion!
> Et pour vous souhaiter tous les malheurs ensemble,
> Puisse naître de vous un fils qui me ressemble!
> (V, 4, 1821-4)

Both Laodice and Cléopatre commit suicide rather than survive without power.

Despite the resemblance of these characters, Thomas gave Laodice
certain traits absent in Cléopatre. The latter was at first open to
negotiation in the matter of choosing a successor. She agreed to crown
the one of her sons who would kill Rodogune. Since neither Antiochus
nor Seleucus was ambitious, their mother would probably have kept
her part of the bargain had one of them accepted her proposition. But
when Laodice makes a similar proposal to Anaxandre, an ambitious
courtier, she has no intention of giving him the promised reward.
Cléopatre seeks the death of her sons as a last resort. Laodice, on the
contrary, conceives the death of Ariarate as a prerequisite to further
plans. Cléopatre lies to Seleucus whereas Laodice indulges in hypocrisy
(Act IV). Finally the most distinctive feature of Laodice and the most
tragic is her incestuous passion; for here, at least, she shows herself
capable of love, a sentiment unknown to Cléopatre. In love Laodice
commits the most ironic absurdity in directing her affection to the
one whose death is essential to the fulfillment of her ambition. Even
this lapse toward a natural feeling of tenderness is not an inconsistency
in her character, for she expresses bitter resentment over it and is
annoyed that affection should interfere in any manner with her in-
dependence (V, 2).

If on the one hand he used the character of Cléopatre as a *point
de départ* for his Laodice, Thomas Corneille did not appropriate many
of the dramatic devices found in *Rodogune*. In *Rodogune* the unknown
quantity on which Cléopatre predicates her scheme is not the identity
of her sons but their age. At the beginning of the play the secret
involving *droit d'aînesse* is a useful suspense-creating device which
invites speculation and review of past events entirely appropriate to

the exposition. In Act II, scene 3 the question of primogeniture is exposed as a sham and thenceforth plays an insignificant role. In *Laodice* Thomas returns to his favorite and most familiar device, the hero incognito. As in *Darius*, the rightful heir to the throne is back after a long absence for the purpose of claiming his throne. Having gained the esteem of the present ruler, in Ariarate's case his mother, his objective is to claim sovereignty as gracefully as possible. Thomas must surely have been tempted to exploit the theme of mistaken identity to the fullest. And in a real sense he did. However, he had the necessary judgment to realize that he had virtually exhausted the dramaturgical possibilities of the identity play in *Pyrrhus* a few years before. It is a tribute to his ingenuity, therefore, that he was able to reduce the aspect of false identity to a functional rather than a self-sufficient role in this new tragedy. This is not to say that any other device could have been arbitrarily substituted for the concealment of Ariarate's identity as a dramaturgical means of producing the effects we see in *Laodice*. On the contrary it is essential to the proper characterization of Laodice that precisely this means and no other be used. What is noteworthy in *Laodice* is that for the first time Thomas succeeded in integrating dramaturgy and character portrayal in effective proportions. The significant difference between this play and his earlier identity plays is that in the latter the revelation of the *alias*, whether gradual or sudden, was in itself the justification for the action as well as the source of dramatic interest. Moreover, the whole process of identification was carried out by one side or "team" in opposition to and without the knowledge of the other side. By contrast, in *Laodice* it is the queen herself who encourages the rumor that her son is alive and bases her strategy on the credulity of this assumption which she herself disbelieves. What irony, therefore, when the spectator is informed almost at the outset of the play (Act I, scene 3), that the genuine Ariarate is indeed very much alive and at his mother's court as if by her hypocritical behest! His mistaken identity is not viewed, then, as a gratuitous imposition of the dramatist in search of an activating device, but as an inherent condition of the initial situation of the tragedy.

Having once established *droit de cité* for the identity theme, Thomas proceeded to use it with discretion, never allowing it to reach sensational proportions as he had in *Timocrate* nor perplex confusion as he had in *Pyrrhus*. The audience and one other character are informed of Ariarate's identity directly by him. No letters are involved. On two occasions Ariarate is on the verge of identifying himself when someone arrives to interrupt him (II, 2 and III, 1). Since this disguise is necessary if Laodice is to fall in love with him, these close calls are laden with suspense. The explanation required to identify him is brief and credible, particularly when compared to the contrived circumstances of Philoxène's survival as described in *Bérénice*. Most important is the fact that whenever Thomas Corneille confronts Laodice with Ariarate, it is always the queen who, by her own aggression, appears to thrust herself into the most equivocal situations possible. Her statements are usually fraught with irony as, upon encountering Ariarate for the first time in the play, she vaunts her maternal affection:

> Tout ce que je regarde est un devoir de mère,
> Qui toujours pour mon fils m'engage à conserver
> Un sceptre dont je vois qu'on cherche à le priver.
> C'est ce que je veux faire avec cette tendresse
> Que demande le sang, que la nature presse.
>
> (II, 2)

In the following act, having heard that Ariarate is just outside the city under Roman escort, the queen changes tunes, asks "Oronte" to assassinate him. The opportunity for irony made possible by this request led Thomas Corneille to indulge in his facile and often used but always effective *quid pro quo*. Ariarate under the guise of Oronte pleads his case to his mother appealing to that "devoir de mère" and "tendresse" which she had professed to him only an hour earlier. But his vain effort to evoke a humane sentiment in her only reveals a turpitude more deep-rooted than ever he had suspected. Yet here a strange thing happens. He refuses to do her will. But instead of infuriating her, Ariarate's refusal ennobles him in her eyes:

> Oui, telle que je suis, aux forfaits enchaînée
> Par le dur ascendant que prend la destinée,
> Je me vois, malgré moi, forcée à respecter
> Ce qu'un fatal penchant me défend d'imiter.
>
> (IV, I)

By endowing his heroine with the capacity to appreciate a positive moral action and showing that her admiration causes her to waver in her evil course, Thomas enriched the portrayal of an otherwise flat character. Laodice's admiration of "Oronte" has turned to love. After the failure of her plans to liquidate Ariarate, she is willing finally to renounce pursuit of him provided "Oronte" will marry her and retire to share her throne in the small kingdom of Lycaonia. Momentarily love seems to have triumphed in this bitter heart. Even after Ariarate identifies himself, his mother is unable to shed her affection immediately. He gallantly invites her to run him through, but her love has not lost momentum:

> Laissez-moi donc, ingrat, le pouvoir de le faire,
> Et quand à vous haïr tout semble m'animer,
> Arrachez-moi du cœur ce qui vous fait aimer.
> Otez-moi cette ardeur qui, quoique je l'abhorre,
> Me fait voir dans mon fils un amant que j'adore.[18]
>
> (V, 2)

Pierre Corneille's Cléopatre lacks the strange antithesis which Thomas gave to Laodice. The latter is at least as perverse as Cléopatre, if degrees of turpitude can be distinguished at this level. But in addition she is given the damning grace of an illicit passion. Ostensibly, therefore, she seems to illustrate more aptly than Cléopatre the concept of hero-villain. Moreover, her momentary redemption through love, which gives her the latent stature of heroine, in the Aristotelian sense, adds a touch of pathos absent in *Rodogune*. The most appealing aspect of Laodice is her utter frankness and realistic approach to situations. Whenever self-interest does not require her to conceal her motives, she goes straight to the heart of the matter. Compared with most of Thomas' heroines, who dress their sentiments in the idiom of propriety and abstractions, Laodice is crisp and incisive. She dismisses Ariarate:

> Allez, vous dis-je,
> Je connais votre cœur, vous le mien, il suffit.
>
> (III, 5)

---

[18] Lockert, who has made the most recent analysis of the play, points admiringly to Thomas Corneille's "sense of psychological realities", with reference to Laodice's inability to change her love instantaneously even after learning the true identity of Oronte.

The interest of the play centers so importantly on Laodice that the other characters, except for Ariarate, have little more than functional roles. Lockert is justified in criticizing Ariarate's fatuous insistence that he can eventually correct his mother's evil ways (*Studies*, p. 233). Otherwise he is effectively portrayed. Aquilius, the Roman ambassador, represents a Rome which, for a change, is a beneficent force in the play. Axiane, princess of Cilicia, is a conventional passive heroine waiting for the events to occur which will determine her fate. Phradate, a friend of Ariarate, and Anaxandre, a second courtier who poses a certain threat to Ariarate, are unusually well differentiated for minor roles of this nature. Essentially, however, Laodice is the play.

THÉODAT

Thomas Corneille must have preserved a fond memory of the success of *Laodice*; for some four years later, despite his trend away from identity situations and toward simplicity, he prepared another play, *Théodat* (1672), whose wicked heroine was very much like the queen of Cappadocia. Meanwhile in 1669 he had given *Annibal* and a year later his comedy, *La Comtesse d'orgueil*, which has been treated above. We shall skip these intervening plays momentarily, as well as *Ariane*, which played a few months earlier than *Théodat*, for a brief glance at the latter. Its general atmosphere recalls earlier romanesque tragi-comedies, but the heroine is closely related to Laodice.

As Lancaster has pointed out, *Théodat* rests ultimately on historical material reported by Procopius, Jordanes, and Cassiodorus (*History*, III, p. 602). Amalasonte, who corresponds to Laodice, is shown to be the ruthless queen of the Goths in love with her favorite courtier, Théodat. The latter, who loves princess Ildegonde, does his best to divert his queen's passion and preserve her good will. This essentially comic situation is complicated by the interposition of Prince Honoric, who is mistakenly assassinated at night in lieu of Théodat, a popular uprising by Théodat's supporters indignant over his supposed death, and finally the demise of the depraved queen.

The play is far inferior to *Laodice* and did not enjoy much success. Although the hero endeavors to reform his queen in much the same manner that Ariarate sought a reconciliation with Laodice, his position involves less tension since he is not dealing with his own mother. This fact as well as the lack of a situation involving false identity prevented Thomas from producing the cruel irony that characterized the former play. Moreover, in *Théodat* he devoted much attention to a conventional struggle of pride and love between Théodat and Ildegonde, which is reminiscent of the contrived obstacles separating the queen and Théodat in Quinault's *Amalasonte* (1657). Except for the portrayal of the villainous queen, *Théodat* is best viewed as a reversion to an earlier type of romanesque tragi-comedy. Yet, ironically, the ingredient conspicuously lacking which would have improved the play most is a situation of false identity.

LA MORT D'ANNIBAL

In November of the year following the presentation of *Laodice*, Thomas Corneille offered *La Mort d'Annibal*, last of the tragedies which concern us in the present chapter. Lancaster has indicated Livy as his source while admitting that Nepos, Plutarch and Justin also present most of Livy's facts (*History*, III, p. 597). The obvious relationship between Pierre Corneille's *Nicomède* and Thomas' play has been noted by Lancaster, Reynier and Lockert but has not been treated in detail. As in his other tragedies where the younger brother's debt to the older is patent, Thomas attempted some significant variations from his model.

The general historical theme — conflict between powerful Rome and outlying kingdoms seeking to preserve autonomy — had been popular with dramatists since early in the century and was yet to be exploited by Racine. Rome's long domination of Europe and the Mideast was studded with hostile outbursts on the part of rulers like Sophonisba, Hannibal, Mithridates, Vercingetorix, and eventually Attila, all of whom figured in tragedies of the time. The subject was a "natural", for not only could the playwright assume the inherent Rome vs. non-Rome conflict, he could also show one character or more of the non-Roman camp to have some degree of affiliation with Rome. Hence it was easy to create conflicting loyalties.

Thomas may have originally taken his decision to deal with Hannibal upon reviewing a peripheral subject of *Nicomède*. In his "Examen" to this play Pierre had observed:

J'ai approché de cette histoire celle de la mort d'Annibal, qui arriva un peu auparavant chez ce même roi [Prusias] et dont le nom n'est pas un petit ornement à mon ouvrage. J'en ai fait Nicomède disciple, pour lui prêter plus de valeur et plus de fierté contre les Romains; et prenant l'occasion de l'ambassade où Flaminius fut envoyé par eux vers ce roi, leur allié, pour demander qu'on remît entre leurs mains ce vieil ennemi de leur grandeur, je l'ai chargé d'une commission secrète de traverser ce mariage [de Laodice-Nicomède], qui leur devoit donner de la jalousie.
(*Œuvres*, V, p. 506)

Thomas placed the action of *Annibal* earlier, "un peu auparavant chez ce même roi", kept Prusias, Nicomède, Attale, and Flaminius.[19] He replaced Laodice with Elise, Annibal's daughter. Attale is no longer Nicomède's step-brother, but his function in the play is very similar to that of Attale in *Nicomède* since in both plays Attale at first rivals Nicomède then befriends and supports him.

Thomas Corneille gave himself the problem of dealing with a hero in humiliating circumstances. Annibal has already been expelled from Ephesus as the distinguished but unwanted guest of Antiochus. Political asylum at Prusias' court at Bithynia proves even less secure. Divested of all effective power save that of his prestige, Annibal is reduced to auctioning his daughter to the suitor who will best serve his interests. Of these, Nicomède, who loves and is loved by Elise, would be his choice, except that he can count on Nicomède's loyalty without the inducement of a marriage. The second, Attale, having recently become king of Pergamus, offers Annibal the more advantageous possibility of asylum and a fresh headquarters in his country. The third candidate is Prusias whose unwillingness to resist Roman pressure makes him suspect to the great Carthaginian.

With no army to support him, Annibal is in a vulnerable position. Unlike Pierre Corneille's Nicomède, he is a hero on the defensive. Thomas chose to portray him making that last stand with little or no

[19] In fact both Thomas and Pierre Corneille telescoped events that had taken place some thirty years apart. Hannibal died in 183 B.C. Nicomède succeeded his father Prusias II, son of Prusias I, in 142 B.C. Prusias II was dethroned in 148 B.C.

hope of success. He must have realized the undertones of the Greek tragic hero in Annibal's situation. Virtually overwhelmed by a series of recent setbacks, Annibal makes a final stalwart effort to deceive fate. He appeals to Prusias' sense of regal self-respect, exhorting him to be rid of Roman bondage. He reiterates his own past successes in thwarting Roman supremacy and paints an impressive picture of himself as Rome's eternal enemy. He is a portrait of courage and inspires our admiration. But, alas, his words fall on ignoble ears. Prusias is hypocritical, selfish and cowardly, a sorry representative of the fate which pursues Annibal. Only the arrogant Flaminius is able to provide some measure of dramatic vigor.

Flaminius and Annibal stand out as individuals of potentially great interest. The former, in an ironic gesture of condescension, allows Attale the rest of the day to decide whether to marry Elise and give asylum to her father. Flaminius is aware, as Attale is not, that the latter has been dispossessed of his throne owing to the revival of Eumènes who, at that moment, has already reclaimed sovereignty in Pergamus. This unexpected change of fortune mars the unity of action, as Lancaster has suggested (*History*, III, p. 598), but it allows Flaminius a moment of sardonic pleasure in dealing with Attale (III, 3), which gives an interesting effect.

Prusias indulges in petty maneuvers of conciliation in an unsuccessful attempt to appease Annibal, ingratiate himself with Flaminius, evict Attale, and win the hand of Elise. He nurtures the incredible delusion that all these courses of action are compatible. Eventually he comes to realize their impossibility:

> O désirs de grandeur, fiers mouvements de gloire
> Amour, Rome, Annibal, qui de vous dois-je croire?
> (IV, 4)

He chooses to betray Annibal in return for Flaminius' promise to grant him Elise. A scheme to this purpose is put into motion. Nicomède manages to free Annibal from the Romans but only after Annibal has taken poison. Prusias is killed in a *mêlée* with Attale and the Roman guards. Annibal is left to die the victim of an awkwardly executed plot.

The frères Parfaict early pointed out that Annibal is inactive except when he poisons himself (*Histoire*, X, p. 425). Even more than the inaction of the hero, it is the excessive attention given to the intrigues carried on by Prusias and Flaminius which weakens the portrayal. What Thomas Corneille really did was to present a court intrigue much in the manner of Pierre's *Othon*. Hence the reader's or viewer's attention is diverted from Annibal to Prusias. Whereas *Nicomède* may be viewed primarily as a play of action with respect to the hero, Annibal is better described as a play of counter-action. Nicomède, the character, embodies the same anti-Roman spirit in both plays, and in both he is in danger of being sent to Rome as a hostage. But in Pierre's play, he is a free agent able to act energetically on his own behalf. In *Annibal* he is the spiritual child of Annibal and acts always as his dutiful subordinate. Furthermore, he appears rarely (8 scenes), and is off-stage throughout the middle of the play.

The character of Elise is noteworthy for combining a noble, proud, and courageous temperament in a role which requires essentially an attitude of submissiveness. She places herself entirely at her father's disposal but in so doing loses none of her self-respect since she is acting from conviction. Witness her declaration of purpose to Prusias:

> Connaissez, Seigneur, toute mon âme.
> Le prince a des vertus qu'on ne peut égaler,
> Mais, quelque feu pour lui dont je puisse brûler,
> Je le dédaignerais si d'une ardeur ouverte,
> Des Romains que j'abhorre il ne jurait la perte.
> De ma haine pour eux mon amour prend la loi,
> Et c'est la seule dot que j'apporte avec moi.
> Ainsi, point de mari capable de me plaire,
> Qui ne venge Carthage, et l'exil de mon père.
> L'univers affranchi de ces cruels tyrans
> Est tout ce qui me flatte; à ce prix je me rends.
> Adieu, Seigneur.
>
> (I, 5)

Lancaster surmises that Racine, in his first preface to *Britannicus*, was referring to Elise where he mentions "une femme qui donnerait des leçons de fierté à des conquérants" (*History*, III, pp. 597-598). On more than one occasion Lancaster has compared a play by Pierre Corneille with one of Thomas. Without exception he has concluded that Pierre infused his plays with greater historical depth and breadth than did Thomas. A typical comment is the following made in reference to *Annibal*: "The political background is far less emphasized than in *Nicomède*" (*History*, III, p. 598). It is in the first place open to discussion whether this statement is accurate in fact. Of all Thomas Corneille's plays it would be difficult to find one dealing more thoroughly with a political problem. The power struggle represented by Prusias in his efforts to curry favor with conflicting forces, Rome and Annibal, is, even more than the death of the hero, the subject of the play. A further dimension of this struggle is provided by the tenuous situation of Attale whose political posture is contingent upon the ebb and flow of Roman support. Moreover, Annibal's background is well delineated. Thomas Corneille tells where he has been, reviews his long career of opposition to Rome and his recent setbacks. Nicomède's discipleship is clearly explained. Flaminius is fittingly presented as an exponent of Roman power politics. To imply that the political background is not sufficiently emphasized is to ignore the whole basis of struggle on which the action depends.

On the contrary one might well argue that Thomas Corneille succeeded in creating a far more realistic impression of political tension in *Annibal* than Pierre did in *Nicomède* because he divested his principal actor, Prusias, of that heroic political idealism characteristic of Pierre's Nicomède which makes of the latter a symbol of supra-political perfection. Pierre dealt with political ideality whereas Thomas dealt with the ugly realities of politics. In so doing Thomas showed somewhat more effectively than his older brother a particular instance of the inherent weaknesses of the Eastern kings, which helps to explain Rome's successful expansion in Asia Minor. Pierre's genius consisted in raising the specific action above the immediate incident and showing it as the embodiment of a broad historical movement.

The structure of *Annibal* offers some explanation for Thomas' failure to generalize on the principles which, in a particular sense, his characters represent very well. The conflict between Rome and Eastern kingdoms is reduced to an imbroglio involving three men in love with the same woman. Since two of these suitors are father and son, there is the additional element of internecine dispute which detracts from the primacy of Annibal's struggle against Rome. Were he dealing primarily with Flaminius, he would be pitted directly against the enemy. But he is forced to spar with an intermediary, Prusias. Indeed the play is as much about the death of Prusias as that of Annibal. We are pulled two ways. Throughout we are led to believe that the discomfiture of Prusias will result in Annibal's safety. But Annibal dies, somewhat fortuitously, in the midst of his party's victory. Thomas Corneille fashioned him as one of his most powerful protagonists, but in so doing he made Annibal incongruously superior to the tragedy bearing his name.

The Cornelian phase of Thomas Corneille is the most important he experienced. His obvious respect for his brother led him to rework many of Pierre's dramatic themes in one form or another. Yet this same respect proved to be an obstacle, too, for he could not merely repeat his brother without adding something of his own. His quest for originality led him to try to intensify the images which Pierre bequeathed him and to couch his stories in varying dramaturgical patterns. *Laodice* is perhaps the most successful of his efforts. Yet he did not renounce a tendency to indulge in romanesque characterizations. For the most part his "good" characters still adhere scrupulously to the *carte de tendre*. On the other hand, his hero-villains, Stilicon, Maximian, and Laodice in particular are worthy studies in pathological behavior and moral crises.

With *Annibal* Thomas Corneille virtually abandoned the use of false identity as a basic device for his tragedies. If we can except *Bradamante*, something of a derelict among his plays, we may conclude that beginning in the 1670's, he was seeking to renew his dramatic art in competition with a new popular dramatist, Racine. In the process he purged himself of all that is extraneous to the portrayal of psychological crises. *Ariane*, *Essex*, and to a lesser extent *Achille* represent Thomas' efforts to do away with the external actions of drama in order to describe the internal dynamics caused by frustrated passion.

IV. THE TRAGEDIES OF FEELING

RACINE AND THOMAS CORNEILLE

It is clear that the plays about to be discussed represent a distinct evolution in Thomas Corneille's approach to dramatic characterizations, but it is far from certain that the change should be attributed wholly to the influence of Racine. For the most part critics have taken for granted that in *Ariane* and *Essex* he was striving consciously to equal Racine in style and dramatic method. Reynier, whose position is typical, groups these two plays in the same chapter as "Tragédies raciniennes". Lancaster was perhaps the first to discount this view but he does not rule out the possibility entirely:

It is not, however, certain that Thomas Corneille was influenced by Racine, for Greek mythology had furnished plots to many authors, Thomas Corneille had already dramatized simple subjects and drawn his events from the emotions of his characters in *Camma* and *Stilicon*, and pity had been the chief emotion he sought to arouse in *Persée et Démétrius*. The subject of *Ariane* was, moreover, probably suggested to him by *le Mariage de Bachus* of his friend de Visé ... It is, of course, possible that the example of *Andromaque* may have encouraged him to treat such a subject and that the simplicity and pathos of *Bérénice* may have influenced his structure and his presentation of *Ariane*, but the facts hardly warrant the confident assertions of M. Reynier and of M. Lanson (*History*, III, p. 599).

More recently Lockert has offered something of a compromise in calling only *Ariane* a Racinian play (*Studies*, p. 240).

As we re-examine the case for Racinian influence, it should be noted that Tristan l'Hermite, Quinault and Thomas Corneille had all anticipated him in many respects. Among others, Daniel Mornet has criticized the easy fallacy of juxtaposing Pierre Corneille and Racine directly without taking into account the contributions of an intervening generation.[1] He instances Quinault's *Mort de Cyrus* as an early example of tragedy in which the essential characteristics of Racinian drama were present:

Si l'on changeait l'absurde et romanesque point de départ des amours de Cyrus et de Thomyris, rien ne serait plus facile que d'imaginer entre lui, elle et le général Odartise, entre l'amour, l'amour jaloux et les nécessités d'Etat une tragédie toute racinienne. On voit donc s'ébaucher parfois, avant Racine, la tragédie racinienne, entendons une action simple, chargée de peu de matière et dont tout l'intérêt vient, ou plutôt devrait venir de l'étude des mouvements du cœur (p. 222).

Earlier in the present study we pointed out, particularly with reference to *Camma*, Thomas Corneille's ability to construct a plot around the fluctuations of a hero beset with a frustrated passion. In both *Commode* and *Camma*, the progression of events was seen to depend on one momentous but simple decision, which set off a chain of repercussions. These plays, which preceded all of Racine's tragedies, provide significant evidence to refute any contention that Thomas Corneille learned a profound lesson in psychology from Racine. In fact, the patterns of psychological reaction we see in *Ariane* and *Essex* were latent in his previous plays.

There is more justification in the conjecture that Thomas may have simplified his action in emulation of Racine whose *Bérénice* appeared two years before *Ariane*. Yet this possibility, too, must be qualified. Whereas complex plots had characterized Thomas' identity plays, he had been moving in the general direction of simplicity. *Antiochus* (1666) and, despite the identity problem, *Laodice* (1668) offered simple situations. Since his *Pyrrhus* (1663-64), Thomas had tended to spend less time on heroic gallantry and the intricate niceties of *précieux* love, and in their place he substituted more direct relationships. Sparing herself a long explanation which his earlier heroines would have found indispensable, Thomas' Stratonice stated simply to her confidant that she had fallen in love with Antiochus for

> L'air galant, l'âme noble, un courage élevé,
> Tout ce qui marque enfin un héros achevé. (I, 4)

[1] *Histoire de la littérature française classique*, 4e éd. (Paris, 1950), p. 220.

And Laodice, who was not one for punctilious verbiage to express a turgid idealism, cut short Ariarate's noble gesture of self-sacrifice with:

> C'est trop, n'en parlons plus, tant de vertu me lasse,
> A moi quelqu'un.

(III, 3)

This heroine may well have been expressing an impatience characteristic of the closing decade. Prolixity and refinement based on a paucity of genuine sentiments had become the target of Boileau's satires as early as 1660:

> Je suis rustique et fier, et j'ai l'âme grossière.
> Je ne puis rien nommer, si ce n'est par son nom.
> J'appelle un chat un chat, et Rolet un fripon.
> De servir un amant, je n'en ai pas l'adresse. (Satire I)

Mornet refers to the fact that the long ten volume romanesque adventures such as Le Grand Cyrus and Clélie were beginning to give way to shorter works: "Même le goût du siècle découvre peu à peu qu'il est plus émouvant de souffrir vraiment d'amour et parfois d'en mourir une fois que de languir mille fois et de mourir par métaphore" (Hist. de la lit. fran. cl., p. 310). The popular Lettres portugaises, appearing in 1669, exalted pure and simple love a year before the ardent pleas of Bérénice were heard at the Hôtel de Bourgogne.

In brief the simplicity and directness frequently associated with Racine's tragedies were in the air at the time and the label "Racinian" has even been used in a retroactive sense to describe tendencies which had taken shape before Racine could have made his influence felt. It is therefore much better not to treat Thomas' final tragedies primarily as Racinian plays. That they have much in common with Andromaque, Bérénice and Phèdre we do not deny, but we see no reason why Thomas Corneille's originality should be sacrificed to the greatness of Racine. To Ariane and Essex we propose to add a brief discussion of a third play, La Mort d'Achille, which shares with the other two many of those qualities commonly identified with the tragedies of Racine.

ARIANE

The simplicity of Ariane suggests Bérénice, which had appeared only a little more than a year earlier, and in some respects Andromaque. It has in common with the latter play the chain of lovers and the themes of love, jealousy and revenge resulting from this relationship. It is, however, different from *Bérénice* in two significant aspects. First *Ariane* focuses on internal motivation to a higher degree than does *Bérénice*, where there is considerable pressure on Titus from the senate, the people, and Roman tradition to abandon the foreign queen. In *Ariane* decisions and actions issue purely from psychological motives unaffected by external events. Thésée's decision to abandon Ariane, unlike Titus' break with Bérénice, is an entirely personal matter. No state policy is involved, he simply loves someone else. Secondly, whereas Racine's play calls for heroic renunciation on the part of hero and heroine, in Thomas Corneille's play the hero is dominated by self-indulgence and the heroine by jealously and revenge. Feeling reigns unchecked by higher considerations.

While Thomas Corneille never admitted indebtedness to Racine as he did to Pierre, it is certain that with *Ariane* he adopted an attitude toward characterization which is closer to that of Racine and different from that of his previous tragedies. Unlike these, for another reason, *Ariane* has practically no plot. A situation is presented: Ariane, in love with Thésée, expects to marry him. Thésée is in love with and is loved by Phèdre. The plot consists of Ariane's discovery through Pirithoüs that Thésée does not love her, her plan to kill her rival, and finally her discovery that this rival is her own sister with whom Thésée has fled. That is all the action. The rest is the painful analysis of motives and emotions.

The high degree of emotional appeal in *Ariane* as opposed to the more nearly logical, rational appeal of Thomas Corneille's earlier tragedies has been the factor most responsible for winning it an honorable mention among French critics. Mme de Sévigné, Donneau de Visé, the brothers Parfaict, La Harpe, Nisard, and finally Reynier have maintained that the play's worth derives from the "beauté de sentiments". Voltaire's comments on the play reveal that his admiration, too, was directed primarily to those passages in which the beauty of sentiment prevailed over the skill of the dramatic craftsman. Reynier has written of *Ariane*:

Il n'y a pas, dans tout notre théâtre classique, de personnage qui inspire, plus qu'Ariane, une pitié complète, absolue, sans mélange d'autre sentiment. Plus sympathique que la Phèdre de Racine, parce qu'elle ne brûle pas d'un amour coupable et qu'elle ne se venge pas de celui qui la dédaigne; plus touchante qu'Hermione, trop violente, trop cruelle; plus misérable que Bérénice, qui "emportera dans la Judée tout l'amour de Titus", elle nous attache à elle par sa candeur, par sa confiance, par sa tendresse en pleurs, parce qu'elle connaît, dans un court instant, toutes les peines, et aussi parce qu'elle est sans force dans un tel excès de maux.

(Thom. Corn., pp. 189-90)

It is true that the role of Ariane calls for the highest skill in rendering the passions, and that the success of the heroine's role is tantamount to the effectiveness of the play. Yet for all that has been said about the pathos inspired by Ariane, it has never been made clear what degree of responsibility she bears in creating her own discomfiture. She has always been looked upon as a victim and nothing but a victim of Thésée's perfidy and Phèdre's deceit. Without prejudice to the primacy of the heroine, both Thésée and Phèdre deserve greater emphasis as characters and a little more sympathy than has commonly been accorded them. Ariane's role need not suffer thereby. She still passes through a transformation from the trusting, happy fiancée to the broken-hearted, disconsolate sufferer and properly claims most of the attention.

While Phèdre, Thésée, Pirithoüs, and Oenarus remain relatively static as agents of interest, Ariane evolves dynamically through a series of attitudes each of which claims renewed attention. Thomas calculated the development of the play on her changing emotions. Absent from Act I she is nevertheless frequently mentioned as the other characters set the stage for her entrance. At the beginning of Act II she appears, enthralled by the mental image of the hero who will soon be hers:

> Parle-moi de Thésée;
> Peins-moi bien quel honneur je reçois de sa foi,
> Peins-moi bien tout l'amour dont il brûle pour moi,
> Offres-en à mes yeux la plus sensible image.
>
> (II, 1)

So profound is her faith in Thésée that she parries the first blows of deception with confident equanimity. In a speech that almost perfectly states the theme of Bérénice, she conjectures that Thésée's trouble is due to state policy:

Je vous comprends tous deux, vous arrivez d'Athènes,
Du sang dont je suis née on n'y veut point de reines,
Et le peuple indigné refuse à ce héros
D'admettre dans son lit la fille de Minos.

(II, 5)

But as Pirithoüs persists in urging her to accept Oenarus' offer of marriage, her trust weakens to suspicion:

Parle plus clairement, ai-je quelque rivale?
Thésée a-t-il changé? Viole-t-il sa foi?

(II, 5)

The propitiously timed arrival of Phèdre at this moment, as if in answer to Ariane's questions, creates a situation of the highest dramatic interest. Ariane pours her heart out to this *rivale inconnue* whom she asks to represent her:

D'un juste et long remords avancez-lui les coups;
Enfin, ma soeur, enfin je n'espère qu'en vous . . .
Hélas! Et plût au ciel que vous sussiez aimer,
Que vous pussiez savoir, par votre expérience
Jusqu'où d'un fort amour s'étend la violence . . .
Au défaut de l'amour, puisqu'il n'a pu vous plaire,
Votre amitié pour moi fera ce qu'il faut faire.

(II, 7)

Two scenes later Phèdre reports that Thésée remains unyielding whereupon Ariane, clinging to the hope that he may be regained, reproaches her sister for not presenting her plight forcefully:

Ma soeur, il ne sait pas qu'il faudra que j'en meure.
Vous avez oublié de bien marquer l'horreur
Du fatal désespoir qui règne dans mon coeur,
Vous avez oublié, pour bien peindre ma rage,
D'assembler tous les maux dont on connaît l'image.

(III, 2)

Unsatisfied with Phèdre's efforts, Ariane decides to confront Thésée in person with all the coercive powers she can muster. She addresses him first in an ironic vein of latent but still controlled rage followed shortly by the stinging reminders of the "labyrinthe ouvert". This approach having no effect, she drops to a more tender, conciliatory tone:

Tu n'as qu'à dire un mot, ce crime est effacé;

C'en est fait, tu le vois, je n'ai plus de colère.
(III, 4)

When Thésée persists in his refusal, all Ariane's suppressed fury
explodes into vociferous indignation: "Ah! c'est trop", and finally
seeing no change in him, "Ôte-toi de mes yeux" (III, 4). This cli-
mactic scene, unfortunately too long to reproduce here, is one of the
best Thomas Corneille ever wrote, summing up as it does the whole
problem of the tragedy and conveying an emotional impact of great
intensity. Having now played her trump card, she can only brood over
her loss. In lines which Voltaire has compared favorably with
Racine's dramatic verse, Ariane deplores her fate:

> As-tu vu quelle joie a paru dans ses yeux?
> Combien il est sorti satisfait de ma haine?
> Que de mépris!
>
> (III, 5)

In Act IV her plan for revenge gives Ariane an ostensible serenity
finally turning to despair in Act V when she learns of Thésée's
elopement with Phèdre.

Reynier's treatment of *Ariane*, which is typical of criticism of
Thomas Corneille, takes as its sole point of orientation the viewpoint
of the heroine, and indeed from a strictly personal point of view
Ariane must have conceived of herself as the most unfortunate victim
of betrayal. However, in his lavish praise of Ariane the character,
Reynier mercilessly sacrifices the other roles to the histrionic apotheosis
of the heroine. His admiration of her is exclusive to the point of
making the other characters seem not only insignificant but unworthy
of figuring among the dramatis personae:

De même qu'il n'y a qu'une seule situation dans la pièce, on peut dire
aussi qu'il n'y a qu'un seul rôle: celui d'Ariane; Thésée, Pirithoüs, son
confident, Phèdre, Oenarus, le roi de Naxos, qui les a reçus dans son
palais, tous les autres personnages enfin sont misérables ou ridicules.
(*Thom. Corn.*, pp. 179-180)

One by one he rails against Oenarus, Pirithoüs, Phèdre and Thésée,
pointing to their moral weaknesses with such scorn as to suggest a
considerable emotional bias. He refers to Oenarus as a hypocritical
consoler lying in ambush for the affections of Ariane. Of Pirithoüs
he exclaims: "Quel pauvre personnage!" and makes him an accomplice

of Thésée's treason. Phèdre, in Reynier's eyes, is a "vicieuse petite personne", an adventuress, a heartless coquette whose love for Thésée is false. Finally Thésée is described as "un seducteur bourgeois" and a "vulgaire égoïste" who resembles "un petit garçon pris en faute" (p. 179 ff.).

Now there is just enough truth in Reynier's epithets to make his treatment of the play interesting to read if for no other reason than to witness a demonstration of genuine emotional involvement in literary appreciation, but some of his statements cannot go un-challenged. In the first place, he has made errors of fact. One of these, already referred to by Lockert (*Studies*, p. 15 ff), involves his condemnation of Phèdre who, says Reynier, "a suivi sa sœur non point par affection, mais bien plutôt par envie de courir les aventures; elle lui vole son amant de l'air le plus dégagé ... Il lui plaît d'avoir fait la conquête ... d'un homme que sa sœur adore" (p. 181). No-where in the play is there evidence to support these assertions. On the contrary Phèdre has fled with Ariane and Thésée reluctantly and only at Ariane's insistence:

> Enfin, ma soeur, enfin je n'espère qu'en vous.
> Le ciel m'inspira bien, quand par l'amour séduite,
> Je vous fis, malgré vous, accompagner ma fuite.
>
> (II, 7)

> Je soupçonnerais Phèdre, elle de qui les pleurs
> Semblaient, en s'embarquant, présager nos malheurs?
> Avant que la résoudre à seconder ma fuite,
> A quoi, pour la gagner, ne fus-je pas réduite?
> Combien de résistance et d'obstinés refus?
>
> (V, 1)

Phèdre's love for Thésée has been involuntary. She has found herself incapable of suppressing it but makes every effort to persuade Thésée to return to Ariane:

> Que de faiblesse! Il faut l'empêcher d'en jouir,
> Combattre incessamment son infidèle audace;
> Allez, Pirithoüs, revoyez-le, de grâce:
> De peur qu'en mon amour il prenne trop d'appui,
> Otez-lui tout espoir que je puisse être à lui;
> J'ai déjà beaucoup dit, dites-lui plus encore.
>
> (III, 1)

One can doubt her sincerity, of course, but not on the basis of what she says and does in the play. Repeatedly she bids Thésée against her own inclinations to renounce her and agrees to flee with him only upon learning that Ariane plans to murder the woman Thésée prefers to her. Even then she is solicitous of her sister and poignantly feels the despair she is about to cause Ariane:

Phèdre: Elle se fie à moi cette sœur, elle m'aime,
        C'est une ardeur sincère, une tendresse extrême,
        Jamais son amitié ne me refusa rien,
        Pour l'en récompenser je lui vole son bien,
        Je l'expose aux rigueurs du sort le plus sévère,
        Je la tue, et c'est vous qui me le faites faire.
        Pourquoi vous ai-je aimé?
Thésée: Vous en repentez-vous?
Phèdre: Je ne sais, pour mon cœur il n'est rien de plus doux;
        Mais vous le remarquez, ce cœur tremble, soupire,
        Et perdant une soeur, si j'ose encore le dire,
        Vous la laissez dans Naxe en proie à ses douleurs.
                                                (IV, 5)

If, as Reynier claims, there is coquetry in Phèdre's reluctance to betray her sister, it must be unconscious. The "Pourquoi vous ai-je aimé", and the "Je ne sais" bear the marks of utter sincerity.

Reynier has referred slightingly to Thomas Corneille's Phèdre as a weak prefiguration of Racine's heroine: "Qui reconnaîtrait en elle la Phèdre d'Euripide et de Racine, la victime désignée de Vénus?" (p. 181). The comparison is invidious because in *Ariane* she is not intended to be "la principale" and hence cannot be measured against a heroine whose guilty passion is made the all-important theme of a play. One could as well compare the role of Andromaque in Giraudoux's *La guerre de Troie n'aura pas lieu* with her role in Racine's *Andromaque*. A fairer comparison, which Reynier also makes in passing, is one between Ariane and Racine's Phèdre. Here he gives Ariane more than fair treatment, but it should be noted that the importance of the respective roles is comparable. Reynier is judging Thomas Corneille's Phèdre with the prejudicial advantage of hindsight. The corpus of appreciative commentary that has grown up around Racine's Phèdre has itself created something of a legend. Finally, even if the comparison is made, nothing in Thomas Corneille's conception of Phèdre is at variance with Racine's character of the same name. As Lancaster so well says of her: "She is neither an heroic character, nor a coquette, rather a preliminary sketch of Racine's Phèdre, a woman who feels she is doing wrong, yet, once started on her course, finds that it is too late to turn back" (*History*, III, p. 601).

Pirithoüs, whose primary function is that of buffer between Thésée and Ariane, admittedly plays a thankless role but an important one. Far from being an accomplice of Thésée, he disapproves his friend's decision to abandon Ariane and cannot bring himself to tell her of it. He compromises by agreeing to speak to Ariane in behalf of Oenarus but objects to Thésée:

> Mais, comme je condamne
> Votre ingrate conduite au regard d'Ariane,
> N'attendez point de moi que, pour vous dégager,
> Je lui parle du feu qui vous porte à changer,
> C'est un aveu honteux qu'un autre lui peut faire.
>
> (I, 3)

To be an accomplice Pirithoüs would somehow have to share the guilt of Thésée's infidelity or encourage him to abandon Ariane. In fact he does not. Only after realizing that his friend is not to be dissuaded does he reluctantly agree to bear the unpleasant tidings to Ariane. Then he becomes, in effect, her adviser. His suggestion that she marry Oenarus, though an entirely unsatisfactory remedy to her despair, is nevertheless good advice, the more so because she had already expressed admiration for the king of Naxos as a worthy recipient of her affection:

> Tant d'ardeur méritait que ce cœur plus sensible
> A l'offre de vos vœux ne fût pas inflexible,
> Que d'un si noble hommage il se trouvât charmé . . .
> Seigneur, tant de vertu dans votre amour éclate,
> Qu'il faut vous l'avouer, je ne suis point ingrate,
> Mon cœur se sent touché de ce que je vous dois;
> Et voudrait être à vous s'il pouvait être à moi.
>
> (II, 2)

Pirithoüs should not be blamed as a person for what he does. Reynier's "quel pauvre personnage!" might better apply to him as a statement of sympathy than as a condemnation of the role in itself.

Reynier's attack on Thésée, in some respects quite sound, is nevertheless exaggerated. He is not alone in his evaluation, for La Harpe too felt that "la conduite de Thésée n'a aucune excuse".[2] In fact a total lack of sympathy for Thésée appears to be the nearly unanimous reaction of those who have analyzed the play. Lancaster, an exception, treats Thésée with forbearance: "Theseus and Phaedra have ungracious roles, but they are not brazen in their attitude towards Ariane. The former is ashamed of his disloyalty to the woman who has saved his life, but he insists that his love for Phaedra is too strong to be resisted" (*History*, III, p. 601). We feel that Thésée's role needs to be re-examined in new perspective. In order to do so, we must inquire further into the role of Ariane and the intimacies of their relationship as well as the total effect of the play.

Lockert has criticized the tragedy on the basis that "a tragedy about love and absolutely nothing else ... is almost certain to lack dignity" (*Studies*, p. 241-242). He classifies Ariane as such a play and makes the generalization that "love does not need to be of subordinate interest in a tragedy as Pierre Corneille maintained, but it cannot be — it never has been in any impressive drama — the only interest" (p. 241-242). One may first object that *Ariane* is not exclusively about love although this is admittedly the primary theme. An extremely important subsidiary, one without which the tragedy would be seriously weakened, is the theme of gratitude. A third is the theme of revenge which becomes prominent beginning at the end of Act III.

A strange hypothesis underlies the thinking of every character in the play. Without exception they believe that Thésée has an obligation to love Ariane. Nowhere in Thomas Corneille's earlier theater was love taken so much for granted as a concomitant of gratitude. A quick survey of his earlier plays does not reveal a single example of a heroine who felt she deserved love solely on the basis of services rendered. This concept marks a distinct change in Thomas Corneille from his former romanesque notions of unselfish, courtly, idyllic love, essentially platonic, toward a conception of love as a domineering passion, self-indulgent and exclusive. In *Ariane* the dramatist's use of the verb *devoir* in speaking of the relationship of hero and heroine becomes a *Leitmotif*, a recurrent reminder of Thésée's constraint and

---

[2] Jean-François La Harpe, *Lycée ou cours de littérature* (Paris, 1818) Vol. 6, p. 166. Hereafter cited as *Cours de littérature*.

Ariane's expectations. He readily acknowledges his indebtedness to her while objecting to the price, his love, that he is expected to pay in return:

> Je la dois [ma vie] à ses soins; mais par quelle rigueur
> Vouloir que je la paye aux dépens de mon cœur?
>
> (I, 3)

He proceeds to develop the idea that his supposed affection for Ariane has been an extortion required by circumstances:

> Qui n'eût fait comme moi?
> Pour me suivre, Ariane abandonnait son père,
> Je lui devais la vie, elle avait de quoi plaire.
> Mon cœur sans passion me laissait présumer
> Qu'il prendrait à mon choix l'habitude d'aimer.
> Par là, ce qu'il donnait à la reconnaissance,
> De l'amour, auprès d'elle, eut l'entière apparence,
> Pour payer ce qu'au sien je voyais être dû
> Mille devoirs . . . Hélas! C'est ce qui m'a perdu.
>
> (I, 3)

An element of self-pity enters into his observation that Ariane has founded her claim to his affection on the gratitude he owes her:

> Rien n'alarme son cœur, tant ce que je lui dois
> Contre ma trahison lui répond de ma foi.
>
> (I, 3)

Nor does Phèdre allow him to forget his obligations to her sister. Three successive reminders of his *devoir* exasperate him:

> Phèdre: Vous lui devez ce cœur dont vous m'offrez l'hommage,
> Vous lui devez la foi que votre amour m'engage,
> Vous lui devez ces vœux que déjà tant de fois . . .
> Thésée: Ah! Ne me parlez plus de ce que je lui dois.
>
> (I, 4)

Pirithoüs candidly illustrates the rationale by which it is universally assumed that Thésée *must* love Ariane. Speaking to the heroine he observes:

> Il vous aime sans doute;
> Et comment pourrait-il avoir le cœur si bas,
> Que tenir tout de vous, et ne vous aimer pas?
>
> (II, 5)

Ariane herself is most vociferous on the subject and makes a point on several occasions of emphasizing her generosity. To Phèdre she complains:

> Oui, ma soeur, après ce qu'il me doit,
> Me quitter est le prix que ma flamme en reçoit.
>
> (II, 7)

Later she speaks to Thésée in a similar vein:

> Par moi, par mon amour, le labyrinthe ouvert
> Vous fit fuir le trépas à vos regards offert;
> Et quand à votre foi cet amour s'abandonne,
> Des serments de respect sont le prix qu'on lui donne!
> Par ce soin de vos jours qui m'a tout fait quitter,
> N'aspirais-je à rien plus qu'à me voir respecter?
> Un service pareil veut un autre salaire,
> C'est le cœur, le cœur seul qui peut y satisfaire.
>
> (III, 4)

There is something unbecoming in the heroine who goes about implying that the only reason she saved a man's life was to procure his affection. When she states her case as a business proposition, insisting that her service to Thésée in Crete was payment in advance for his love, she forfeits some of the respect she would otherwise deserve:

> Qu'aurais-tu fait, parjure,
> Si quand tu vins du monstre éprouver l'aventure,
> Abandonnant ta vie à ta seule valeur,
> Je me fusse arrêtée à plaindre ton malheur?
> Pour mériter ce cœur qui pouvait seul me plaire,
> Si j'ai peu fait pour toi, que fallait-il plus faire?
>
> (III, 4)

When she expects pity from Phèdre, she again invokes the notion of merit:

> Je sais que vous m'aimez, et vous le devez faire.
> Vous m'avez dès l'enfance été toujours si chère,
> Que cette inébranlable et fidèle amitié
> Mérite bien de vous au moins quelque pitié.
>
> (II, 7)

Is this not dangerously close to saying: Since I've always loved you, you must love me; I deserve your pity. Ariane fails consistently to appreciate the very important element of gratuity in matters of love and friendship. There is every good reason one could imagine for Thésée to love Ariane; but the only reason that matters is absent. Thésée does not feel that ineffable but indispensable ingredient of the love relationship that Montaigne in his essay on friendship sought to describe variously as "quelque ordonnance du ciel" or, "je ne sais quelle force inexplicable et fatale". Ariane proffers her own love in the most gratuitous fashion, but she cannot accept the absence of this same gratuitousness in Thésée as a reason to withhold his affection from her.

It may be argued that regardless of his feelings toward Ariane, he should have worked to cultivate an affection for her and married her out of sheer gratitude, as Phèdre suggests:

> Ce qu'il doit à ma soeur méritait que sa foi
> Se fît de l'aimer seule une sévère loi.
>
> (III, 1)

But is this what Ariane wants? She has been careful to distinguish in herself between love and gratitude and has acted in accordance with the principle that love should prevail. She rejects Oenarus' love on the grounds that her feeling toward him, one of gratitude and respect, cannot prevail over her love for Thésée. And yet she would deny Thésée the same standard of behavior. To Oenarus she says:

> Seigneur, tant de vertu dans votre amour éclate,
> Qu'il faut vous l'avouer, je ne suis point ingrate,
> Mon cœur se sent touché de ce que je vous dois;
> Et voudrait être à vous, s'il pouvait être à moi;
> Mais il perdrait le prix dont vous le croyez être,
> Si l'infidélité vous en rendait le maître.
> Thésée y règne seul, et s'y trouve adoré.
>
> (II, 2)

Ironically, one could substitute "Madame" for "Seigneur" in the first line, "Phèdre" for "Thésée" in the last, and with the appropriate changes in gender the whole speech would be perfect for Thésée to address to Ariane.

Contrary to Reynier's belief that "il n'y a qu'un seul rôle, celui d'Ariane" and that the others are "ennemis", we would contend that the dramatic effectiveness of Ariane's role is largely dependent on the fact that the other characters do indeed sympathize with her. If, as

Reynier suggests, Phèdre and Thésée had deliberately mounted a conspiracy to deceive her, then the viewer or reader of the play would quite naturally be divided between pity for Ariane and contempt for her tormentors. These two reactions are not incompatible, as Reynier's analysis plainly reveals. But how much more poignantly one views Ariane's distress upon recognizing that it is caused reluctantly and without malice on the part of Phèdre and Thésée.

Reynier, in his attempt to simplify the tragedy by making Ariane "all good" and Thésée and Phèdre "all bad", has avoided all mention of Ariane's plan of revenge, as if Act IV did not exist. In fact the interest shifts in this act from Ariane's misfortune as victim to an active role as vindictive schemer. In order to force disclosure of her rival, she agrees to marry Oenarus provided that Thésée at the same time marry his beloved. Ariane intends to stab the latter before Thésée's very eyes. To Phèdre's horror, she revels in anticipation of her *coup*:

> Vous figurez-vous bien son désespoir extrême,
> Quand, dégouttante encor du sang de ce qu'il aime,
> Ma main offerte au roi dans ce fatal instant,
> Bravera jusqu'au bout la douleur qui l'attend?
> C'est en vain de son cœur qu'il croit m'avoir chassée,
> Je n'y suis pas peut-être encor tout effacée;
> Et ce sera de quoi mieux combler son ennui,
> Que de vivre à ses yeux pour un autre que lui.
>
> (IV, 3)

It is not difficult to see why Reynier, eager to portray Ariane sympathetically, studiously avoided this uncomplimentary aspect of her personality. This omission is symptomatic of a more general failure to distinguish properly between the roles as creations of dramatic fiction and the characters as real human beings. His harsh treatment of Phèdre and Thésée are presumably attacks *ad hominem* based squarely on the moral issues involved. But what of their roles as creations of dramatic artistry? To say that Thésée, Phèdre and the others are poorly conceived because of their moral weakness is to wish away the very substance of the tragedy as a work of art. One might equally condemn Titus for having encouraged Bérénice's affections, Pyrrhus for renouncing Hermione, Phèdre for falling in love with Hippolyte — the list is endless. Such conditions are inherent in the elemental situation of the play and form the hypothesis of its action. Thomas Corneille chose to portray "Thésée parjure". Reynier seems to criticize Thésée precisely because he *is* faithless.

Ultimately, however, perhaps Reynier's partisan defense of Ariane at the expense of the other characters is complimentary to the play as a whole. For the first time Thomas Corneille managed to create an illusion in which the spectator's attention is directed almost exclusively to the emotional tribulations of the characters. One is not immediately aware of the artistic medium, of dramaturgical devices or the presence of a self-imposing playwright wrestling with the particular problems of his art. The effect is a more nearly pure artistic production achieved by means of self-effacing art. Reynier's involvement with the characters as opposed to characterization is indicative of Thomas Corneille's success in encouraging the willing suspension of disbelief. An anecdote, reported by Reynier himself, attests to Thomas Corneille's new found competence:

Un soir que Mlle Gaussin jouait ce rôle, au moment où Ariane essaye de deviner le nom de sa rivale:
  „Est-ce Mégiste, Aeglé, qui le rend infidèle?"
un jeune homme lui cria, tout éploré: 'C'est Phèdre, c'est Phèdre.'
(*Thom. Corn.*, p. 190)

ACHILLE

A year after his next tragedy, *Théodat* (1672), Thomas Corneille offered *La Mort d'Achille* to the troupe of the Guénégaud. Despite a eulogistic advance billing by de Visé, who reported the duc de Richelieu as having said that the new tragedy "surpasse son *Ariane*",[3] *Achille* enjoyed scant success with only ten performances. Although it is not necessary to analyse the play in detail, certain observations about it are pertinent to the later phases of Thomas Corneille's dramatic art.

Lancaster has briefly outlined the resemblance of *Achille* to Racine's *Mithridate, Andromaque* and Thomas' *Ariane* (*History*, IV, p. 147). He might also have added the latter's *Commode*. The action occurs

---

[3] Reported in Parfaict, *Histoire*, Vol. 11, pp. 346-347.

during a truce before the walls of Troy shortly after the death of Hector. Briseis, feeling she has unlimited powers of persuasion over Achille, promises to bring about the marriage of Polyxène with Pyrrhus, who are in love with each other. Briseis is unaware that Achille, who had promised to marry her, now loves Polyxène and insists on marrying her as the price of ending the war against the Trojans. At Polyxène's request, seconded by Briseis, Hector's body has been delivered to Priam who, in the interests of peace, consents to give Polyxène to Achille. As the latter appears in the temple he is slain by Paris. At this, Briseis vows to seek vengeance on Paris while Polyxène returns to Troy.

The resemblance to *Andromaque* is conspicuous. The action of both plays centers around the Trojan War. Both Andromaque and Polyxène are forced into a political marriage with a ruler who renounces a former fiancée. Even after their death, the faithless suitors, Pyrrhus and Achille, continue to evoke expressions of love from their rejected fiancées, Hermione and Briseis. *Achille* contains a chain of lovers which approximates that of *Andromaque*: Briseis loves Achille who loves Polyxène who loves Pyrrhus. Racine's manner of having Pyrrhus killed by Oreste is dramatically superior to Thomas Corneille's unaccountable (in the play) introduction of Paris who never appears on stage and whose motivation to kill Achille is a bit remote from the internal circumstances.

One cannot help feeling that Corneille was striving with special ardor to create a masterpiece in *Achille*. He packed the play with as much material evocative of the *Iliad* as was consistent with the particular situation of the main characters. In the background are Cassandre, Hecuba, Paris, Helen, Menelaus, Ajax, Nestor, Hector, Patrocles, Troilus, Priam, Agamemnon and Ulysses. Of these the last three are directly accessible to the characters on stage, for Achille and Briseis consult with Priam, Pyrrhus with Agamemnon and Briseis with Ulysses. One is made to feel the urgency and tenuousness of the truce, due to end the following day, and the uneasiness attendant upon an impending crisis. The fate of Troy depends on Achille; and his fateful decision, whether to inflict carnage on an already suffering population or to grant peace, is made to appear an event of truly momentous proportions. In no other play did Thomas Corneille create so well a mood of latent tragedy. Polyxène alone has the power to assuage Achille's wrath. She need only acquiesce in his desire to marry her. Her moral struggle is well though briefly presented but is by no means the only one of the tragedy. In fact all the major characters suffer some discomfiture. Pyrrhus, finding a rival in his father, must renounce Polyxène. Briseis, betrayed by Achille, struggles to win him back. Achille himself is torn between love and duty. Surely here were the ingredients for a brilliant tragedy. Nor is it devoid of interest. The gradual crescendo of emotional turmoil as characters pass from a state of blissful ignorance to disillusionment is brought about with skill and sensitivity.

The activating device of the first three acts is a *quid pro quo* based on the proposition that the blood of Priam must be united to the blood of Achille to guarantee peace between Troy and Greece. Polyxène and Pyrrhus are the logical ones to unite for this purpose. But Achille, while appearing to consent to this alliance, really has himself in mind to represent "le sang d'Achille". Hence he can equivocate by the familiar tactic of casuistry as, in speaking to Briseis, he refers to the "alliance d'Achille" without disturbing her impression that he is speaking of a marriage between Pyrrhus and Polyxène:

Briseis: Cet hymen aux Troyens assure un sort si doux,
         Que Priam recevra ...
Achille: Je le crois comme vous,
         Il voit pour lui la guerre en trop de maux fertile
         Pour oser dédaigner l'alliance d'Achille.

                                                        (II, 2)

Act IV features a scene in which Briseis attempts to win back Achille much in the manner of Ariane's campaign to salvage Thésée's affection, Hermione's effort to regain Pyrrhus by intimidation and Bérénice's struggle for Titus. This type of encounter had become a well established source of dramatic tension, always effective if well done. Technically speaking the first four acts are well managed. Thomas Corneille focused interest on Achille's decision to marry Polyxène, showed how the others reacted and worked events toward a climax, the marriage ceremony. But Act V is disappointing. After a few scenes during which preparations are made for the ceremony, a confidant reports that Paris has entered the temple in a rage. The next report is of the death of Achille. Paris' sudden involvement has the effect of a *deus ex machina* quite inconsistent in a play which otherwise has self-contained motivations. Moreover, the fate of the characters after Achille's death is not clear. While we know that Polyxène returns with Priam to Troy, we hear of Pyrrhus only that he has disappeared. Nothing is said to suggest that his situation has been resolved. Briseis, who is last to leave the stage, sets out on a plan of revenge against Paris as if stepping into the beginning of a sequel tragedy.

Perhaps the greatest single weakness lies in the role of its title character. Although he is not depraved in the same manner as Commode, Achille nevertheless displays a kinship of temperament with the Roman emperor. There is something irreconcilable in the fact that as the most famous and bravest warrior of Greece, Achille can be so petty and selfish in a domestic matter. If he were portrayed convincingly as a passionate lover, as Racine succeeded in portraying Pyrrhus in *Andromaque*, his behavior might elicit sympathy. But he is not. His every decision appears as a spiteful calculation to alienate those who surround him. With Troy at his mercy, he can afford to play the tyrant and does. Hence upon reaching the central event of the play, his death, the spectator is not saddened but relieved. Not evil enough to be a *bona fide* villain nor sufficiently admirable to be a sympathetic hero, Achille misses the mark as a central tragic figure. Nor is the failure of his role compensated by the pathos of Pyrrhus, Polyxène or Briseis. The result is a general diffusion of interest.

It is tempting to view this play as a noble failure resulting from the dramatist's desire to enjoy the best of two worlds. From his brother he took the concept of the unfaltering, willful, uncompromising hero exemplified by Horace, Polyeucte and others. Greek mythology supplied him with a character who, without adaptation, was more nearly akin to the Cornelian hero than any he had treated except Laodice whose spiritual relationship to Medea qualifies her for similar consideration. But having started with a heroic type suitable for the most intense political drama and endowed with those "sentiments mâles" which Pierre had posed as the very basis of tragic characterization, Thomas proceeded to infuse his play with a Racinian morality. It is difficult to know whether to consider Achille as a warrior or as a lover. Racine himself may have experienced a similar perplexity in portraying Mithridate and Alexandre. In any case, the characterization of Achille, with all its shortcomings, confirms the presence of Thomas Corneille's new orientation to the sense of tragedy. He now sees the tragic event not so much as the misfortune caused by circumstances but as the anguish of pure psychological conflict. This is not to say that he ignores the importance of events as circumstances, without which a dramatist cannot function; but it is clear that his characters now absorb his attention more than ever before for their own sake. His last significant tragedy, *Le Comte d'Essex*, gives full evidence of his conversion to a concept of tragedy which reduces time and event to a place of minimum importance and asserts the triumph of character as a dramatic absolute.

LE COMTE D'ESSEX

Queen Elizabeth's affection for Robert Devereux, second Earl of Essex, proved to be a popular subject in French drama. The story was first presented in France by La Calprenède in his *Comte d'Essex* of the 1630's. He was followed some forty years later by Thomas Corneille whose play prompted the abbé Claude Boyer to compose a tragedy of the same title for presentation two months after the first performance of Corneille's version. Subsequently the Essex story was revived in 1829 by Ancelot under the title of *Elisabeth d'Angleterre*, then as the libretto of an opera by Donizetti, *Roberto Devereux, Conte d'Essex* in 1838 and in plays by Edouard Marteau, Ali Vial de Sabligny and Couturier.[4] In April, 1912 Sarah Bernhardt acted the title role of Emile Moreau's *La Reine Elisabeth* and later in the year appeared in a successful film version of the same play. Of all these productions Thomas Corneille's enjoyed the most enduring success.

Le Comte d'Essex appeared almost exactly one year after Racine's *Phèdre*. Its initial success, mentioned in the *Mercure galant* and by Thomas in his "Au lecteur", must have been gratifying to the author after the failure of *Achille*. In fact *Essex* proved to be the most popular

[4]   See Alfreda Hill, *The Tudors in French Drama* (Baltimore, 1932), pp. 132-153.

of all the author's tragedies and in 1790 ranked ninth among all seventeenth century French tragedies with respect to the number of performances at the Comédie Française. Casual references to it by Diderot, Rousseau, and Voltaire indicate how well it was known in the eighteenth century.[5] This tragedy, along with *Ariane*, has been the one most often reproduced in the combined re-editions of the *Œuvres* of Pierre and Thomas Corneille which ran well through the nineteenth century. The most recent revival of *Le Comte d'Essex* in a live performance took place at the festival Corneille at Barentin near Rouen on June 16, 1961.

The play recounts the following events. Essex, upon returning from a mission in Ireland, has attempted, unsuccessfully, to prevent the marriage of his beloved Henriette to the duc d'Irton by surrounding Queen Elisabeth's palace with a group of his followers, but this imprudent gesture of a lover has all the aspects of an attempt to seize the throne. When the play opens, Essex' political enemies, Raleigh, Cécile and others, have taken advantage of his indiscretion and accused him of treason. Elisabeth, who is in love with Essex, is unaware of the latter's affection for Henriette, who had married Irton to make herself unavailable to Essex, since she felt that it was in Essex' best interests to remove herself as a barrier between him and his sovereign. But Essex is bitterly resentful at losing Henriette and refuses to speak in self-defense or ask for his queen's clemency. She would gladly pardon him his apparent political disloyalty in exchange for a show of repentance, a flicker of affection or a mere gesture of humility, none of which Essex deigns to make in spite of appeals by friends, his mistress and the queen herself. Meanwhile his enemies try him, find him guilty and rush to execute him before Elisabeth, after many changes of mind, decides, only too late, to grant him his life.

The story as Thomas Corneille dramatized it is basically the same as La Calprenède's tragedy. Lancaster has pointed out several structural similarities,[6] but Corneille's characterization of Elisabeth differs

---

[5]   Diderot in the *Paradoxe sur le comédien*, Rousseau in his *Lettre à d'Alembert*, and Voltaire in *Candide*.

[6]   The subject in each case is the arrest, trial, and execution of Essex in spite of Elizabeth's love for him. To each of Thomas Corneille's seven characters — Elizabeth, her confidant, Essex, his friend, the woman he loves, one of his enemies, a captain of the guards — there is a corresponding character

from his predecessor's in portraying her as a jealous woman impeded by her emotions from the forceful exercise of her regal functions. La Calprenède's queen shows no jealousy and, despite her love for Essex, maintains a level-headed attitude toward justice and her responsibilities as head of state:

> Qu'on n'ayt aucun esgard aux honneurs qu'il receut
> Qu'on juge ce qu'il est, et non pas ce qu'il fut,
> Et que pas un de vous si la pitié l'arreste
> Ne me pense obliger en espargnant sa teste.[7]
>
> (II, 1)

In her *Tudors in French Drama* Miss Hill makes the following generalization: "In the forty years which elapsed between La Calprenède's production and Corneille's, the French theater had changed, writers of classical tragedy had come to accept Racine as their model, and consequently Thomas Corneille's *Comte d'Essex* falls into this new category" (p. 138). There is an arbitrariness to this statement owing to a complete neglect of the developments in the forty years intervening. The temperament of Corneille's play is Racinian in the usual sense of this epithet, — that is, by its structural simplicity, the psychological development of situations issuing directly and almost exclusively from the emotions, and the featured treatment of love and jealousy. Yet Corneille did not imitate Racine in any specific details. Voltaire's observation that Essex' situation resembles that of Bajazet does not prove influence, for Thomas found this relationship already delineated in La Calprenède's play. Lancaster has contended that Elisabeth's passion is not Racinian, for she would settle for a purely platonic relationship with Essex. Could one imagine Hermione, Roxane, or Phèdre uttering such a speech as Elisabeth's:

> Ce qu'il faut qu'il espère? Et qu'en puis-je espérer
> Que la douceur de voir, d'aimer, de soupirer?
>
> (II, 1)

---

in the old tragedy and the attitude of these persons towards one another is much the same. In each play Elizabeth and Essex meet only once, he is arrested on the stage at the end of an act, he refers ironically in II, 5, to his great deeds as crimes, and at the end the queen expects soon to die (*History*, IV, p. 149).

[7] Quoted from Lancaster, *History*, II, p. 180.

Such a maudlin aspiration is neither the expression of "la fierté cornélienne" nor "une âme racinienne" which Lanson imputes to Thomas Corneille's Tudor queen.[8] It is rather the atavistic romanesque idyl of the earlier dramatist. Nevertheless the Racinian qualities persist in one's general impression of this play. Elisabeth, like Hermione and Bérénice, like Roxane and Phèdre, is beset with a consuming passion. Her love for Essex, platonic though it may be, usurps all the moral powers implicit in her personal and political sovereignty.. As portrayed Elisabeth is not a queen but a woman. That he should so conceive her is a clear indication that Thomas Corneille had drifted away from his brother's concept of the resolute, self-respecting heroine. On the other hand the drift carried Thomas to the point of hypercorrection, for Elisabeth reaches the proportions of a caricature. Her role has greater interest than Essex'. It is more prominent psychologically as well as physically (she appears in eighteen scenes, Essex in twelve). Yet she is not impressive. Her real weakness lies in the fact, already observed by Voltaire, that even within the framework of her emotional upset and due allowances made for her right to vacillate, she is still inconsistent. She violates the logic of her passion.

One rarely sees a tragic heroine as well informed as Elisabeth. Her opening lines are indicative:

> En vain tu crois tromper la douleur qui m'accable,
> C'est parce qu'il me hait, qu'il s'est rendu coupable;
> Et la belle Suffolk refusée à ses voeux,
> Lui fait joindre le crime au mépris de mes feux.
>
> (II, 1)

In these few lines Elisabeth acknowledges three significant beliefs: that Essex is guilty of a political crime, that he scorns her affection and that he loves another. Here and in subsequent speeches Elisabeth shows herself too self-conscious, too condescending to Essex, too much aware of his indifference and treason to persist so long in a patient effort to extract a sign of repentence from him. She defies her own perspicacity, for she presses for Essex' love, fully aware that, if he should yield to her, she would win a tribute born of duress. Unlike Ariane, who had something brand new to learn about Thésée, Elisa-

---

[8]   Gustave Lanson, *Esquisse d'une histoire de la tragédie française* (New York, 1920), p. 79.

beth knows only too well of Essex' aloofness toward her. Yet she remains strangely fascinated by this creature whose pride is a worthy pendant to her own. As the play begins we learn that she has already banished her supposed rival in the hope of monopolizing Essex. Her vain precaution only makes him react violently, but she is not discouraged from trying to win him over. Finding this impossible, she resorts to threat, using his supposed political guilt as a pretext. However it quickly becomes apparent that she has not the slightest conviction about his political misbehavior. She does not weigh the merits of his survival on the scale of justice but on the scale of emotions. Sending him to be judged by Raleigh and the others is an empty gesture, for Elisabeth has already determined his guilt: he does not love her. Hence the alleged insurrection, the supposed alliance with Tyrone, the counterfeited documents, the trial, imprisonment and finally the execution of Essex prove to be peripheral decoys. *Raison d'état* is incidental to the queen's *raison du cœur*. But since she uses the former to vindicate the latter, one might expect her to observe at least a formal objectivity. She assumes at the outset that Essex is guilty of treason, that he has plotted her demise in order to crown Suffolk. This she assumes in complete gratuitousness without inquiry into the allegations. Yet after Essex is judged guilty, she assumes with equal arbitrariness that he is politically innocent. She is consistently indifferent to the legal situation which she refuses to take seriously.

It would seem that Elisabeth's knowledge of Essex' scorn might convince her of the futility of trying to gain his affection. The fact that it does not suggests that her passion is indeed overwhelming. She persists against every reasonable hope. One cannot escape the impression that her willful self-delusion is the product of *amour-passion*. Yet this queen, who has vowed never to marry, would be satisfied with a platonic relationship with Essex. There is a discrepancy in her character which is discomfiting. Despite the depth of her love, she evinces a strangely cerebral affection. How can one explain otherwise her long patience with the obstinate courtier, her eventual reconciliation to the prospect of letting him marry elsewhere and the equanimity with which she treats Henriette upon learning that this trusted woman, not Suffolk, has been her rival. If we accept Elisabeth's statements on the intensity of her love and jealousy, it is natural to expect a major outburst when we see her learning the true identity of her rival. Yet when Henriette reveals herself as the object of Essex' love, the queen directs most of her irritation toward Essex:

> Ai-je bien entendu? Le perfide vous aime,
> Me dédaigne, me brave, et contraire à moi-même,
> Je vous assurerais, en l'osant secourir,
> La douceur d'être aimée et de me voir souffrir?
> Non, il faut qu'il périsse, et que je sois vengée,
> Je dois ce coup funeste à ma flamme outragée,
> Il a trop mérité l'arrêt qui le punit,
> Innocent ou coupable, il vous aime, il suffit.
> S'il n'a point de vrai crime, ainsi qu'on le veut croire,
> Sur le crime apparent je sauverai ma gloire.
>
> (III, 4)

She then enlists Henriette's support in an effort to coax Essex to live and later reaffirms her faith in Henriette's good intentions:

> Oui, Suffolk fut un nom emprunté,
> Pour cacher un amour qui n'a point éclaté.
> La duchesse l'aima, mais sans m'être infidèle,
> Son hymen l'a fait voir, je ne me plains point d'elle
>
> (V, 1)

This reasonable composure in dealing with Henriette contrasts harshly with her erratic treatment of Essex.

Lockert admires the realism of Elisabeth's role on the grounds that her mental torment brings her to "go over and over the same ground, as tortured people who do not know too clearly their own minds are wont to do" (*Studies*, p. 246). Human experience tells us that emotional crises can and often do subvert our rational processes and powers of judgment. But surely there is a limit to the number of times a character in a sober tragedy can reverse decisions without weakening dramatic effect. After the fourth or fifth time Elisabeth changes from a decision to execute Essex to an attitude of clemency, the spectator realizes that she is indeed hard put to settle on his fate. But when in the course of three acts she changes her mind eleven times on such a crucial matter, the impact of her decision is seriously diminished. When Elisabeth and Essex meet in II, 6, the queen is predisposed to forgive her favorite courtier if he will confess. In the same scene she threatens to have him executed and then pardons him and again threatens. Two scenes later Essex is arrested and put on trial. When in III, 1, the queen hears of his haughty behavior at the trial, she erupts with "il paiera de sa tête", commands his seizure and takes steps to prevent a popular uprising in his favor. In the following scene she confirms her resolution but talks herself out of it. In scene 3 she reaffirms her order of execution. Scene 4 shows her reconsidering, reconfirming and again relenting. In Act V, after all efforts to move Essex to humility have failed, Elisabeth, with monotonous regularity recants once again only to revert to her vindictive cry "qu'il périsse". Ultimately, despite all her efforts to justify his execution in her own mind, love and pity prevail over her political sense and she orders "qu'il vive". One is reminded of Lewis Carroll's Queen of Hearts of *Alice in Wonderland* casually tossing off her sentence "Off with his head". Elisabeth also shares with the Queen of Hearts a desire to pronounce the "sentence first — verdict afterwards". A list of the lines showing the Tudor queen's vacillation cannot fail to show how, after a certain point, the impact of this device diminishes in proportion to the frequency of its repetition. To Essex, speaking of herself in the third person Elisabeth says:

> Tout ce qu'elle demande est un aveu sincère . . .

and again to Essex:

> Va, c'en est fait, il faut contenter ton envie,
> A ton lâche destin j'abandonne ta vie . . .
> Tandis qu'encor pour toi je veux bien l'écouter, [sa bonté]
> Le pardon t'est offert, tu le peux accepter.
>
> (II, 6)

She continues in the same vein throughout the play:

> Il me pousse à l'éclat, il paiera de sa tête.
>
> (III, 1)

> Enfin, perfide, enfin ta perte est résolue; . . .
> Plus de grâce, tes voeux vont être satisfaits . . .
> Qu'il fléchisse, il suffit, j'oublierai le passé.
>
> (III, 2)

> L'arrêt est prononcé, Comte; . . .
>
> (III, 3)

> Il faudra le sauver aux dépens de ma vie;
> M'y voilà résolue . . .

Non, il faut qu'il périsse, et que je sois vengée,
Je dois ce coup funeste à ma flamme outragée...
Duchesse, c'en est fait, qu'il vive, j'y consens.

(III, 4)

Jusque sur l'échafaud je voulais l'envoyer,
Pour dernière espérance essayer ce remède,
Mais la honte est trop forte, il vaut mieux que je cède...
C'en est trop; puisqu'il aime à périr, qu'il périsse.

(V, 1)

Upon learning that he is on his way to the scaffold she concludes:

Qu'on l'empêche, cours, vole, et fais qu'on le ramène.
Je veux, je veux qu'il vive.

(V, 2)

It should be stated, however, that it is not on the grounds of inconsistency in this particular aspect of her behavior that we criticize the role of the queen; for, in the final analysis, her capriciousness comprises the unifying trait of her character as well as the chief motive factor of the play. The basic question is one of dramatic effectiveness, dulled by excessive repetition.

In contrast to Elisabeth's fluctuating nature Essex stands as the unyielding, proud, self-confident hero. Lockert admires his role for its portrayal of "something so human and yet so little treated elsewhere in literature that this tragedy would be notable ... if for no other reason" (*Studies*, p. 247). He refers to Essex' bitterness of heart and adds: "He dies to satisfy his savage desire to hurt those who love him but have wronged him and hurt him — to make them suffer, as he can because they love him" (p. 247). There is, however, an irritating quality in the manner in which Essex expresses his bitterness which Thomas Corneille may or may not have intended. It may be argued that the proper way to convey to an audience the sentiment which a character feels is to make the audience feel toward the character that same sentiment. This is not the same thing as sympathy, which is rather a parallel and corresponding reaction on the part of the spectator to a situation faced by a dramatic character. In the latter case, we "feel for" the character, share his emotion and, temporarily, adopt his viewpoint; in the former case our attitude toward the character is inspired not by a vicarious response to his situation but by the mood we adopt in reaction to the manner in which he meets the

situation. This inevitably involves our tacit judgment of his qualifi-
cations to elicit sympathy rather than a direct sympathetic involvement
with his problem.

Essex earns some degree of sympathy for having suffered the loss
of the woman he loves. For this, one can appreciate his sense of disappointment. But his manner of expressing resentment and anger
contrasts all too strikingly with the feeling of sympathy which the
spectator is predisposed to render in his behalf. Encountering Essex
for the first time only after he has learned of Henriette's marriage,
we see only the acrimonious part of his character. We are assured that
he is brave, patriotic and admirable in every sense, but too many of
his speeches belie this grand reputation. From one end of the tragedy
to the other he can be heard uttering truculent, antagonistic, and vain-
glorious assertions which eventually detract from his heroic stature
rather than corroborate it. To Salsbury he boasts:

> Un homme tel que moi, sur l'appui de son nom,
> Devrait comme du crime être exempt du soupçon;
> Mais enfin cent exploits et sur mer et sur terre,
> M'ont fait connaître assez à toute l'Angleterre;
> Et j'ai trop bien servi, pour pouvoir redouter
> Ce que mes ennemis ont osé m'imputer . . .
> Tout a tremblé sous moi, vous voulez que je tremble.
> L'imposture m'attaque, il est vrai, mais ce bras
> Rend l'Angleterre à craindre aux plus puissants états.
>
> (I, 1)

When Henriette suggests the possibility of his arrest:

> On n'oserait, Madame,
> Si l'on avait tenté ce dangereux éclat,
> Le coup qui le peut suivre entraînerait l'état.
>
> (I, 2)

He speaks of Cécile, Coban and Raleigh as "hommes sans foi",
"traîtres", and "flatteurs à gages", an expression which Voltaire found
lacking in nobility. When confronted with the accusation of treason,
his only defense is a boastful allusion to his past glory and his
courage:

> Et toute ma vertu contre leur lâcheté
> S'offre en vain pour garant de ma fidélité.
>
> (II, 6)

At the moment of arrest he yields his sword without a struggle but as if this gesture entailed the collapse of England:

> Prenez.
> Vous avez dans vos mains ce que toute la terre
> A vu plus d'une fois utile à l'Angleterre.
> Marchons; quelque douleur que j'en puisse sentir,
> La reine veut se perdre, il faut y consentir.
>
> (II, 8)

Again and again he protests his innocence without proving it and accuses his enemies of imposture without substantiating his charge. Repeatedly he refuses to ask for grace on the grounds that to do so would be to admit guilt. Here his righteous indignation is perhaps noble and justified. But he does not preserve it, for he would betray his vaunted innocence:

> Si vous [Henriette] aviez flatté l'espoir qui m'abandonne,
> Si, n'étant point à moi, vous n'étiez à personne,
> Et qu'au moins votre amour moins cruel à mes feux
> M'eût épargné l'horreur de voir un autre heureux,
> Pour vous garder ce cœur où vous seule avez place,
> Cent fois, quoique innocent, j'aurais demandé grâce.
>
> (IV, 5)

Undeniably this lament has a touching effect, but it also bespeaks a strong element of self-pity incompatible with the heroic image that Essex has painted of himself. In the final analysis, for all his pride, nobility and courage, Essex is tainted as a dramatic figure by his negativism and despondency. He, and his queen, doggedly refuse to face up to the realities of the situation. Hence they are to an unfortunate degree irritating as human beings. This is not to deny that their emotional impasse is a fair representation of the way real people often act. Indeed the play's saving grace lies precisely in the true-to-life image Thomas Corneille manages to create of irrational yet psychologically sound behavior.

It is tempting to view the characterization of Essex as a peculiar variation on Corneillian heroism. This disenchanted hero is not really so different in spirit from Horace and Nicomède. He differs mainly in the fact that the outlet into which he chooses to channel his energies is not one worthy of his greatness. The discrepancy between his vaunted heroism and the mean task of saving his life by playing on the affection of a queen he does not love calls forth in him an understandable reaction of spite and resentment. It is interesting to speculate what Racine might have done with Essex. In fact he never portrayed anyone quite like him. Pierre Corneille's *Suréna* comes closest to Essex in the characterization of a hero who, for want of a challenge, martyrs himself to his own superiority. Suréna, Essex, and to a lesser extent Thomas Corneille's Annibal testify to the fact that the indomitable hero, if deprived of the opportunity to resist a worthy challenge commensurate with his heroic stature, could find refuge only in an indifference to life itself.

Elisabeth herself comes very close to experiencing a similar disenchantment, for she too is caught in a struggle between the ideal of personal sovereignty and sentimental surrender. However, she is able to reconcile the two forces, at least theoretically, in a doctrine of platonic love which would leave her sovereignty intact. But it is difficult to reconcile the disparities of these characters. Voltaire, who would have excused the most flagrant inconsistencies caused by the emotions provided they were expressed in a noble style, treated *Le Comte d'Essex* with reserved disfavor. In general we find his evaluation of the play to be fair. One of his comments sums up his principal objections:

Il me semble qu'il y a toujours quelque chose de louche, de confus, de vague, dans tout ce que les personnages de cette tragédie disent et font. Que toute action soit claire, toute intrigue bien connue, tout sentiment bien développé; ce sont là des règles inviolables. Mais ici que veut le comte d'Essex? que veut Elisabeth? quel est le crime du comte? est-il accusé faussement? est-il coupable? Si la reine le croit innocent, elle doit prendre sa défense; s'il est reconnu criminel, est-il raisonnable que la confidente dise qu'il n'implorera jamais sa grâce, qu'il est trop fier? La fierté est très convenable à un guerrier vertueux et innocent, non à un homme convaincu de haute trahison. *Qu'il fléchisse*, dit la reine. Est-ce bien là le sentiment qui doit l'occuper, si elle l'aime? Quand il aura fléchi, quand il aura obtenu sa grâce, Elisabeth en sera-t-elle plus aimée? *Je l'aime*, dit la reine, *cent fois plus que moi-même.* Ah! madame, si vous avez la tête tournée à ce point, si votre passion est si grande, examinez donc l'affaire de votre amant, et ne souffrez pas que ses ennemis l'accablent et le persécutent injustement sous votre nom, comme il est dit, quoique faussement, dans toute la pièce (*Œuvres*, Vol. 32, pp. 335-336).

Voltaire further objected, as is suggested by the "quoique faussement" of the last sentence quoted above, to Corneille's failure to observe historical fact in Essex. This question has frequently been raised in relation to the play. While there is no doubt that *Essex* lacks the persuasive authority of history accurately recorded, this lack did not prevent it from having a series of successful performances in 1678 and surviving on the stage for a century and a half. La Harpe and later Reynier had the leisure to condemn Thomas' play as history; they did not thereby appraise its success as drama. La Harpe was most adamant on the subject, which is primarily one of critical point of view.

Voltaire's commentaries on *Essex* reveal a curious dualism. In the capacity of dramatist he did not begrudge Thomas the right to impose an historically inaccurate image of Elizabeth and Essex in the play. As a historian, however, with a special interest in England, Voltaire was disturbed by the discrepancies which he was aware of: "Quand les événements qu'on traite sont ignorés d'une nation, l'auteur en est absolument le maître. Presque personne en France, du temps de Thomas Corneille, n'était instruit de l'histoire d'Angleterre: aujourd'hui un poète devrait être plus circonspect" (*Œuvres*, Vol. 32, p. 328). His own enjoyment of *Essex* was significantly diminished by his knowledge that Elizabeth was sixty-eight years old at the time represented in the events of the tragedy. Having made particular investigations for the purpose, Voltaire knew also that Thomas Corneille had grossly exaggerated Essex' historical role by portraying him as a pillar of the English nation. But since Thomas Corneille nowhere indicated Elizabeth's age and took great pains to eulogize Essex as a national hero, Voltaire could find no internal evidence on which to base an accusation of *invraisemblance*. When he expressed dismay over Thomas' neglect of fact, he was careful to add that his criticism applied only for one versed in English history, that is, "le spectateur éclairé" or "le lecteur instruit".

La Harpe was less indulgent. His remarks on *Essex* begin: "D'abord l'histoire est étrangement défigurée; et comme il s'agissait d'un peuple voisin et d'un fait assez récent, cette licence n'est pas excusable" (*Cours de littérature*, Vol. 6, p. 158). He proceeds to point out some of the incongruities and suggests that the novel is a more suitable medium than tragedy for distorted history. Finally he calls for a full-scale censure of Thomas and anyone else who might disfigure history under the guise of tragedy:

C'est aux hommes équitables et éclairés, à ceux qui respectent la vérité et la justice, à décider si un poète a le droit de flétrir la mémoire d'une grande princesse, de lui attribuer une faute grave qu'elle n'a pas commise, de faire d'un rebelle ingrat et d'un conspirateur insensé un héros innocent et un citoyen vertueux, et de représenter comme une œuvre d'iniquité ce qui fut la punition d'un crime public et avoué; s'il a le droit de nous donner pour de vils scélérats des juges qui firent leur devoir, et nommément Robert Cécil, ministre intègre et estimé, et le vice-amiral Raleigh, un des grands hommes de l'Angleterre, qui rendit tant de services à sa patrie, et dont le nom y est encore respecté; enfin si, violer ainsi l'histoire, ce n'est pas en effet déshonorer la tragédie, qui ne doit s'en servir que pour en rendre les exemples plus frappants et les leçons plus utiles (pp. 160-161).

La Harpe could scarcely overcome his moralistic view of tragedy in order to appraise *Essex* as drama. He would easily have found matter for criticism if he had but looked. Making the sixty-eight year old queen appear younger was an obvious requirement of verisimilitude and hence a judicious lie. Would he not have strengthened the play further by inventing a more plausible set of circumstances to explain Essex' involvement in the Irish problem? Grasping half-heartedly for a historical reference, Thomas remained vague and generally unconvincing about Essex' political activities, which are the ostensible cause of his predicament.

The structure of the tragedy is generally satisfactory by contemporary standards with one notable exception. Act IV takes place in Essex' prison cell which was probably some distance from the palace where the other four acts took place:

L'unité de lieu y est incontestablement violée, puisque le *Mémoire* des décorateurs de l'Hôtel de Bourgogne demande pour cette pièce "un palais et une prison qui paraît au quatrième acte". Cette violation flagrante de la règle n'a pas empêché la tragédie d'avoir un grand succès; ni le public ni les auteurs n'étaient donc convaincus, à l'apogée même de la période classique, de la nécessité de l'unité de lieu (Scherer, *Dramaturgie*, p. 183).

The simplicity of action makes for repetition which in some instances contributes very little to development. In Act IV, for example, Essex' friends, Tilney, Salsbury, and Henriette try each in turn to cut through his obstinacy. Salsbury does little more than reiterate what Tilney has just said. Although Elisabeth and Essex meet only once, the play is essentially a duel between them. The characters may be divided according to whether they officially support his political guilt (Elisabeth, Cécile; and, not appearing on stage, Raleigh and Coban) or support his innocence (Essex, Henriette, Salsbury). Dramaturgically *Essex* is the simplest of all Thomas Corneille's tragedies. The single use of a device, a *quid pro quo* produced by the fact that Elisabeth believes Suffolk rather than Henriette to be her rival, has no important effect on the action within the play. It is even less complicated internally than *Ariane* although the frequent reference to political events in Ireland, the presence of a band of Essex' supporters in London, the off-stage council meeting, and the prison scene suggest a greater complexity and depth than is immediately evident in the isolated setting and particularized events of *Ariane*. Voltaire somewhat glibly reduced the play to a simple argument: "Je veux qu'il me demande pardon; je ne veux pas demander pardon; voilà la pièce" (*Œuvres*, Vol. 32, p. 340).

Here and there can be glimpsed a turn of phrase clearly reminiscent of Racine. Much in the manner of Racine's frequent use of a series of rapid questions is Elisabeth's retort to Tilney:

Tilney: Chacun tremble pour lui, mais il ne mourra pas.
Elisabeth: Il ne mourra pas, lui? Non, crois-moi, tu t'abuses,
              Tu sais son attentat, est-ce que tu l'excuses;
              Et que de son arrêt, blâmant l'indignité,
              Tu crois qu'il soit injuste ou trop précipité?
              Penses-tu quand l'ingrat contre moi se déclare,
              Qu'il n'ait pas mérité la mort qu'on lui prépare;
              Et que je venge trop, en le laissant périr,
              Ce que par ses dédains l'amour m'a fait souffrir?
                                                         (III, 2)

Her reaction to the report of Essex' death reminds us of a mild version of Hermione's "Qui te l'a dit?":

Elisabeth: Ne m'apprends point sa mort, si tu ne veux la mienne.
              Mais d'une âme égarée inutile transport!
              C'en sera fait sans doute?
Tilney: Oui madame.
Elisabeth: Il est mort,
              Et tu l'as pu souffrir?
                                                         (V, 6)

The three plays treated here share with each other and with several of Racine's plays the theme of imperious love, a theme virtually absent in Thomas Corneille's earlier tragedies. The lovers in these plays are invested with an insatiable urge to be loved by a person who is indifferent or antagonistic toward them. 'Love me or else' is the condition which Elisabeth makes to Essex, Essex in turn to Henriette, Briseis to Achille, Achille to Polyxène, and Ariane to Thésée. This is a far cry from the heroes and heroines of Corneille's identity plays in which the concept of love featured the cultivation of merit as if the essence of love consisted in a long preparation for its incipient manifestations. Ariane, Briseis and Elisabeth are not so patient. Their love is of the self-indulgent variety which is not long denied without dire consequences. Hence the source of interest in *Ariane, Achille* and *Essex* is to be sought directly in the emotional experience of the characters as they react to internal crises.

With *Essex* Thomas Corneille had achieved something of a psychological maturity. He dared turn his back on the romanesque tradition in the theater which he had himself helped to foster some twenty years before. A minor but perhaps symbolic indication of his growth away from *précieux* predilections may be seen in the fact that in *Essex* he refused to use the episode of the ring that Elizabeth is said to have given Essex as a guarantee of her protection in an emergency. One assumes that for the author of *Timocrate* and *Antiochus* such a touch was the devil's own temptation to resist.

BRADAMANTE

Thomas would have done well to conclude his tragedies with *Essex*, for in this play he had achieved a degree of intensification and simplicity not likely to be matched. However, an atavastic force compelled him to try his hand once again in the genre which had made him famous. By his own admission his final play *Bradamante* (1695), was an anomaly. He turned, irresistably it would seem, to the familiar situation of mistaken identity as the basis of his plot. This time a proud heroine, Bradamante, believing her lover, Roger, to be dead, agrees to marry only if another suitor can prove his worthiness by defeating her in a duel. Roger, very much alive, is imposed upon by the young Greek prince, Léon, to engage in the duel wearing Léon's armor for concealment. He does so and reluctantly defeats his beloved. From this initial situation events succeed one another in rather predictable fashion through scenes of recognition, self-sacrifice, and reconciliation. Woven into the background are the threads of a story involving the cessation of hostilities between Greece and Bulgaria. Ambassadors from the latter country request Roger to be their ruler, and everyone lives happily ever after.

The novelty of the play lay in the confrontation of hero and heroine in physical combat as if, after filling his plays with verbal combats of generosity, Thomas Corneille could no longer resist giving material representation to such a struggle. In his "Au Lecteur", he admitted that a lover fighting against his mistress on behalf of his rival "est une chose si éloignée de nos mœurs, qu'on a demandé pourquoi Roger n'a pas combattu Léon, en lui déclarant qui il était, plutôt que d'être si religieux observateur de sa parole". The situation is indeed singular but not much more so than the circumstances of *Timocrate*. In any case Thomas Corneille had the perspicacity to realize that the glitter of romanesque tragedy had lost some of its brilliance in the public eye and that his own creative faculties were waning. Having written *Bradamante* some fifteen years before it was produced, he claims to have been reluctant to have it performed, but the persuasiveness of friends and probably his desire for a final flourish prevailed. The play's mediocre success convinced its author that his career as dramatist was drawing to a close. With a sense of generous resignation, Thomas Corneille took leave of his public and in the "Au Lecteur" to *Bradamante* concluded modestly: "Mais enfin il y a des temps pour tout, et s'il est un âge qui semble permettre ces sortes d'amusements, il en est un autre qui demande que l'on songe à la retraite."

V. CONCLUSION

STYLE

In the preceding chapters we have referred to Thomas Corneille's perceptiveness, his powers of assimilation, his technical competence, his sense of timeliness, in brief, his ability to produce plays calculated to please and in large measure derivative of the fleeting predilections of the society in which they were performed. We have said little of his worth as a poet. Those who have commented on his poetic style have been generally unimpressed. Lockert feels that he was the least inspiring of his major contemporaries.[1]

He is unanimously acknowledged as a facile writer, an agile versifier capable of rapid but not brilliant composition. A well known anecdote, first reported by Voisenon in his *Anecdotes littéraires*, holds that, when Pierre and Thomas occupied adjoining apartments in Paris, Pierre would open a trap door and consult Thomas whenever he needed to complete a troublesome rhyme. Thomas, it is alleged, invariably supplied a ready answer.[2] The volume of his dramatic production, which is fourth greatest in the century after Hardy, Rotrou, and Dancourt, clearly suggests that he was not one to linger over stylistic niceties. He is said to have spent only forty days writing *Ariane*.

---

[1] "The average quality of his verse is probably inferior to that of any other dramatist included in this volume, except Campistron" (*Rivals*, p. 322). The group includes Mairet, Rotrou, DuRyer, Tristan l'Hermite, LaFosse, Crébillon, and Voltaire.

[2] For a somewhat skeptical view on the veracity of this story, see François Bouquet, *Points obscurs et nouveaux de la vie de Pierre Corneille* (Paris, 1888), pp. 192-193.

Yet his facility for composing dramatic pieces did not involve a corresponding prolixity as narrator. On the contrary, in his economy as raconteur he showed a preoccupation for orderliness and clear delineation of situations worthy of a scrupulous journalist. Ironically his logical clarity is most evident in the complex plots of Spanish inspiration and in the identity plays where a high degree of accuracy was indispensable to comprehension. His primary concern seems to have been one of communication.

Those who have labeled Thomas as little more than a facile versifier have usually supported their contentions by comparing him with Racine — a comparison by which any seventeenth century poet is likely to suffer. Thomas did not have the powers of lyric expression of his more gifted contemporary. He failed to take advantage of the evocative powers of proper names to infuse his tragedies with a sense of historical depth, and he never entirely outgrew a *précieux* tendency to describe emotional turmoil as a battle of abstract nouns. Nevertheless in the later plays, notably in *Laodice*, *Ariane* and *Essex*, one can trace a progression toward simplicity and directness of style commensurate with his effort to intensify the psychological crises of his characters. Occasionally he rose to an exalted level of expression as, for example, in Stilicon's great speech quoted above (p. 113). But in general his style reflects a desire to convey the specific impressions necessary to the immediate effects of a given plot.

PERSPECTIVE VIEW

To the extent that Thomas Corneille succeeded in pleasing only a contemporary audience, so the honored formula has it, he failed as a dramatist of enduring reputation. By consensus those who have judged his plays, with the exception of Lockert, have divided his contribution to the theater into four areas each of which, they claim, is better represented by another dramatist. He has been overshadowed by Pierre Corneille, Molière, Racine and, to a lesser extent, Quinault. Since Reynier inaugurated the division of his plays into *comédies espagnoles*, *comédies françaises*, *tragédies romanesques*, *tragédies cornéliennes*, and *tragédies raciniennes*, no one has made a significant revision. Only recently did Miss Brée suggest that in Reynier's treatment an "artificial division of theater into 'types' prevents any organic view of development of the work as a whole".[3] While we have found it convenient to preserve some of Reynier's terms as working labels, Miss Brée's viewpoint is well taken. The compartmentalized view of Thomas Corneille has tended to make him entirely derivative and obscured a modest but genuine originality. We propose to conclude this study by an attempt to synthesize the diverse elements of Thomas Corneille's long career into a unified whole in an effort to disengage his peculiar merits. Having treated the plays in some detail, we shall now make a necessarily impressionistic survey in the hope of achieving a perspective. Four principles suggest themselves as guidelines to his dramatic art. These principles are drawn directly from the plays without consideration for the influence of contemporary dramatists. That such influence existed is undeniable. Nevertheless an interrelationship among these principles indicates that Thomas Corneille exercised an autonomy of creative spirit which his critics have generally failed to recognize. Finally we shall attempt to characterize the psychology of his dramatic art.

Thomas Corneille's career as dramatist represents an evolution characterized by several interrelated phases that may be traced through his productions. One can readily detect a progression from paradox toward dilemma accompanied by a structural change from complexity toward simplicity, which in turn is reflected by a shift from highly self-conscious dramaturgy toward the dramatic and finally reaching the tragic. His conception of characters, so often said to mirror the changing moods of his century, evinces a growth in his own psychological vision.

Having been initiated into the vogue of the Spanish *comedia*, around mid-century, Thomas Corneille early learned the manipulative aspects of dramatic craft. His early plays constitute what we might call today a workshop session and gave him the opportunity to develop an approach to drama. Although the quality of the early comedies is admittedly mediocre, the importance of the formative aspects of this early experience should be appreciated. From it Thomas Corneille

---

[3] *A Critical Bibliography of French Literature*, Vol. III, "The Seventeenth Century" (Syracuse, 1961), p. 188 (no. 1767).

derived his first principle of drama which we shall call the principle of external dynamics. For above all his early plays abound in sheer movement. His valets, Clarin, Philipin, and Cliton romp with delight in the antics of their equally scatterbrained masters. A closet, a "coiffe abattue", an intercepted note, in short, any pretext sufficed to create instantaneous glee and superfluous motion largely for its own sake. The term *extravagant* which is placed in the title of one of his comedies is a telling attribution of his early conception of theater art. Here is not the place to seek the profound inanities of Molière but the frivolous complications conjured up by an apprentice still enamoured of the techniques of theater. Yet two significant accomplishments emerge from this otherwise inauspicious début. One, formal in nature, was the acquisition of a stylistic mould into which to pour subsequent themes of greater depth. The second, substantial in nature, was the production of two plays, *Don Bertrand de Cigarral* and *Le Geôlier de soi-même* which, we believe, deserve recognition in their own right. The success of these two plays appears to have guided Thomas toward the second of his principles which embodies the notion of focus.

From the galimatias of conventional characters involved in trivial situations, Thomas Corneille had quite naturally failed to produce a striking play. But in these two comedies he concentrated attention on a single role for which all the others were primarily foils. Hence the recognition that a strong central character might serve as the best nucleus of interest. By an extension of this principle, it is easy to explain why Thomas was attracted to the identity play. For what better way to concentrate interest on the hero than to shroud his identity in mystery? The early comedies had trained him in the use of those devices which were precisely the ones needed to disguise the hero, not momentarily but through several acts. The transition from "coiffe abattue" to "prince déguisé" was a natural one. The possibilities of *quid pro quo*, so often exploited in his comedies, were perfectly adaptable to the new genre. The identity play probably occurred to Thomas as a compatible, indeed glorious alliance of his two principles. There was ample opportunity for external dynamics which could be used to enhance the importance of the mysterious hero. The reassuring success of *Timocrate* was sufficient confirmation for its author to encourage a full scale application of his talents in this direction. The years 1656-1663, which encompass his identity plays, were the most productive and representative of his career.

Yet the identity play, Thomas discovered, was not inexhaustible. The hero incognito, fashionable though he was in the tales of Mlle de Scudéry and La Calprenède, was, beneath it all, an imposter. One could be titillated by him but could scarcely be expected to sympathize or identify with him. He owed his theatrical viability to an enormous mistake wrapped in a series of highly contrived circumstances. For a time Thomas Corneille's audiences loved Timocrate and his like, and indeed the type of hero he represents has never entirely disappeared from vogue. But to a maturing dramatist the challenge of creating a progeny of Timocrates must have appeared a monotonous task of dreary proportions. Beneath the glitter of ingenious dramaturgy lay a vacuum of psychological dishonesty. This hero was not ultimately responsible for himself or his actions. The bewilderment of Philoxène shows vividly the lacking sense of self-identification which made this hero an ineffectual plaything of fortune:

> Dieux, quel astre fatal éclaira ma naissance,
> Si sans m'en éclaircir le funeste embarras,
> L'on m'apprend seulement ce que je ne puis pas?
>   (*Bérénice*, V, 10)

Philoxène's malaise is symptomatic of the general sense of unreality in Thomas Corneille's identity plays. But even as he was reveling in the heroics of *Timocrate*, he was developing a new dimension to his art based on a new principle. This third principle may be labeled internal cohesion.

In the identity plays the essential activating forces, starting with the initial situation and continuing through the denouement, were largely external and coincidental.[4] No inevitability and very little credibility obtain in the action of the disguised prince. By contrast *Commode, Stilicon* and the plays which follow in this group portray characters in situations which are self-sufficient. Actions evolve in psychological harmony with the nature of characters in certain defined

---

[4] Lockert's charge that Thomas Corneille relegates "crucial plot details to the intervals between the acts" is perhaps less valid as a criticism of dramaturgy than it is one of psychology which, in the identity plays, is left in the wings.

predicaments. Stilicon's conspiracy, for example, may be readily understood as a direct reaction to Placidie's haughty refusal of his son. In order to produce plays with internal cohesion, Thomas Corneille sought to portray forceful characters compelled by some overpowering sentiment. Whereas Timocrate, Darius, and Pyrrhus are rather symbolic figures than real, Stilicon, Maximian, Laodice, and Annibal are living individuals with a core of reality about them that enabled Thomas Corneille to treat them in accordance with natural rather than artificial events. He did not need to superimpose a scheme of external events to justify the denouements of *Maximian* and *Camma*, for the denouements of these plays have latent form within the psychological factors known and exposed in Act I.

In abandoning the hero incognito, Thomas Corneille was not really changing subjects. The identity plays dealt with dynastic succession, political marriage, and conspiracy just as his Cornelian plays did. But he did make an all important change in technical approach and in his attitude toward characters. The moral problem itself emerges as his central preoccupation in *Stilicon* and *Maximian*. The dramaturgical virtuosity required to sustain *Timocrate* was neither necessary nor appropriate for *Commode*. Thomas Corneille was refining his technique through simplification.

One play in particular stands out as a tribute to his maturing talents. *Laodice* combines psychological depth with serious moral import in a plot activated by the device of the disguised hero. Here lay the triumph of Thomas Corneille's dramatic art and the climax of his syncretic method. In *Laodice* are fused his three principles, and the result is striking. A closer look at the play reveals the hint of a fourth principle which eventually found full expression in *Ariane* and *Essex*. It may be best described as intensification and represents the logical conclusion of Thomas Corneille's dual evolution toward dramaturgical simplicity and psychological penetration. His implementation of the story of Laodice still depended significantly on external dynamics, but his attention seems to have been converted in this play to a fascination with the heroine's self-awareness. The remarkable trait of Laodice is her lucidity with respect to her own nature. In creating a character capable of keen self-analysis, Thomas Corneille was well on the way to discovering the potentialities of pure psychological tragedy.

His earlier characters, Commode, Stilicon, and Maximian, were aware to some degree of their own motivations and capable of making generalizations which justified their conduct; but Laodice is a pitiless self-critic. Her most immediate predecessor is Sinorix of *Camma* who, as early as 1661, stands out as a highly self-conscious hero whose sense of guilt leads him to explore the recesses of his troubled mind with a masochistic indulgence in self-recrimination.

PSYCHOLOGY OF CHARACTERIZATIONS

As Thomas Corneille came to recognize that the human psyche itself could be used as the primary source of dramatic action, he devoted himself more intently to the portrayal of characters in emotional conflict. In the later tragedies deeds yield in importance to the state of mind which they provoke. Hence Thésée's abandonment of Ariane and Essex' refusal to accept the love of his queen unleash a series of psychological reactions requiring a minimum of dynamic accompaniment. The characters sustain themselves, for they need no further pretext to declaim than the original one and their own peculiar sense of misfortune. The arrival and departure of characters on the stage serve merely to create a variation of tableaux as the background of inexorable, painful self-analysis. The intensification of emotional struggle and concomitant diminution of external action involved an automatic neglect of his first principle, that of external dynamics. But Thomas Corneille surely gained by sacrificing this principle for the sake of penetration in character analysis, for only in this way could he hope to create artistically the experience of tragedy.

What exactly was the tragic experience as Thomas Corneille came to conceive it? It is important to notice that the tragic sense in his plays arises not from an accident, not directly from an unfortunate event, not even from the spontaneous outburst of grief occasioned by such an event, but finally from the victim's lucid comprehension of his failure. Thomas Corneille's most striking heroes and heroines die fully appreciating the causes which have brought about their destruction. We have only to recall the last words of Maximian, Stilicon, Laodice, or Ariane to recognize that in his better plays Thomas

Corneille conceived of the tragic as the full consciousness of futility.

The psychological make-up of his tragic figures is varied, for they do not all elicit the same quality of sympathy nor react by fixed formulae. As his ill-fated heroes and heroines take a final inventory of their despair, we can discern an individuality in their psychological stance. Strangely enough, those who die "best", that is with Stoic grace, are the ones whose moral depravity has made them least sympathetic in the play. Laodice and Maximian, having exhausted their resources for evil, summarily choose death and express no rancorous malevolence toward those who have defeated them. On the other hand the "good" heroes and heroines, upon reaching the moment of ultimate frustration, remain full of vindictive wrath or self-pity. With poison already working inside him, Annibal never ceases cursing Rome and exhorting those around him to work for its destruction. Elisabeth and Ariane indulge in the most doleful lamentations.

There is a curious psychological validity in Thomas Corneille's treatment of the defeated hero and heroine. The ones who had dedicated themselves to the destruction of another and failed in their quest find a sense of satisfaction in turning their hatred inward toward the perverse ego which has led them to defeat. Death is to them a means of self-realization. The suicide of Commode, Stilicon, Maximian, and Laodice are their noblest gestures. Having failed in all else, here at least was a victory and a release.

On the other hand Ariane and Elisabeth survive their grief and give vent to it in self-pity. Their unsuccessful efforts had been directed toward the restoration of themselves as objects of love. It seems a natural response to their particular kind of failure that they should seek inwardly what had been denied them by recusant lovers. Self-pity was a form of self-appreciation, indeed, of self-love and the only sentiment that could compensate for their loss. In the final analysis their reaction to profound disappointment finds expression in a victory of egotism. They are therefore quite different from Racine's defeated protagonists who sound the depths to emerge under a new light. His Phèdre views her death as an act of purification:

> Et la mort, à mes yeux dérobant la clarté,
> Rend au jour, qu'ils souillaient, toute sa pureté.
> *(Phèdre*, V, 7, 1644-5)

She is sorry but no longer for herself as she was earlier in the play. She has reached a state of self-recognition which will not allow her egotism to survive. Defeated in the fulfillment of her passions, she can find her only victory in self-renunciation.

Thomas Corneille's tragedies show an interesting trend toward a realism in the portrayal of human experiences. After the fantastic world of the early productions, he worked gradually to bring into his plays situations closer to everyday experience. In *Ariane* and *Essex* he portrays with stark simplicity the psychological reactions produced by frustrated passion. To do so he did not stress the regal magnificence of his characters but their basic frailty. Ariane is just a broken-hearted girl; Elisabeth is a woman who is used to having her own way but, for once, cannot impose her will. Thomas Corneille's strength lay in the realistic portrayal of the misfortunes of these heroines as individual predicaments.

THOMAS CORNEILLE THE MODERN

His lack of emphasis on the universal dimensions of particular human experience is perhaps the most significant feature distinguishing him from Racine. Thomas was resolutely a Modern whose inherent optimism was incompatible with a genuinely tragic view of life. His tragedies seldom give the impression that the suffering of his heroes and heroines reflects the injustice of a world gone awry. The plight of Annibal, as we have shown, is represented against a highly realistic background of political corruption. But it is also one which might have been entirely different with only minor changes. Thomas did not envision the death of the great Carthaginian as an inevitable and irreparable misfortune to Annibal's partisans, to the ideal he stood for, or even to Annibal himself. Like a stalwart and loyal soldier, Annibal goes down fighting having been caught, so to speak, by a stray bullet but in his last breath bidding his followers to keep up the good fight.

Even more than in his tragedies, Thomas shows himself as a Modern in the late comedies where, as in *La Devineresse*, he focused on current situations to illuminate the foibles of his contemporaries in a restricted context. In this respect and in his predilection for describing specific reactions to the human condition rather than the human condition itself, he anticipated certain tendencies which were to characterize the eighteenth century. It is curious how many of Thomas' qualities are to be found, for example, in Voltaire: a concern for stagecraft and cleverly contrived situations, facile rather than profound characterizations, a fondness for situations which play on the sensibilities of the spectator rather than on his deepest emotions, and the use of verse in drama primarily as a means of communication. This uncle of Fontenelle did not live long enough to see a performance of Voltaire's *Zaïre* or *Mahomet*; but if he had, he would have recognized in them the implications of a *Weltanschauung* to which he himself subscribed.

We have stated that Thomas Corneille was a clever assimilator. Others have claimed that he was little more than an imitator. He is judged by general consent to be a mediocre stylist. For the sake of parody one is tempted to draw a parallel between Thomas and one of his less fortunate heroes, Sinorix. The latter, it could be argued, was a usurper just as Thomas was a would-be usurper of his brother's reputation. Recognizing his inability to fill the role of his predecessor, Sinorix prostrated himself before Camma in an act of sentimental surrender in much the same way that Thomas succumbed to the precious sentimentality usually associated with Quinault. And finally, despite his efforts, Sinorix was killed by the one he adored just as Thomas' hopes for pre-eminence in the theater were dashed by the success of Racine whom he emulated.

The foregoing comparison is contrived, intentionally so. It represents, nevertheless, the average judgment of Thomas Corneille's critics, and it is not altogether invalid. Appearing as he does in a play by the younger brother of the great Corneille, Sinorix represents a fallacy both strangely appropriate and ironic. For Sinorix is an anachronism. He is an essentially Quinaultian personality placed in a situation which demands a Corneillian temperament. He is the gallant lover forced to play the incompatible role of usurper. The mixture yields an interesting result.

This kind of anachronism is far more pronounced in the tragedies of Quinault, who invariably placed an oversensitive hero in a situation requiring acts which he is not suited to perform. The result is usually

an extended sigh, a lament, a pronouncement on the bittersweet qualities of unrequited love. It is a tribute to the tenacity of French classical dogmatism, but more especially to Pierre Corneille, that the basic
hypothesis of the tragic plot, some form of political crisis, could
survive into a generation whose predilection for the gallant hero must
have suggested the use of less rigorous moral crises. It may be fairly
contended that Thomas Corneille, more than any of his contemporaries,
helped to preserve the Cornelian ethic and to prevent tragedy from
becoming comedy through lack of moral importance.

Thomas Corneille never reached the extremes of Quinault. The
coquettish abnegation which characterizes Quinault's royal lovers, their
eagerness to make any sacrifice to win a lady already in love with them,
their fatuous insistence on dispelling the remotest unlikely objections
to their love before presuming to deserve the consideration of the
beloved — these were the ludicrous aspects of characterization which
Thomas successfully outgrew. His works are not exempt of many of
the *précieux* influences which Quinault epitomizes, but he never
pushed them to a point of caricature. Witness a typical sentiment of
Quinault's characters such as this one by the "villain" Odartise of
Cyrus who moralizes:

> L'amant le plus injuste et le moins excusable,
> Lorsqu'il devient heureux, cesse d'être coupable,
> Et du feu le plus noir parût-il animé,
> Il n'est plus criminel sitôt qu'il est aimé.
>
> (I, 2)

Quinault attributed to love the same ennobling qualities that Pierre
Corneille reserved for political ambition. But Quinault's lovers are
nothing but lovers. The mighty Cyrus leading his army to battle
catches a glimpse of the enemy queen, Thomiris, on horseback and is
immediately hypnotized into powerlessness. His only wish is to be
captured so that he may tell her of his flame:

> Auprès de Thomiris voulant trouver la mort,
> Je pris des fers sans peine et cédai sans effort . . .
> Je ne souhaite plus d'autre bien dans ma peine
> Et voudrais seulement pour mourir satisfait,
> Que son cœur sût les maux que ses beaux yeux m'ont fait.
>
> (II, 1)

Now even Sinorix, whose kinship with Quinault's heroes is greater than most of Thomas' characters does not surrender his moral identity in exchange for a sigh. Even in *Timocrate*, Thomas was not guilty, as Quinault was in most of his tragedies, of sacrificing the basic moral fiber to unctuous sentimental embroidery. Yet even more movingly than Pierre Corneille's royal lovers, those of Thomas manage to show the inner suffering caused by dynastic responsibilities.

Thomas Corneille has an originality of his own. His protean imagination prompted him to write a remarkable variety of dramatic pieces. But what is more, the range of his psychological portraits bespeaks a more imposing versatility than he is given credit for at times and reveals a definite originality of conception not unworthy of his brother.

It is questionable whether Thomas Corneille's descendants, now active in reviving one or two of his plays each summer, will effect a broad revival of interest in his theater. However, if a few of the better plays are salvaged from near oblivion, our perspective of French classical theater stands to be enriched. The apotheosis of Corneille, Molière and Racine as the sacred triumvirate vested with exclusive trusteeship of seventeenth century French dramatic traditions surely has obscured our vision of the period as a whole. They were its finest exponents, but the edifice of their theater was constructed on the efforts of many dramatists. The variety of his dramatic art and a persistent dedication to his craft mark Thomas Corneille as one of the most significant and interesting contributors to these efforts.

APPENDIX

CHRONOLOGICAL LIST OF THOMAS CORNEILLE'S PLAYS

The following information is provided for each of the plays: the date of the first performance, the name of the play, the genre to which it belongs, the collaborating author or authors if any, the troupe which first performed it, and the place and year of original publication. Where the dates are highly conjectural we have given those suggested by Lancaster with a question mark. The following abbreviations are used: Ac. de Mus. — Académie de Musique; Gué. — Guénégaud; H. de B. — Hôtel de Bourgogne; M. — Théâtre du Marais; T. F. — Théâtre Français.

1649	*Les Engagements du hasard*, comedy, H. de B., Rouen Maurry for A. Courbé, Paris, 1657, 12°.
1650	*Le Feint astrologue*, comedy, H. de B., Rouen, Maurry, and Paris, C. de Sercy, 1651, 4° and 12°.
1651, May	*Don Bertrand de Cigarral*, comedy, H. de B., Rouen, Maurry, and Paris, Le Petit, 1652, 12°.
1651	*L'Amour à la mode*, comedy, H. de B., Rouen, Maurry, and Paris, de Luyne, 1653 and 1654, 12°.
1652	*Le Berger extravagant*, comedy, H. de B., Rouen, Maurry for de Luyne, Paris, 1653, 12°.
1655	*Les Illustres ennemis*, comedy, M., Rouen, Maurry for A. Courbé, Paris, 1657, 12°.
1655	*Le Geôlier de soi-même*, comedy, M., Rouen, Maurry for A. Courbé, Paris, 1656, 12°.
1656?	*Le Charme de la voix*, comedy, H. de B., Rouen, Maurry for Courbé and de Luyne, Paris, 1658, 12°.
1656, Dec.	*Timocrate*, tragedy, M., Rouen, Maurry for Courbé and de Luyne, Paris, 1658, 12°.
1657	*Bérénice*, tragedy, M., Rouen, Maurry for Courbé and de Luyne, Paris, 1659, 12°.

1657   *La Mort de l'empereur Commode*, tragedy, M., Rouen, Maurry for Courbé and de Luyne, Paris, 1659, 12°.

1659   *Darius*, tragedy, H. de B., Printed at Rouen and published at Paris, de Luyne and Courbé, 1659, 12°.

1660, Jan.   *Stilicon*, tragedy, H. de B., Paris, Courbé, 1660, 12°.

1660, Jan.   *Le Galant doublé*, comedy, H. de B., Paris, Courbé, 1660, 12°.

1661, Jan.   *Camma*, tragedy, H. de B., Rouen and Paris, Courbé and de Luyne, 1661, 12°.

1662, Feb.   *Maximian*, tragedy, H. de B., Paris, Courbé, 1662, 12°.

1662, Dec.   *Persée et Démétrius*, tragedy, H. de B., Paris, Quinet, 1665, 12°.

1663?   *Pyrrhus*, tragedy, H. de B., Paris, Quinet, 1665, 12°.

1666, Jan.   *Antiochus*, tragedy, H. de B., Rouen, Maurry for Billaine, de Luyne, Jolly and Quinet, 1666, 12°.

1667   *Le Baron d'Albikrac*, comedy, H. de B., Paris, Quinet and Barbin, 1669, 12°.

1668   *Laodice*, tragedy, H. de B., Printed at Rouen for Barbin and Quinet, Paris, 1668, 12°.

1669   *La Mort d'Annibal*, tragedy, H. de B., Paris, Barbin and de Luyne, 1670, 12°.

1670   *La Comtesse d'Orgueil*, comedy, H. de B., Paris, de Luyne, 1671, 12°.

1672, Feb.   *Ariane*, tragedy, H. de B., Paris, de Luyne, Barbin and Trabouillet, 1672, 12°.

1672, Nov.   *Théodat*, tragedy, H. de B., Paris, de Luyne and Barbin, 1673, 12°.

1673, Nov.   *Le Comédien poète*, comedy (with Montfleury), Gué., Paris, Promé, 1674, 12°.

1673, Dec.   *La Mort d'Achille*, tragedy, Gué., Paris, Barbin, 1674, 12°.

1674, Dec.   *Don César d'Avalos*, comedy, Gué., Paris, Jean Ribou, 1676, 12°.

1675, Mar.   *Circé*, lyric tragedy (with de Visé), Gué., Paris, Pierre Promé, 1675, 12°.

1675, Nov.   *L'Inconnu*, comedy with machines (with de Visé), Gué., Paris, Ribou, 1676, 12°.

1676, Aug.   *Le Triomphe des dames*, comedy with machines (with de Visé), Gué., unpublished: MS lost. Libretto reproduced in Parfaict, *Histoire*, Vol. XI, pp. 457-490.

1677, Feb.   *Le Festin de Pierre*, comedy of Molière versified by Thomas Corneille, Gué., Paris, Th. Guillain, 1683, 12°.

1678, Jan.   *Le Comte d'Essex*, tragedy, H. de B., Paris, Ribou, 1678, 12°.

1678, April   *Psyché*, opera (music by Lulli), Ac. de Mus., Paris, René Baudry, 1678, 4°.

1679, Jan.   *Bellérophon*, opera (with Fontenelle and Boileau; music by Lulli), Ac. de Mus., Paris, Christophe Ballard and Mlle de Beaujeu, 1679, 4°.

1679, Nov.   *La Devineresse*, comedy with machines (with de Visé), Gué., Paris, Blageart, 1680, 12°.

1681, Feb.   *La Pierre philosophale*, comedy with machines (with de Visé), Gué., unpublished. Libretto reproduced in Parfaict, *Histoire*, Vol. XII, pp. 225-265.

1685, Feb.   *L'Usurier*, comedy (with de Visé), T. F., unpublished. Brief account of de Visé's remarks concerning it reproduced in Parfaict, *Histoire*, Vol. XII, pp. 457-461.

1686, Jan.   *Le Baron des Fondrières*, comedy, T. F., unpublished; MS lost.

1693, Dec.   *Médée*, opera (music by Charpentier), Ac. de Mus., Paris, Christophe Ballard, 1693, 4°.

1695, Feb.   *Les Dames vengées*, comedy in prose (with de Visé), T. F., Paris, Michel Brunet, 1695, 12°.

1695, Nov.   *Bradamante*, tragedy, T. F., Paris, Brunet and de Luyne, 1696, 12°.

LIST OF WORKS CONSULTED

NOTE ON THOMAS CORNEILLE'S WORKS

For various reasons no single collective edition of the plays is satisfactory for all purposes. The edition of 1722, which is listed by
Lanson (*Manuel bibliographique*), lacks the dedicatory "épîtres". The
edition of 1738 contains the same plays as the 1722 edition and most
of the "épîtres" as well but lacks the "Au Lecteur" to *Bradamante*.
Neither edition contains *La Devineresse*. The latest publication of
Thomas Corneille's works is a one volume collection misleadingly
entitled *Théâtre complet* (Paris, 1881). It contains *La Devineresse* but
lacks *Le Berger extravagant, Darius, Pyrrhus, Théodat*, and *La Mort
d'Achille* and has none of the author's prefatory material. Hence we
have used the 1738 edition to document all quotations from the plays
and prefatory material except in the cases of *La Devineresse* and
Bradamante where we have used the separate original editions. (For a
listing of the successive editions see Reynier, *Thom. Corn.* and
Francis Bar, éd. *Le Berger extravagant.*)

Adam, Antoine, *Histoire de la littérature française au XVIIe siècle*. Part I,
    1948; Part II, 1951; Part III, 1952; Part IV, 1954; Part V, 1956 (Paris,
    Domat.), 5 vols.
Bar, Francis, ed., *Le Berger extravagant* by Thomas Corneille (Paris, Droz,
    1960).
Bernardin, N. M., *Un Précurseur de Racine: Tristan L'Hermite* (Paris, Picard
    et fils, 1895).
Boileau-Despréaux, Nicolas, *Satires*, ed. Albert Cahen (Paris, Droz, 1932).
Bouquet, François Valentin, *Points obscurs et nouveaux de la vie de Pierre
    Corneille* (Paris, Hachette, 1888).
—, *La Troupe de Molière et les deux Corneille à Rouen en 1658* (Paris, A.
    Claudin, 1880).

Brasillach, Robert, *Pierre Corneille* (Paris, A. Fayard, 1938).

Bray, René, *La Formation de la doctrine classique en France* (Paris, Hachette, 1927).

Canfield, Dorothea Frances, *Corneille and Racine in England* (New York, Columbia University Press, 1904).

Chappuzeau, Samuel, *Le Théâtre François* (1674), ed. Paul Lacroix (Bruxelles, A. Mertens et fils, 1867).

Cherpack, Clifton, *The Call of the Blood in French Classical Tragedy* (Baltimore, Johns Hopkins Press, 1958).

Corneille, Pierre, *Œuvre de Pierre Corneille*, ed. Charles Marty-Laveaux (Paris, Hachette, 1862-1868), 12 vols.

Corneille, Thomas, *Bradamante* (Paris, Michel Brunet and G. de Luyne, 1696), Original edition.

—, *Poèmes dramatiques de T. Corneille* (Paris, David, 1722), 5 vols.

—, *Poèmes dramatiques de T. Corneille* (Paris, Nion fils, 1738), 5 vols.

—, *Chefs-d'Œuvre de T. Corneille*, ed. Le Corney (Paris, Pourrat, 1833).

—, *Théâtre complet de T. Corneille*, ed. Edouard Thierry (Paris, Laplace, Sanchez et Cie, 1881).

—, and Donneau de Visé, Jean, *La Devineresse ou les faux enchantements* (Paris, Blageart, 1680).

Couton, Georges, *Corneille et la Fronde* (Clermont-Ferrand, G. de Bussac, 1951).

—, *La Vieillesse de Corneille (1658-1684)* (Paris, Maloine, 1949).

Deierkauf-Holsboer, S. Wilma, *Le Théâtre du Marais* (Paris, Nizet, 1954), 2 vols.

Despois, Eugène, *Le Théâtre Français sous Louis XIV* (Paris, Hachette, 1874).

Edelman, Nathan, ed., *The Seventeenth Century*, Volume III of *A Critical Bibliography of French Literature*, general editors David C. Cabeen and Jules Brody (Syracuse, Syracuse University Press, 1961).

Fontenelle, Bernard Le Bouvier de, *Œuvres complètes* (Paris, A. Belin, 1818), 3 vols.

Fournel, Victor, *Les Contemporains de Molière; Recueil de comédies rares ou peu connues jouées de 1650-1680* (Paris, Firmin-Didot, 1863-75), 3 vols.

—, *Petites comédies rares et curieuses du XVIIe siècle* (Paris, Quantin, 1884), 2 vols.

Giraud, Jeanne, *Manuel de bibliographie littéraire pour les XVIe, XVIIe et XVIIIe siècles français, 1936-1945* (Paris, Nizet, 1956).

Gros, Etienne, *Philippe Quinault: sa vie et son œuvre* (Paris, Edouard Champion, 1926).

Herland, Louis, *Corneille par lui-même* (Paris, Ecrivains de toujours, aux éditions de Seuil, 1954).

Hill, L. Alfreda, *The Tudors in French Drama* (Baltimore, Johns Hopkins Press, 1932). Vol. XX of the Johns Hopkins Studies in Romance Literatures and Languages.

Jasinski, René, *Vers le vrai Racine* (Paris, A. Colin, 1958), 2 vols.

Joannidès, A., *La Comédie Française de 1680 à 1900; Dictionnaire général des pièces et des auteurs* (Paris, Plon, 1901).

—, *La Comédie Française de 1680 à 1920: Tableau des représentations* (Paris, Plon, 1921).

La Harpe, Jean-François, *Lycée ou cours de littérature ancienne et moderne* (Paris, Deterville, 1818). 16 vols.

Lancaster, Henry Carrington, *A History of French Dramatic Literature in the Seventeenth Century* (Baltimore, The Johns Hopkins Press, Part I, 1929; Part II, 1932; Part III, 1936; Part IV, 1940; Part V, 1942), 9 vols.

Lanson, Gustave, *Esquisse d'une histoire de la tragédie française* (New York, Columbia University Press, 1920).

—, *Manuel bibliographique de la littérature française moderne* (Paris, Hachette, 1925).

Levy, Raphael, "The Sources of Thomas Corneille's *Darius*", *Romanic Review*, XX (1929), pp. 35-41.

Lockert, Lacy, *The Chief Rivals of Corneille and Racine* (Nashville, Vanderbilt University Press, 1956).

—, *Studies in French Classical Tragedy* (Nashville, Vanderbilt University Press, 1958).

Loret, Jean, *La Muze historique ou Recueil des lettres en vers*, ed. Ch.-L. Livet (Paris, P. Daffis, 1878), Vols. II, III, IV.

Lough, John, *Paris Theatre Audiences in the Seventeenth and Eighteenth Centuries* (London, Oxford University Press, 1957).

Lowenstein, Robert, *Voltaire as an Historian of Seventeenth-Century French Drama* (Baltimore, Johns Hopkins Press, 1935), Vol. XXV of the Johns Hopkins Studies in Romance Literatures and Languages.

Magendie, Maurice, *Le Roman français au XVIIᵉ siècle* (Paris, Droz, 1932).

Magne, Emile, *Scarron et son milieu* (Paris, Emile-Paul frères, 1924).

Mahelot, Laurent et al., *Le Mémoire de Mahelot, Laurent et d'autres décorateurs de l'Hôtel de Bourgogne et de la Comédie-Française au XVIIᵉ siècle*, ed. H. C. Lancaster (Paris, Champion, 1920).

Martinenche, Ernest, *La Comedia espagnole en France de Hardy à Racine* (Paris, Hachette, 1900).

May, Georges, *Tragédie cornélienne, tragédie racinienne* (Urbana, University of Illinois Press, 1948).

Mélèse, Pierre, *Un Homme de lettres au temps du grand roi: Donneau de Visé* (Paris, Droz, 1936).

—, *Répertoire analytique des documents contemporains d'information et de critique concernant le théâtre à Paris sous Louis XIV, 1659-1715* (Paris, Droz, 1934).

Michaelis, Georg, *Die sogenannten "comédies espagnoles" des Thomas Corneille, ihr Verhältnis zu den spanischen Vorlagen und ihre eventuellen weiteren Schicksale in dem Schrifttum anderer Nationen* (Berlin, Emil Ebering, 1914).

Mornet, Daniel, *Histoire de la littérature française classique*, 4th ed. (Paris, Armand Colin, 1950).

Nisard, Désiré, *Histoire de la littérature française*, 12th ed. (Paris, Firmin-Didot, 1884), 4 vols.

Parfaict, François et Claude (frères), *Histoire du Théâtre François depuis son origine jusqu'à présent* (Paris, André Morin et Flahault), Vol. I; le Mercier et Saillant, Vols., II-XV, 1734-1749. 15 vols.

Petit de Julleville, Louis, ed., *Histoire de la langue et de la littérature françaises* (Paris, A. Colin, 1896-99), 8 vols.

Petit de Julleville, Louis, ed., *Le Théâtre en France*, 6th ed. (Paris, A. Colin, 1906).

Peyre, Henri, "Common Sense Remarks on the French Baroque", *Studies in Seventeenth Century French Literature*, ed. Jean-Jacques Demorest (Ithaca [New York], Cornell University Press, 1962), pp. 1-19.

Picard, Raymond, *La Carrière de Jean Racine*, 3rd ed. (Paris, Gallimard, 1956).

Privitera, Joseph F., "The Sources of Thomas Corneille's *La Comtesse d'Orgueil*", *Modern Language Notes*, LVI (March, 1941), pp. 211-214.

Quinault, Philippe, *Le Théâtre de Mr Quinault* (Amsterdam, Pierre de Coup, 1715), 2 vols.

Racine, Jean, *Œuvres de J. Racine*, ed. Mesnard (Paris, Hachette, 1885), 2nd ed., 10 vols.

Renynghe de Voxvrie, Louis van, *Descendance de Thomas Corneille* (Bruges, Tablettes des Flandres, 1959).

Reynier, Gustave, *Thomas Corneille: Sa vie et son théâtre* (Paris, Hachette, 1892).

Schaffer, Aaron, "Thomas Corneille's Reworking of Molière's *Don Juan*", *Modern Philology*, XIX (1921-1922), pp. 163-175.

Scherer, Jacques, *La Dramaturgie classique en France* (Paris, Nizet, 1950).

Scudéry, Georges de, *Le Prince déguisé*, ed. Barbara Matulka (New York, Columbia University Press, 1929).

Smith, John Harrington, "Thomas Corneille to Betterton to Congreve", *Journal of English and Germanic Philology*, XLV (April, 1946), pp. 209-213.

Smith, Winifred, "The Earl of Essex on the Stage", *PMLA*, XXXIX (1924), pp. 147-173.

Spycket, Sylvie, "Thomas Corneille et la musique", *Bulletin de la Société d'Etude du XVIIᵉ Siècle*, XXI-XXII (1954), pp. 442-455.

Steiner, George, *The Death of Tragedy* (New York, Knopf, 1961).

Van Roosbroeck, Gustav L., "A Commonplace in *Mélite*: the Madness of Eraste", *Modern Philology*, XVII (1919-1920), pp. 141-149.

Voisenon, Claude Henri de Fusée, abbé de, *Anecdotes littéraires*, ed. P.-L. Jacob (Paris, Libraire des Bibliophiles, 1880).

Voltaire, *Œuvres complètes*, ed. Louis Moland (Paris, Garnier, 1877-1883), 52 vols.

Wogue, Jules, *La Comédie aux XVIIᵉ et XVIIIᵉ siècles* (Paris, Henri Paulin et Cie, 1905).

Yarrow, P. J., "*Timocrate* 1656: A Note on French Classicism", *Orpheus*, III (September, 1955), pp. 171-182.